The Emergence
of the
Modern Capital Ship

The Emergence
of the
Modern Capital Ship

Stanley Sandler

Newark
University of Delaware Press
London: Associated University Presses

Associated University Presses, Inc.
Cranbury, New Jersey 08512

Associated University Presses
Magdalen House
136–148 Tooley Street
London SE1 2TT, England

Library of Congress Cataloging in Publication Data

Sandler, Stanley, 1937–
  The emergence of the modern capital ship.

   Bibliography: p.
   Includes index.
    1. Armored vessels—History—19th century. 2. Naval architecture—
History—19th century. 3. Great Britain. Navy—History—19th century.
4. Reed, Sir Edward James, 1830–1906. I. Title.
V799.S26   359.8′3   76-21271
ISBN 0-87413-119-7

for Marion

Contents

Preface

While the introduction of the ironclad warship and the Era of the *Dreadnought* have been studied at length, the intervening decades have not been made the subject of studies of comparable exhaustiveness. The 1860s in particular—the most fertile period in the history of naval architecture—have been strangely neglected.

The researcher into naval archives of the early ironclad era (ca. 1860–70) will find no embarrassment of riches regarding naval design. A mass of detail regarding the daily movements and activities of the fleets will indeed be located, but this material must be sifted carefully and patiently to locate items of historical significance. Journals and newspapers of the time were deeply concerned with design and detail, but generally ignored the larger questions of strategy, sea power, tactics, and ships' organization. Much of the writing is sheer polemic, of value simply as a way to understand the inventive ferment that characterized the 1860s.

Acknowledgments

I would like to begin this litany of indebtedness with a tribute to my intellectual mentor, Professor Michael Howard, F.B.A., then chairman of the Department of War Studies, King's College, University of London, and currently Chichele Professor of the History of War, Oxford University. Without his gentlemanly scholastic rigor this work might well have foundered.

I further wish to express my gratitude to the staff of the Admiralty Library, Ministry of Defense, London, and to the military and naval records staffs of the Public Record Office, London, as well as to the Library and the Manuscript and Plans divisions of the National Maritime Museum, Greenwich, and to the Reference Division, British Library.

American material was located in the National Archives, the Manuscript Division of the Library of Congress, and the Office of Naval History, all in Washington, D.C., and I am grateful for cordial staff assistance. Special acknowledgement must be extended to the staff of the Smithsonian Institution, and to the Armed Forces Museum Advisory Board of that remarkable Institution, to N.A.F.M.A.B.'s director, Mr. James Hutchins, and to Mr. James Stokesberry, former staff member. Research on the United States Navy ironclads was financed by an American Council of Learned Societies—Smithsonian Postdoctoral Research Fellowship; the author is thus doubly indebted to the Smithsonian and deeply grateful to the A.C.L.S. Illustrative material was provided through the cooperation and diligence of Ms. Agnes Hoover and Mr. Robert Carlisle of

11

the Photo Collection, Naval Historical Center, United States Navy.

Other cordial expressions of gratitude are due the Cowper Coles family for their kind permission to peruse material pertaining to Capt. Cowper P. Coles and his inventiveness. The staffs of the Buckinghamshire Record Office, the National Registry of Archives, the Hughenden Archives (Disraeli MSS), and the New York Historical Society proved most helpful. The Associated University Presses, Inc., and in particular Ms. Susan Stock Means, proved most helpful with suggestions and in the spotting of errors and infelicities. My thanks go also to the Bureau of Personnel, U.S. Navy, and to Capt. J. Edward Snyder, for permitting me to ship aboard U.S.S. *New Jersey* (BB-62) for a fortnight's familiarization with what may prove to be the last battleship called to active duty.

Mrs. Mary Lee Chase George merits a particular note of gratitude for her kindness and hospitality in making her fourteenth-century cottage a haven from the rigors of research and London life.

A special acknowledgment must go to my wife, Marion, who did not type the manuscript, but whose indefatigable support, interest, and encouragement were essential for the completion of this work.

The Emergence
of the
Modern Capital Ship

1

The Shape of Ships

I

In a placid backwater at Pembroke, Wales, lies a stripped wrought-iron hulk, still graceful despite her lowly work as an oil-line pipe pier. Beneath the grime of a half century of neglect, the broken iron letters of her name can still be picked out. She is H.M.S. *Warrior*, the first and now the last of the ironclad capital ships (the first-class warship of navies) that were the most obvious affirmation of Great Britain's industrial might. The wheel has come full turn, for all subsequent ironclads have vanished into the scrap merchant's acetylene maw and only the *Warrior* remains.[1]

The armored warship lasted for one hundred years, from the launching of the *Warrior* in 1860 to the scrapping of H.M.S. *Vanguard* in 1960. Incredibly, within the first ten years of that century, the capital ship had shed its wooden chrysalis and had rid itself of reliance upon sails and broadside smoothbores. It emerged as a war engine mounting four giant rifles in revolving turrets, bunkered with sufficient coal for oceanic voyages. From 1860 to 1869 a final farewell was bidden to most of the traditional material of the ships of the world and a strong beginning was made in the new age of steam, iron construction, armor, heavy ordnance, and turrets.

Of all the warlike technology of the zenith of the Industrial Revolution and of the Age of Progress, none

15

loomed more impressively, generated more public controversy, or captured the general imagination of powers with
naval pretensions than the ironclad warship. By its very
bulk the ironclad compelled admiration and apprehension,
and although secrecy was even then a serious consideration
(cf. chap. 2), an ironclad could scarcely be hidden even
while under construction. Further, it might on occasion be
visited, inspected, or even embarked upon. Finally, each
maritime power had its peculiar reasons for ironclad programs, reasons that gave that handful of expensive, egregious weapons a focus of patriotism. France of the Second
Empire began the era of steam, iron hulls, the ironclad, and
rifled naval artillery in order to "level up" its fleet with that
of the Royal Navy of Great Britain, while the Royal Navy
naturally felt impelled to retain its enormous supremacy in
material by surpassing France in each of these fields. The
United States Federal Navy was forced into the ironclad
era by the depredations of the Confederate steam-ironclad
ram *Virginia*, and Italy, Russia, Sweden, and Austria-
Hungary almost simultaneously armored their fleets against
their neighbors. All naval powers, great and small, looked
upon their own ironclads as symbols of their national great-
ness and genius. All of this is fairly obvious, but what is
surprising about the coming of the ironclad and the commencement of the century of armored warships is that it
was so long in coming and that the basic innovations necessary for the emergence of the battleship were introduced in
so brief a period of time.

As James Phinney Baxter III has pointed out, Drake's
seadogs would have experienced little difficulty in manning
the federal sailing sloop U.S.S. *Cumberland* when she was
sunk by the C.S.S. *Virginia* at Hampton Roads over two-
and-one-half centuries after the Spanish Armada.[2] Yet
aboard the U.S.S. *Monitor,* which arrived the following
day, these seamen would have felt completely lost amidst
a mass of complicated machinery and a total absence of the
familiar masts and sails. Naval architecture had moved

with glacial slowness from the sixteenth to the nineteenth century. The situation would be radically altered in the 1860s.

The earliest British seagoing ironclad, H.M.S. *Warrior*, retained the basic configuration of the traditional sailing frigate, and was distinguishable from her timber-built consorts and predecessors only by her enormously increased length, made possible by iron construction. Previously, a ship's length had been limited by the size of the bole of the tallest available tree. Until the appointment of Edward James Reed as Chief Constructor of the Admiralty, ironclads of the Royal Navy had varied only slightly from the *Warrior* pattern. Ram bows were added, for the combination of iron construction and steam made this ancient weapon feasible once again. In later designs, iron armor was extended from the *Warrior's* patch, protecting the guns, to a waterline belt from stem to stern rising to enclose the battery amidships. Hoisting screws were installed on some ironclads to enable them to improve their performance under sail, an important consideration then because of the cost of coal, the relative inefficiency of engines, and a conservative attachment to masts and sails.

The apogee of this early development was reached with the *Minotaur* class, gigantic iron warships four hundred feet in length, of ten thousand tons displacement, and with no fewer than five masts—all this merely to carry an increase of one inch of armor plate and stem-to-stern plating. But they bunkered less coal and were no faster under steam than the *Warrior*.[3]

Previous to the *Minotaur* class, four timber-built ironclads had been constructed from the partially completed hulls of wooden line-of-battleships, strictly as a temporary measure to maintain Britain's lead in capital ships, a lead that was constantly challenged by the French. Because of their bluff wooden construction, these ships were of more moderate dimensions than were those of the *Warrior* and *Minotaur* classes, although they carried the same size guns

H.M.S. *Warrior*. First seagoing, iron-built ironclad. OFFICIAL U.S. NAVY PHOTOGRAPH.

H.M.S. *Warrior*, 1964. PHOTO BY AUTHOR.

H.M.S. *Warrior.* Four-and-one-half-inch wrought-iron armor and eighteen-inch teakwood backing. PHOTO BY AUTHOR.

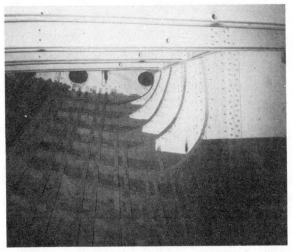

H.M.S. *Warrior.* Interior of stern counter, showing detail of construction and well for hoisting of screw. ("Down funnel, up screw.") PHOTO BY AUTHOR.

and the same thickness of armor plating over a far greater area. The drawbacks of this system were, of course, the short-lived nature of the wooden hull, the impossibility of watertight subdivisions' working between armor and wood, the heavier weight of a wooden hull, and the danger of fire.[4]

However, neither increased dimensions nor conversions from wooden line-of-battleships could provide the answer to the question of the design of the next generation of ironclads. Heavier gun power and the thick armor necessary to protect the guns indicated that a long row of small-bore ordnance arranged along the broadside would be inefficient. For with the new ordnance the number of guns could be cut in half and still achieve far greater fire power. But it would be impossible to arrange the new twelve-ton muzzle-loading rifles along the entire broadside of a warship of the dimensions of the *Warrior*, along with the six-inch armor required to keep out the shot thrown by such ordnance. To protect such a lengthy gun deck with six-inch plates would destroy the ship's stability or raise its waterline to an alarming height. Obviously, new design concepts were needed.

The Duke of Somerset, First Lord of the Admiralty, recognized this need. On the "strong recommendation" of Adm. Sir Robert Spencer Robinson, controller of the Navy (chief naval officer responsible for materiel), Somerset appointed Edward James Reed as Chief Constructor of the Navy in July 1863.[5] Only thirty-three years old at the time, Reed was to enjoy a meteoric and turbulent rise to fame, and at the height of his success was to resign his position under strange circumstances connected with the *Captain* tragedy. During his seven years in office, according to the authoritative Lord Brassey, he provided a "new and remarkable impetus" to naval architecture.[6] Another authority, Fred T. Jane, editor of *Jane's Fighting Ships*, lauded Reed as the "first man to conceive of the ironclad as a separate and distinct entity. Previously to him the ironclad was merely an ordinary steamer with some armour-plating on

Edward James Reed. Chief Constructor, Royal Navy, 1863–70.
NATIONAL MARITIME MUSEUM, LONDON.

her."[7] During his entire career Reed was to design a total
of ninety-five warships, of which twenty-five were ironclad.

The *Warrior* and *Minotaur* classes had relied on their
long, thin hulls for speed, since this design would permit a
multiplication of boilers and clean lines. But Reed believed
that shorter, broad ironclads, by a moderate addition to
their engine power, might be driven just as fast as the long
ships and that in turning-power and handiness under both

steam and sail they would be quite superior. The growing acceptance of the ram strengthened the attraction of such maneuverability. Most important, the new design could carry heavier armor and guns. In addition, shorter iron-clads were cheaper to build and man. Reed felt that the maximum proportions had been reached in the *Minotaur* class because of increased friction aggravated by fouling and because of lack of docking facilities. A year before his retirement Reed summarized his ideas of ironclad design:

> As far as our experience goes, then, I am warranted in making the assertion that in armoured ships as the extent and thickness of the armour to be carried are increased, the proportion of length to breadth should be diminished, and the fullness of the water-lines increased; and that the shorter, fuller ship can be propelled at as great a speed as the longer, finer ship with about the same, or only a little greater horsepower. The constants of performance will undoubtedly be lower in the shorter ship; but they are only hypo-thetical standards of merit, and the benefits in point of first cost, handiness, and maintenance, resulting from moderate proportions, are tangible facts, far out-weighing in importance the small economy of steam-power resulting from the adoption of greater proportion and fineness of form.[8]

Reed held tenaciously to these views during his seven years in office as chief constructor. In fact he was so success-ful in forcing their adoption that he later came to complain bitterly of the tonnage restrictions imposed on him by an economy-minded Admiralty, which cramped work on almost all of his designs, particularly the *Devastation*.[9] However, his ideas on the limitation of tonnage seem to have taken root only after his accession to office. Just prior to his ap-pointment, Reed outlined his desiderata for the modern ironclad. He called for armour of some kind for every war-ship that could carry it, a minimum of a complete waterline belt. The many small guns should be replaced by a few large pieces that would be given as wide a range of fire as possible —a system later to be known as the *box-battery*. Bows should be strengthened for emergency ramming. Efficient sailing rig was to be carried on a moderate freeboard. Ship-building should be in iron wherever possible. At this time Reed made no mention of the benefits to be derived from moderate tonnage.[10] Yet by the end of his first year in office he had voiced in detail his objections to lengthy ships of war: the difficulty in steering (seventy seamen needed at the helm and relieving tackles), the hull strains set up, the numerous masts necessary, and the poor sea-keeping ability of a long ironclad.[11]

Reed was later to give the credit for the introduction of moderate dimensions to Admiral Robinson.[12] Since Reed's ideas of ordnance and armor could not be carried out in a warship of the *Minotaur* class, he would thus have been most receptive to the Duke of Somerset's concepts of smaller, handier ironclads. In time the limitation of tonnage was to degenerate into an inflexible dogma, heartily supported by economizing politicians, and was to be the root cause of many of the unsatisfactory qualities of later ironclads. But in 1863 this concept seemed to represent à healthy reaction to the impractical mastodons of the first generation of ironclads. It should be noted that John Scott Russell defended the *Warrior*, which he had helped to design, by asserting that its length was solely the result of an original plan, suggested by Admirals Milne and Dundas, to enable the pioneer ironclad to steam six thousand miles for, among other duties, the blockade of ports "which shall be nameless." Russell never explained why the bunkerage was reduced to a level sufficient for only 1,420 to 2,100 miles radius, or, for that matter, why subsequent ships such as the still larger *Minotaur* class were fitted with even less coal capacity.[13]

Reed's first ships, designed before he was appointed as chief constructor, were three wooden sloops, converted on the stocks into lightweight ironclads. They are significant as the first representation of Reed concepts of concentration of armament and moderate tonnage. Also for the first time, the main guns could be shifted to provide axial fire. This arrangement appeared to be of vast significance as the concept of ramming warfare gathered strength. A powerful part of the ironclad's artillery could be utilized in laying down fire ahead while charging in to ram.[14] However, this early trio of converted wooden hulls was not destined to enhance Reed's reputation. The arrangements for shifting the guns for axial fire were efficient only on paper. In any sort of seaway the operation would have been impossible. The dimensions were also too cramped to make an efficient fighting ship. Reed was no seaman, and in details of his designs he sometimes displayed a preference for theory over nautical experience.[15]

In order to use up the vast stacks of timber that had been purchased as much as twenty years previously, Reed designed, from the keel up, three other wooden warships. They are chiefly of interest as the farewell to wooden shipbuilding for war. His designs were not completely retrograde steps, however, for the *Lord Warden* had eight- and nine-inch guns, and she and her sister ship, the *Lord Clyde*, were given an inch-thicker armor plating than Reed's first three ships. The third wooden-hulled ironclad, the *Pallas*, carried compound engines. Of these three, only the *Lord Warden* can be considered a success, for the *Lord Clyde* early fell victim to a fungus rot and lingered *in extremis* for a mere ten years. The *Pallas* was too small to develop her potentialities in either speed or armament. But then, Reed had designed her primarily as a ramming vessel, not as an ocean cruiser.[16]

The first ship that Reed built while he was chief constructor was a far more successful venture. With it he stamped his pattern of naval architecture upon the ships of the Royal Navy for over two decades. Reed himself compared his new warship, the *Bellerophon,* launched in 1865, with the *Achilles*, generally considered the best of the old type of long ironclads. According to him, the *Bellerophon* was far more handy and could carry heavier armor and a more powerful armament on a hull 1,270 tons lighter and

H.M.S. *Lord Warden*. Typical timber-built ironclad of the 1860s.
OFFICIAL U.S. NAVY PHOTOGRAPH.

£106,000 cheaper.[17] However, an increase of about 800
indicated horsepower was necessary to drive the *Bellerophon's* stubby hull at a somewhat slower speed than the
Achilles.

Reed's method of construction in the *Bellerophon* was
unique. William Fairbairn, himself a pioneer in iron shipbuilding, called the *Bellerophon* "the first ship built upon
what we could consider sound principles."[18] This new system
of construction was termed the *bracket-frame* method, in
which the longitudinal girders were deepened and the trans-
verse members replaced by bracket-frames plated top and
bottom, thus forming a double bottom along the ship's
entire length. Reed claimed that the new system of hull
construction would save weight, simplify workmanship, and
add to the strength and safety of the ship.[19] That Reed's
successors agreed with him in the main is seen in the fact

that the system has been retained to the present day in the form of the cellular double bottom. By 1880 the method was so universal that a member of the Council of the Institution of Naval Architects could call it "almost the stereotyped system of construction for the bottom of iron-clad ships all over the world."[20] Reed was also alive to the new torpedo menace from under the seas, and in the *Bellerophon* he introduced the double bottom as much for defense as for structural strength.

H.M.S. *Bellerophon*. First application of E. J. Reed's design principles to a first-class ironclad. OFFICIAL U.S. NAVY PHOTOGRAPH.

But Reed's main pride in his new ship lay in her maneuverability. Increased engine power, reduced length, and the newly introduced balanced rudder combined to make the *Bellerophon* a powerful ram. After a slow beginning, the new chief constructor was rapidly establishing his reputation. The first lord of the Admiralty, favorably impressed with Reed's work, wrote to Lord Palmerston (who still fidgeted over the state of Britain's naval defense) that the *Bellerophon* would serve as a model for private yards in England that were working on foreign contracts for iron-clads.[21]

The increase in the thickness and extent of armor, upon which Reed always insisted, compelled a change in the design of the extremities of ironclads. A heavy load of armor plate on the fine lines of the *Warrior* or *Minotaur* would cause these ships to pitch heavily, burrowing their bows in heavy seas and rendering bow gunnery and ramming impossible. Reed combined bluffer extremities with a large ram bow. For increased maneuverability, he designed his warships so that they were more deeply immersed at the stern rather than riding on an even keel. Such construction served to give a better "bite" to the large single screw that he pre-ferred and to cause the ship to answer her helm easily.[22]

Reed's ideas were debated in the reports of the Channel Fleet trials in 1867 and 1868. Although Rear Admiral Warden, Commander of the Channel Fleet, had lauded the *Achilles* as "the finest ironclad ship that has ever been built," Admiral Robinson pointed out that ships of the *Achilles* pattern were superior to the Reed-built ironclads in speed only; in armor, armament, and handiness, they would remain inferior. The Second in Command of the Channel Fleet, Admiral Yelverton, admitted that for all its qualities the vaunted *Achilles* "would have to go out of action to turn around"—a crippling disability in the age of the ram. Robinson, as a firm supporter of Reed, discounted Admiral Warden's opinion of the *Achilles*, and concluded: "I can see no encouragement whatever in these reports to return to the construction of unhandy, long, and compara-tively slightly-armoured ships; on the contrary, these reports of Admiral Warden, in so far as they go, thoroughly con-firm the propriety of the changes that have been made in the forms of ships recently constructed—less length and

H.M.S. *Bellerophon*. Section showing bracket-frame construction, armor belt, and backing. T. Brassey, *The British Navy*.

greater fighting-power, combined with handiness having been secured to them." [23]

The Channel Fleet trials of the following year reinforced Reed's position. Admiral Warden now praised the power of the *Bellerophon* and her ordnance, handiness, and protection, while deprecating her lack of axial fire and upper-deck armament, and what he considered her overly compact arrangement of guns. His praise of the *Achilles* was more muted. Rear Adm. A. P. Ryder expounded on the virtues of the *Bellerophon's* ramming and general fighting ability. He concluded that the *Achilles* and the *Minotaur* could be considered first-class warships only if guns and armor had not increased in size and thickness. It is not surprising that Reed asserted to the Admiralty: "I know of no desire on the part of anyone to return to the dimensions and the proportions of the ships that preceded the *Bellerophon*." [24]

Reed could well be confident of Admiralty support, for he enjoyed the encouragement and active cooperation of the controller of the navy, the Admiralty official responsible for the entire materiel of the navy. Admiral Robinson must be given full credit for guiding the Royal Navy through a time of unprecedented change, an experience perhaps the more trying in that it came in time of peace, when funds for the reequipment of the fleet had to come from often unsympathetic governments. [25] Nathaniel Barnaby, Reed's successor, generously remarked before the Royal United Service Institution that Robinson's office at the Admiralty from 1862 until 1871 "has been marked by an amount of success in novel and grand enterprises in naval construction which is without parallel in our history." [26] In turn, Barnaby's successor, the brilliant William White, credited Admiral Robinson with regaining for England the lead in ironclad construction, which had for a time seemed in doubt. [27] It is difficult to evaluate the controller's contributions a century afterward, to see where his work ended and Reed's began. Reed's was an egotistical personality, while Robinson's seems to have been just the opposite. The chief constructor wielded a prolific pen while the controller published only a few pamphlets and letters. But the important fact is the partnership between the two, the harmony that permitted Reed to design the new ironclads needed to cope with the growth of guns and armor, confident that he would have the backing of most of the Admiralty. Of this partnership Robinson testified before the Committee on Designs: "I do not think I have once differed from Mr. Reed in any conclusion he had formed advisedly."[28] When Reed was forced from office by his disagreements with the first lord at that time, Hugh Childers, Robinson termed the resignation almost a "national calamity."[29] And while in office, Robinson endeavored to give the chief constructor a free hand with his designs.[30] The full Board of Admiralty seemed to share Robinson's opinion of Reed, expressing their appreciation that he had "enabled the Admiralty to greatly increase the offensive and defensive powers of ironclad frigates,[31] while diminishing their size and cost compared with the earlier vessels."[32]

Reed certainly had need of such a secure base, for immediately upon his appointment in July 1863 he attracted opposition, first from the devotees and builders of the older elongated ironclads and soon afterward from partisans of Captain Coles and his turret system. In fact, violent opposition dogged Reed's career from its beginning. Eventually it drove him from office under a cloud of recrimination and held him at least partially responsible for the most ghastly naval disaster of the nineteenth century. When he first came to office, a member of Parliament demanded the reason for the preference given at the expense of the incumbent Admiralty constructors to "one who had never built a ship." Reed rashly excoriated his denigrator, was promptly called to the Bar of the House of Commons on a breach of privilege, and was forced to make a complete apology.[33]

Perhaps Reed's high opinion of his services or his florid insistence upon the primacy of science had much to do with the venom of his opponents. But even when allowance is made for vested interests, partisanship of rival designs and designers, and Reed's own fiery personality, the reason for the continuing, intense denigration that he had to endure throughout his career remains elusive. The mere announcement that he was to succeed Isacc Watts as chief constructor was enough to drive one service periodical to violent polemic: "Anything, we repeat, more extraordinary, is not recorded in the history of modern times." [34] Because of Reed's influence at the Admiralty, Richard Cobden publicly doubted his impartiality in considering other designs, particularly those pertaining to turret ships. [35] Sir John Pakington denounced the removal of Watts and his subordinates in order to make room for the youthful new chief constructor and described one of Reed's earliest converted ironclads as "built in some respects on such erroneous principles," and another as "not fit to be sent to sea." [36] Scott Russell decried the heterogeneity of the ironclad fleet designed "as chance, party or personal predilection, or whim happen to gain the ascendancy in our Board of Admiralty." [37] From less exalted sources the abuse of Reed barely remained on the right side of the libel laws. The *Naval and Military Gazette* wondered if the ideas of other more original inventors were "sweated" for Reed's benefit. [38] The *Times* and *Globe* dilated on his official power and salary and compared these with the cool reception afforded Captain Coles and his turret ships. The *London Review* simply described Reed's appointment as "the act of a madman." [39]

Some of the opposition to Reed can be ascribed to a reluctance to accept change. Russell's strictures seemed to fall into this category; the most he could offer in place of Reed's ships was "a faster, larger, stronger *Warrior*" with a battery composed of many large caliber guns, only a few rifled, arranged in the traditional broadside fashion. [40] But soon the turret controversy eclipsed all previous opposition to Reed (cf. chap. 7). Many advocates of the turret were genuine friends and collaborators with Capt. Cowper Coles, its chief protagonist in Britain. Others simply found his invention a useful stick with which to beat the Admiralty.

Reed's replies reveal growing exasperation as the attacks on him and his work mounted over the years. But they never reached the depths of vituperation and invective that his opponents plumbed. During his first year in office, Reed pleaded for cooperation in "the great and anxious work," rather than for agitation "against official persons in the interests of novel, untried, and doubtful schemes."[41] Two years later he complained of those who denounced him for "not doing what they themselves could not do," and in 1868, goaded into a fury by the attacks of the *Standard*, he inveighed against "cowardly scribbling in newspapers," intimating that they flowed from the pens of only two flag officers, presumably Coles and his confidant, Captain Sherard Osborne. Reed's temper was undoubtedly not improved by the teasing he had to endure from *Punch* and *Judy* during these years.[42]

In summary, it may be asserted that these controversies did little to further naval architecture; they merely compounded the confusion that existed concerning the proper forms of the new ironclads. It is not surprising that the *United Service Gazette* could wistfully wonder if it would not be possible to "have the best points of every individual designer combined in one good design, forming the model man-of-war, on which all men-of-war should afterwards be constructed."[43] To balance this picture, the *Times* was relatively favorable to Reed for his first few years in office, while the *Army and Navy Gazette* and *Colburn's United Service Magazine* selectively supported Reed throughout.

With the hindsight of a century it seems apparent that Reed's designs were indeed a brilliant answer to the problems of an ever-changing technology. He may be justly criticized for retaining his box-battery system after the advantages of the turret ship were obvious; but his final design as chief constructor, H.M.S. *Devastation*, was a turreted, mastless, seagoing ironclad, the forerunner of the modern battleship.

II

The new technology of iron shipbuilding demanded far more sophisticated methods of design and construction than the traditional rule-of-thumb system that had served the Royal Navy so badly in the past. The metallurgist and laboratory would have to replace the shipwright and adze. A new science to move familiarly among such abstruse subjects as stability, strains of ships, and hull resistance, was required. Not only were the ironclads unique, but also the ordnance, armor, and fittings that determined in large measure an ironclad's final design. It seems nothing less than astounding that two schools of naval architecture that had been founded prior to 1860 to deal with the improvements in warships that were even then evident had been liquidated.[44] Throughout the period of the introduction of the ironclad there was no school of naval architecture in Britain. Because of such official antiscientific bias, aspiring naval designers were compelled to go to the palatial École Polytechnique in France for their scientific education.[45] In Britain, a dockyard apprenticeship was deemed sufficient to produce a skilled shipbuilder. The motto for both naval and private marine architects might well have been *experientia docet.*

The lasting break with this unsatisfactory situation came when a private organization, the Institution of Naval Architects, was organized in 1860 to fill the obvious gap in naval architecture. This magnificant institution, whose *Transactions* form the best single guide to the progress of naval and mercantile design, flourishes to the present day. The mere naming of the institution's founders—John Scott Russell, E. J. Reed, Dr. Joseph Wooley, and Nathaniel Barnaby—will suffice to demonstrate the firm foundation on which it was based. From the first the institution prospered, and a perusal of the authors of the papers printed in the *Transactions* shows that most of the prominent shipbuilders and naval officers of the time participated in its affairs.[46]

It was only fitting that so successful an organization should take the lead in agitating for the reestablishment of a school of naval architecture. Scott Russell in 1863 presented a paper at the institution's fourth annual meeting in which he spoke startlingly of the "mutilated profession" of naval architecture in Britain, with its "holding up in sight to the British public the stump of its right arm" cut off by official myopia.[47] Both he and John Laird, vice president of the institution and founder of Messrs. Laird, one of the foremost iron shipbuilders in Britain, had had to send their sons to France for scientific training. Russell's paper seems to have forced the issue, for the president of the Institution, Sir John Pakington, First Lord of the Admiralty at the time of the laying down of H.M.S. *Warrior*, spoke in favor of the idea in Parliament and privately brought pressure to bear upon the current first lord, the Duke of Somerset.[48] The Admiralty responded generously and by the following year, 1864, had established a School of Naval Architecture at South Kensington. The unnautical site was chosen in order to take advantage of London's scientific talent and to attract scholars and support from the private shipbuilding firms, which would be reluctant to cooperate with a school "too much under the shade of the Admiralty," which would be the case if the school was located in a dockyard. In general terms the Admiralty's policy was to offer "a more advanced and liberal education than the present dockyard schools are capable of furnishing."[49]

Naturally a concept so at variance with the traditional mode of producing shipwrights (if not naval architects) was derided. Captain Jervois in Parliament denounced the school as "mere rubbish" and insisted that "the pupils did not want mere theoretical knowledge." The Admiralty's Parliamentary secretary patiently explained in reply that half of the students' year would be spent in Royal dockyards absorbing practical knowledge of shipbuilding.[50] Most of the critics of the new school concentrated their criticism (with the exception of those who boggled at the cost of

£4,300 per annum) upon the issue of the location of the school. The value of anything as abstract as the mathematics and science taught at Kensington was difficult to prove to old sailors. The Service periodicals passed over the school's establishment with what could be termed contemptuous silence, the exception being the vituperative *Naval and Military Gazette*, which denounced the school as a piece of jobbery, extolled the private shipbuilders' rule-of-thumb successes, and delivered itself of the opinion that a worthwhile shipbuilder was the result of "pure ingenuity, seamanship, and the grounding in the first principles of shipbuilding."[51] Even those quite familiar with the shipbuilding industry found it difficult sometimes to cast off the old ways. One authority went so far as to assert that "what shipbuilding really stands in need of is complete and perpetual emancipation from mathematics."[52] The Admiralty and the Institution of Naval Architects must certainly be given full credit for breaking so clearly with tradition in the new school. It is probable that the pressure of E. J. Reed upon the Admiralty and his influence with the controller and with the first lord also helped the Board of Admiralty to found such a school for the third time.[53]

The school, later absorbed by the Royal Naval College, Greenwich, flourished in the ensuing years. Lectures by Scott Russell, Sir George Airy (the Astronomer Royal), and E. J. Reed were some of the more outstanding academic events of the school's earlier years.[54]

The only cause for regret was to be found in the reluctance of the young men from private yards to enter the school. Thirteen years after its founding not a single private student had come from the first-class shipbuilding firms, although two or three builders had sent their sons. All private students, as opposed to those who came from the Admiralty dockyards, were sadly deficient in mathematics, a comment on the education generally available at the time. The reason given for this failure to interest private shipbuilders in the school was that they still retained an invincible aversion to the theory of naval architecture, preferring their apprentice system, trusting to practice, night classes, and luck to instill the art into their young men. Since many of the ironclads of the Royal Navy of this period were constructed in private yards, it is instructive to see how one contemporary authority described the lack of scientific method prevailing there.

> A lad goes into the office, copies drawings, makes some of the more simple yet indispensible [sic] calculations, and generally acquires a knowledge of his profession as best he can—the more observant and industrious he is, the more versed he becomes in his art. But direct instruction in the higher branches of the subject is rarely accorded him. . . . Hence, when called upon to design a vessel, he must rely upon some good type of the ship required, and make his own as like it as circumstances will allow. This, in general, is as good a plan as can be pursued, but when some novel design is required—and the exigencies of modern commerce and progress will make this more common than formerly—he cannot fall back on scientific theories to fortify the conclusions which his experience may enable him to arrive at, and however firm may be his *belief* that he has compassed his end, yet he lacks more certain modes of testing it.

The actual building of the ship was often no more precise than its planning. In some cases a half-model would be used, altered here and there in the light of practical experience. No drawings would be made, no calculations as to tonnage, displacement, or draught of water. Sections would be taken from the model, rather than laid off in a mold loft, and then measured to scale for the proposed vessel.[55] Not surprisingly, the *Transactions* of the Institution of Naval Architects were regularly interspersed with expressions of regret over the loss of a merchant vessel, and influential writers such as Reed, William Fairbairn, and Robert Murray inveighed strongly against ships poorly built or poorly designed, or both. In many cases successful merchant ships were the result of chance, of the duplication of a good ship, or of the elimination of the more obvious faults from a bad one.[56] William White noted that as late as the early

1880s he was unsuccessful in his quest for theoretical information from private yards for his famous *Manual of Naval Architecture* because they had none to give him.[57]

The conclusion is inescapable that much of the progress in naval and commercial shipbuilding at this time was the result of the efforts of the Institution of Naval Architects. It attracted the most progressive private builders, such as Scott Russell, Napier, Scott, Denny, Rennie, Maudslay, and Penn, as well as Lloyd's chief officers. Four chief constructors—Isaac Watts, Reed, Barnaby, and White—were among its earliest members, as well as naval officers of the caliber of Admirals Milne and Robinson. The institution was not a school for training naval architects and shipbuilders, but it had the foresight to persuade the Admiralty to make a final, and this time a successful, attempt to establish such a school. And here its efforts were lasting and profound, bearing fruit in the latter part of the century. Not only was White a graduate of the school, but so also were the heads of the shipbuilding and design departments of such firms as Laird's, Brown's, Fairfield's, and Elswick. The chief constructors of the United States and Danish navies were also graduates. Without the School of Naval Architecture and the Institution of Naval Architects, it is difficult to visualize British shipbuilding and design, both in the Admiralty dockyards and in the private yards, as retaining any lead in the design and construction of iron ships for commerce and war. As William White remarked in his presidential address before the Institution of Civil Engineers in 1903: "The supply of men competent to do the new work and thoroughly trained as naval architects, has been mainly due up to the present time to the enlightened policy of the Admiralty in establishing and maintaining Schools of Naval Architecture."[58] He could have added that this "enlightened policy," so different from the previous antipathy to scientific education, was the result of agitation by the distinguished founders of the Institution of Naval Architects.

III

What processes were followed in the drawing-up and acceptance of a warship's design in the 1860s? There is agreement among contemporary authorities that the initiative for a new warship would usually come from the Board of Admiralty rather than from the constructor's or controller's departments. This situation was fitting, for the first lord was a political official, a member of the Cabinet, and thus privy to discussions of national policy. He would be expected to forward vigorously the claims of the navy upon the nation's purse, but to implement loyally and just as vigorously Cabinet decisions that might well have determined upon half a loaf in place of the first lord's requested whole. Because no Cabinet minutes were taken at this time, policy discussions will never be fully known. The political leaders of both parties were obviously aware of the rapid changes in naval architecture taking place from month to month. Despite such awareness, however, or perhaps because of it, they never seemed to have proposed a systematic scheme of shipbuilding to keep Britain ahead of her foreign rivals and to defend her commerce and honor. Instead, they apparently relied on a simple policy of out-building the French or the Americans, of furious activity when attachés or the popular press and Parliament declared England's lead diminished or nonexistent, and of quiescence when that superiority seemed safe. Neither the Palmerston, Derby, Disraeli, nor Gladstone regimes appear to have had any definite shipbuilding program, and the last two prime ministers of this period treated the navy as an expensive nuisance. Disraeli, who might be considered to have been slightly more sympathetic to the needs of the navy, drew up the navy estimates for 1868 without even consulting First Lord of the Admiralty H. L. Corry. Realizing that any attempt to interfere with these *in camera* proceedings would be "perfectly idle," Corry concluded: "I cannot, therefore, pretend to accept your ultimatum either cordially or cheerfully, but I

frankly accept the situation, and you need be under no
apprehension of the scenes of last year being renewed by
me."[59] The chancellor of the Exchequer apparently wielded
authority almost equal to that of the Prime Minister in these
matters. In 1875 the first lord's estimates calling for six
cruisers were entirely deleted by the chancellor, who neither
informed nor consulted the Board of Admiralty.[60] Sir John
Briggs, Chief Clerk of the Admiralty for forty-four years,
wrote that during his entire term of office only Sir James
Graham had had any Cabinet support as first lord.[61]

The first lord, who was always a civilian, would know
from Cabinet discussions and decisions just how much of the
service estimates, approved by Parliament, he could spend
upon new ironclads, and often what type of warships the
Cabinet would favor. With these guides before him the
first lord would then call together his board, composed
mostly of naval officers. The full Board of Admiralty would
decide on the type of ship, her size, speed, armament,
armorplating, rig, and other general particulars. Then the
chief constructor, who like the controller, was not a member
of the board at this time, would attempt to fulfill the conditions laid down by his superiors. This was a difficult task,
for the board, following the lead of the Cabinet, would
often attempt to pack as much offensive and defensive power
as possible into the minimum displacement, in the interests
of economy. The chief constructor worked in conference
with the engineer in chief and the director-general of naval
ordnance, although the War Office controlled the actual
design and construction of naval ordnance. A preliminary
sketch would be submitted to the board to be either approved or modified. The chief constructor and his assistants
then completed the design, after which it was given to the
board secretary, who circulated it individually among board
members prior to its consideration at the regular board
meeting. It would then be brought into the first lord's room
for consideration. All of the naval lords, the civilian Parliamentary secretary, and very often the controller would

discuss the designs before them. The plans could be handed back so that new suggestions might be incorporated. The constructor would then return them to the board along with a model of the proposed warship.

When the plans received the board's stamp, they could not be altered except by the concurrence of the whole board. Drawings, specifications, and a bill of particulars were sent to the dockyard and "laid-off" in a mold loft; working drawings were made, subject to the approval of the controller, the director of naval ordnance, and possibly the first sea lord. Costs, previously worked out by the constructor, were replaced by a more detailed statement prepared by the officers of the yard. At the same time contracts had been arranged at the Admiralty for the collecting of materials and equipment at the site.[62]

This system of procurement of ironclads was quite flexible, depending on the administrative methods of the incumbent first lord. The most abrupt break with the routine established by Sir James Graham in 1832 came with the administration of Hugh C. E. Childers. Board meetings became almost extinct and were replaced by personal, private consultation with the first lord in his office. Some responsible officers attributed the *Captain* disaster to this lack of board consultation and, upon the resignation of Childers, the old system was revived.

The arrangements were somewhat different in the case of warships built by contract in private yards. The drawing up of plans was the same as with dockyard-built ships. After the plans had been approved, the constructor would suggest to the controller what firms should be invited to tender. These companies would have had their works inspected by officers from the constructor's department, which had also scrutinized the tenders submitted. Unlike dockyard arrangements, the private yard reached a full agreement on the entire cost of the projected warship before a rivet was clinched. Resident overseers from the constructor's department supervised workmanship, materials, and design, and were also stationed at the chain and armor works involved. This department finally determined when the warship was ready for service.

The arrangement whereby the chief constructor would recommend only certain firms to submit tenders was early denounced by John Laird. Laird also made a plausible case for permitting private builders to submit their own designs for ironclads.[63] It is ironical that the first and only British capital ship to be planned by a private firm, Messrs. Laird, was H.M.S. *Captain.* Admiral Robinson defended the practice of selected tenders on Admiralty designs by pointing out that the lowest bid did not always ensure the best warship, that experience and building time must also be given weight.[64]

The Admiralty, as well as the chief constructor, endured savage criticism during this time of rapid change. Wearily the Duke of Somerset remarked (anonymously) that "the human memory cannot recall the period when the department of the Admiralty was not the subject of accusation and complaint."[65] His predecessor, Sir John Pakington, asserted that "there seems to be a feeling that any man who wants to write a pamphlet or make a speech cannot do better than attack the Admiralty."[66] For example, the *Naval and Military Gazette* denounced with gusto the Admiralty's refusal to buy an ironclad designed by E. J. Reed for the Prussian Government; "Such drivelling, bungling incompetency, observable not only in this but in numerous other matters, is a positive disgrace and injury to the country; and how the country has patience to stand it so long is to us a marvel."[67] The *United Service Gazette* termed the Admiralty "as remarkable for incapacity as for intrigue."[68]

The criticisms and complaints were similar to those leveled against the chief constructor: want of initiative, conservatism, a stifling of other people's genius, and incompetence. By its very structure the Admiralty invited attack, for it alone among the large departments of state was controlled by an executive subject to the fortunes of political war.[69] Between 1834 and 1871 the average tenure of a Board of Admiralty was a fraction over three years. Even Sir John Pakington, while first lord, termed the Admiralty administration a "clumsy machine." [70] After leaving office, Hugh Childers admitted that "The cry for Admiralty reform was at the time universal in the country." [71] The important point, however, is that the lords of the Admiralty and the controller's and constructor's departments were compelled to be very sensitive to a public opinion gravely suspicious of official ability and integrity. This situation necessarily colored major decisions on ironclad designs. Service and general papers bear out the fact that a majority of literate opinion seemed to be against the Admiralty, no matter which party happened to be in office.[72] Not only would a projected ironclad need to master its foreign counterpart and the natural elements; it would also have to run the gauntlet of a public opinion always alert to suspect a "job" in any new design.

IV

Whatever the quality of the ironclads designed by Reed and his predecessors, the quantity of British armored ships did not permit any euphoria as to Britannia's ruling of the waves with a rod of iron. The building program of the French was always uncomfortably close upon the heels of the Admiralty, and if the American and Russian fleets were added to France's (a possibility dwelt upon by the more lurid publicists), the balance of sea power would tell against Britain. An obvious expedient to restore that threatened balance would be the conversion of wooden ships-of-the-line into ironclads. These plans represented an obvious dead end in naval architecture, and some of the converted ironclads were obsolete before they took to the water. But their procurement helps to shed some light on the naval policy of the time.

At the beginning of Reed's Admiralty career, the question of wood versus iron for the construction of capital ships had still not been completely resolved. Lord Clarence Paget, Admiralty spokesman in the Commons, asserted: "The fact is, that the question of wood *vs.* iron is one which may argued any way (a laugh)." [73] Wooden ironclads possessed several advantages: their construction could be more easily modified, advanced, or delayed on the stocks than that of iron-built ironclads. Since the French built most of their armored fleet on wooden hulls, these converted ironclads would not be at a disadvantage. [74] Timber hulls also would not foul as did iron hulls, which, if not scraped regularly, suffered from bottoms that resembled a "lawyer's wig." The only successful check to marine fouling in iron ships was provided by the "composite" method, in which a layer of wood separated the iron of the hull from the copper sheathing. But copper was expensive, and only a few ships were so protected. [75] The Admiralty was besieged with inventions (one from Captain Coles) for checking the ravages of fouling but "all were alike useless" during this period and recourse had to be made to docking, scraping, and divers. [76] So serious was the situation in the early 1860s that Lord Clarence Paget was driven to assert that wooden construction would almost be preferable. [77]

The major reason for the conversion of wooden warships into ironclads, however, was the simple one of economy. Here was an inexpensive method of keeping Britain's lead in armored ships. Public pressure had much to do with this, as in so many other Admiralty decisions. Palmerston, while now agreeing that iron was obviously the superior material for warship construction, admitted that "great pressure was exerted upon the government to get an iron-cased fleet equal in number and power to the iron-cased fleets of other powers." [78] To create such a fleet in iron would have compelled a substantial rise in the estimates. But the dockyards at this time still groaned under the weight of timber that had been accumulated for the grand line-of-battleship program of the late 1850s, and the wooden-hulled ironclads were a convenient method of using up the stocks. Thus, the yards were put to work converting the line-of-battleships that had been laid down only a few years previously at Palmerston's insistence to match the French Emperor's ironclad building program.[79] In 1865 Lord Clarence had to acknowledge that "we were positively driven by the House of Commons, and I will admit, by public opinion, not to confine ourselves to iron armored ships, but to convert what wooden ships we had in the dockyards into armored-plated vessels." [80]

One of the strongest cases for wooden ironclad building was advanced by Admiral Robinson. Considering the unstinting support that the controller gave to the progressive Reed, Robinson's denunciation of iron hulls in 1863 is difficult to understand. He agreed that iron hulls could be of unlimited dimensions, but brushed aside this argument by assessing that locally in the hull the wooden ship was the stronger. Iron hulls made possible watertight doors and compartmentation, but Admiral Robinson turned this argument on its head, insisting that these "complicated arrangements" were unnecessary in a wooden ship. He speculated that progress in ordnance and warfare in general might render the iron ship's admittedly superior longevity a liability, thus reversing another of the arguments in favor of iron ships. Robinson further dilated on the iniquities of the private iron shipbuilders, denouncing their increased costs, slovenly workmanship, and tardiness in delivering completed warships. He apparently made no allowance for the obvious fact that these builders were working in a new and difficult medium, that few of them could make a profit on their early ironclads, and that at least one of their number fell into bankruptcy through an ironclad contract. Robinson concluded his strangely reactionary views by recommending that "it seems decidedly preferable, *at the present time*, to build these ships in our dockyards of wood, rather than in private yards and of iron." [81] His prediction as to the great progress of ordnance was certainly fulfilled, but it is difficult to imagine just what type of ship he had in mind to bear the new guns and to resist their effects. The controller must have changed his opinion soon after this denunciation of iron ships was issued, for he later consistently supported Reed's design policy, which was based upon the bracket-frame method of iron hull construction and which viewed wooden ironclads as a mere temporary expedient.[82] This latter opinion seemed to be general in the Service as well as in Whitehall.[83]

Opposition to this method of retaining parity with France was inevitable, both from the Admiralty's critics in Parliament and from those who looked upon wooden warship building of any kind as a distinctly retrograde step. Sir John Pakington, who acted as the conservative spokesman on naval matters, pointed out that the Whigs had explained away the apparent French equality in armored ships by contending that the British ironclads were of much higher quality, being constructed of iron. Where would this qualitative margin be if the Admiralty also opted for wooden construction? Later Pakington condemned all the wooden ironclads as unfit for the sea, as well as being firetraps.[84] John Laird personally remonstrated with Disraeli against the "deplorable administration" of the Admiralty in cobbling up wooden ships into ironclads.[85] The fact that Laird's was one of the foremost constructors of iron ships reveals that John Laird was as assiduous a businessman as patriot. The Duke of Somerset also objected to the pressure on him to convert completed wooden line-of-battleships into ironclads, but for somewhat different reasons from those of Pakington or Laird. Primarily he feared France's wooden fleet, which could cause mischief in commerce raiding and in attacks on colonial stations. He also felt that the timber-hulled ironclads were useful only for coastal work, probably because of the working between wood and armor plate. Finally, cutting down and adding armor to a wooden warship added enormously to its costs, unmitigated by any corresponding reduction in material or men required.[86]

The timber-hulled ironclads, contrary to the Duke of

Somerset's opinion, enabled the Royal Navy to station ironclads around the world, reserving the first class iron-hulled warships for home waters. They served a temporary purpose; not one of them, either those converted from wooden line-of-battleships or those built expressly as wooden warships from the keel up, survived the decade of the 1860s on the active list, and all were scrapped by the end of the 1880s.

V

During the decade of the 1860s, the Admiralty con-structor's department and the controller were compelled to deal with the problem of warship design at a time of change unparalleled in rapidity and complexity. The steady growth of ordnance, the increased demands for overseas colonial protection and for coast defense at home, the insistence of the turret party on "fair play," and changing tactical con-cepts, complicated the task of Reed and Robinson almost beyond endurance.[87] The record is clear that they both con-scientiously attempted to adopt new ideas and concepts to warships that would be sound in construction and thoroughly seaworthy. This policy was one of steady development, bringing together current inventions and ideas to improve existing ironclad models. As Robinson declared in 1866: "It is a wise and judicious compromise and balance of those qualities (each by itself of value) which make the best ship of war,"[88] or as Reed asserted: "My own opinion is, that the only wise policy for the country at a period of change, like the present, is to be always sure—not that you are doing something like what you did last year, but that you are doing something superior to what your neighbour is doing."[89] The results of such a policy are apparent in the ironclads of the time, from the *Bellerophon* to the *Devas-tation*. Some of the progress was obvious enough: concen-tration of guns, improvement of armor, the development of axial fire, and the introduction of twin screws. Less visible was the steady improvement in engines that gradually enabled steam to become more practical and eventually to oust sail power. However, between Reed's earliest ironclads and his last (while in office), H.M.S. *Devastation*, there is more than just steady evolution and keeping ahead of the French. The *Devastation* represented a complete break with the past; it marks Reed as a designer of genius.

With Reed's philosophy of steady progress in design, his warships naturally revealed little similarity with each other. Thus he was vulnerable to the charge that he had created a "fleet of samples," or in the words of a pro-Coles journal, "an extraordinary series of experiments." [90] That warships constructed during a time of rapid technological change would be dissimilar to each other is obvious today, but in Reed's time it was often considered proof of bungling and lack of method. Reed replied to such criticism by asserting that the French fleet was even more individually varied in design (a debatable point); he insisted that a far greater danger was that naval architecture "tended to run in grooves, out of which it is most difficult to move it even in times of the greatest emergency." [91] Admiral Robinson's reply was more practical. He stated that, whatever their differences in structure, ironclads could maneuver and fight as a single unit if divided into certain classifications. First came the ironclads that represented the vanished line-of-battleships, then those intended for the duties of the old frigates or corvettes, and finally those devoted to coast defense and offense and to cruising—in fine weather—in the Channel. The first class comprised, in 1863, the great ironclads of the *Warrior* and *Minotaur* classes, the *Bellerophon*, and larger timber-hulled ironclads; the second class was composed of the smaller wooden ironclads designed by Reed; the third class was made up of the Coles type of turret ships, *Royal Sovereign* and *Prince Albert*, and the purchased "Laird rams," *Scorpion* and *Wivern*. According to Robinson, the ships within each class could maneuver together with little difficulty. The frigate and coastal classes could work together fairly efficiently, but the battleship class must stand alone. This group was handicapped severely by the great length of most of its component warships, which not only precluded their maneuvering with the frigate class, but also made it impossible for them to be dry-docked anywhere outside England. Robinson's system of classification compiled over a three-year period was drawn up specifically to refute the "fleet of samples" charge.[92]

Much of the energy of Reed and the controller in the later years of their official careers was directed to obtaining and perfecting what was known at the time as *end-on-fire* from an ironclad. Their reasons for such a policy are complex. Probably of first importance was the weight attached to such axial firing (parallel with the ship's keel) in time of battle. End-on-fire was intimately associated with the ram, and some naval tacticians asserted that a warship's bows, pierced for artillery, heavily armored, and equipped with an underwater snout was the *sine qua non* for victory. Even in naval battles fought without recourse to ramming, "the escape of many a chase and the history of many a disaster may be attributed to the absence of this *desideratum*." [93] But it was the drawing up of a memorandum on the subject by Captain Astley Cooper Key, captain of the gunnery school H.M.S. *Excellent*, that brought this question before the Admiralty, and it was to have far-reaching effects. Key followed the general tactical thinking of the time in assuming that future naval battles would consist of closely fought melees. There a ship had to have command of the whole horizon with its guns; no longer could the unprotected ends of ships designed to fight in line-ahead formation be permitted. For the new line-abreast, or the *peloton* arrangement, the bow would become the most important part of the warship. Key noted that gun ports had been fitted into the bows of British ironclads since the launching of the *Warrior*, but that this armament was strictly secondary. He proposed to reverse the armament of ironclads, giving them greater power ahead than on the broadside. These arguments carried the navy with them. Reed, who from the first provided for bow guns, greatly increased the forward fire of all his subsequent ironclads. The principle was, in fact, carried to the point of absurdity with such ships as the *Belleisle* and *Orion* (purchased during the war scare of 1877), which were completely lacking in broadside fire. But in a day when the ram reigned supreme, this seemed of little moment.[94]

H.M.S. *Hercules*. Typical Reed era, masted ironclad, with ram bow and provision for broadside and fore-and-aft fire. T. Brassey, *The British Navy*.

The acceptance of the principle of end-on-fire provided a new rationale for the opponents of seagoing turret ships. If turret ships were to be safe for ocean cruising, they must be fitted with at least a forecastle and possibly a poop, in order to give them increased buoyancy and to make them habitable. But such structures, along with masts, would block

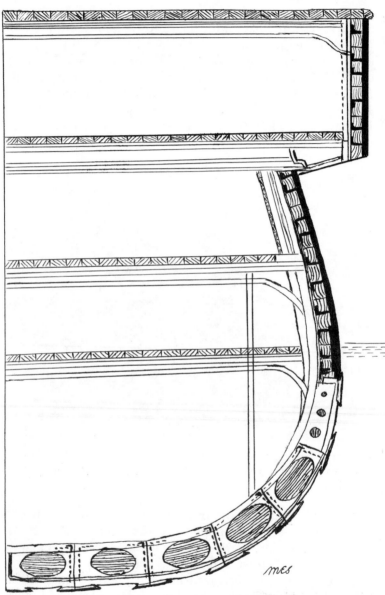

Section of *Audacious* class. Illustrates sponsoned box-battery, and arrangement for the securing of forward fire.

the end-on fire from the turrets. Reed carefully pointed out that in battle or in chase the turret ship would be compelled to yaw from fifteen to twenty degrees in order to bring a gun to bear on the enemy ahead. This would entail loss of speed, and loss of the enemy as well. The warship possessing strong ahead-fire, however, could proceed at full steam toward its quarry and, after disabling him with shot thrown from the bows, perhaps destroy him by ramming. Furthermore, a well designed box battery ironclad could fire three or perhaps even four, guns parallel to the keel, whereas a turret ship could bring only two to bear fifteen to twenty degrees away from the center line. Finally, the new mechanical gun carriages developed by Captain Scott ensured that the heaviest guns could be worked in the box-battery as easily as in a turret, and that eight or ten guns could be simultaneously engaged in a naval battle of the melee variety. If the clash developed into a ramming duel or a general chase, the heavy bow guns would come into use.[95] This concept of the value of end-on-fire helps to account for Reed's designs and provides some answer to those who found in his opposition to Coles's ideas proof of a dull antipathy to innovation.

Reed was able to incorporate the concept of end-on-fire into his subsequent warships by several expedients: guns mounted forward in the bows, or sponsoned from the hull, or mounted on tracks. However, only the last of his ships were equipped with twin screws, which greatly increased his ironclads' maneuverability. Reed objected to twin screws because they were a severe handicap for rigged warships. It was almost impossible to perfect a method of hoisting twin screws, which consequently acted as drags on a ship's progress under sail. But Reed's box-battery warships were not inferior to the only seagoing full-rigged turret ironclads ever built in England, the *Monarch* and *Captain*. In many ways they were superior. Until the turret ship could be divested of its masts, something that was almost completely out of Reed's hands, the box-battery ironclad, utilizing axial fire, rightly reigned supreme.

2

Foreign Competition

The introduction of the ironclad had leveled all major naval powers to a position of approximate equality. For with all her fleet of wooden walls swept away, Britain had to face a situation in which France, America, Russia, and other powers could inaugurate ironclad building programs that might leave no country in a position of dominance. This challenge by foreign powers—and it must be emphasized that France, and to some extent the United States, preceded Britain in building ironclad warships—was doubtless exaggerated by nervous Admiralty officials and by popular opinion. Britain in the mid-nineteenth century possessed the industrial capacity and momentum to outbuild the French and Americans with ease. Both of her closest rivals were distracted by military considerations that competed for funds with their navies, and both possessed as yet immature industrial and technological bases for their great programs of naval armaments. As a result, Britain was able not only to outbuild France and America, but also to design and construct ships that were individually superior.[1]

But this relatively favorable situation was not so evident at the time, and on paper America's horde of monitors, or France's numerous wooden ironclads, or even Russia's fleet looked formidable indeed, fatally so if any two of these powers were combined. With no well-thought-out strategic doctrines, and still hypnotized by the old bogey of invasion,

52

the Admiralty could often think of no better naval policy than one of outbuilding the foreigner.

The new ironclads were expensive, and slow in completion. Each one was considered a priceless asset, an individual guarantee of Britain's very survival in an uncertain and rapidly changing world of naval rivalry. This was a ship-for-ship rivalry. The two-power standard was an impossible goal until after America turned her energies inward to develop a continent and until the French painfully began to rebuild their army after the disasters of 1870–71. The situation was succinctly described by Sir Alexander Milne in a confidential minute to First Lord of the Admiralty H. L. Corry:

> Before the introduction of armour-clads, it was an accepted rule that we required, and we actually maintained, a navy not far short of double that of France in order to place ourselves on relative equality with her; but at present our armourclad navy is inferior to her; and it is impossible that this can be consistent with our national safety.[2]

I

Since the new armorclads were of such short range, and since the Americans and Russians concentrated upon coastal defense and offense, it was natural that France, which had begun the ironclad revolution in naval architecture, would loom as Britain's dread naval rival. Ever since the days when steam was supposed to have "bridged the Channel," nightmares of invasion haunted the more imaginative of Admiralty and government officials. Now that France possessed both steamships and armorclads in numbers and quality apparenty equal to Britain's fleet, the specter of revenge for Trafalgar and other defeats seemed ever more threatening. Admiral Robinson, from the beginning of his position as controller of the navy, frankly and understandably worried about French naval power. In 1862, according to Robinson, the balance of ironclad power was absolutely even—four French and four British ironclads "available for hostilities" and two ships on each side almost ready. But Robinson felt that the French would predominate, for their speed, artillery, armor, and homeogeneity were superior.[3] The following year the Duke of Somerset, First Lord of the Admiralty, indicated that ironclad supremacy over France was still a goal, not an accomplished reality.[4] Such doubts were not for public consumption, however, and Lord Clarence Paget declared to the Commons in February 1863 that the navy had never been in a better state than at the present. He presented estimates calling for a cut of £245,000 in shipbuilding and for the laying-down of no new ironclads.[5] Consistent reductions failed to dampen the economizing of the Cobdenites, who on naval matters seemed to put economy above considerations of efficiency and strength. W. E. Baxter, for example, not only deprecated the French threat but also insisted that Britain's wooden frigates, line-of-battleships, and merchant fleet would make up for any inferiority in time of war.[6] In fairness to Baxter, it must be remembered that at this particular time, February 1864, Britain seemed far more likely to become embroiled in a war with the Federal American states over the *Trent* and *Alabama* affairs than with France, merely because the Emperor was building ironclads.

But Admiral Robinson was not particularly interested in the diplomatic situation. He saw his duty as one of making Britain the strongest naval power in the world. Robinson's fears cannot be dismissed as panic of the moment, for, as he wrote several years after his dismissal from office in 1871, "in 1864 the Navy of England was not superior to that of France for fighting purposes; and . . . it was inferior to a combination of any two powers of which France was one."[7] At the end of 1864 the Royal Navy possessed eleven completed ironclads, five less than the number originally hoped for by that date in April 1863.[8] The interminable delays occasioned by the unfamiliarity of private shipbuilders and dockyards with iron construction did little to improve Robinson's peace of mind. The *Agincourt*, estimated in 1865 to be completed by October of that year, was not, in fact, commissioned until December 1868. A similar delay retarded the *Valiant* and the *Northumberland*. The prime cause of delay was attributable either to the slow delivery of the new muzzle-loading ordnance or to the need for rapid changes in design to accommodate the ever-growing size and complexity of the gun. As a result, estimates made to Parliament of construction time for ironclad ships erred usually on the side of optimism, since the Admiralty was not anxious to publicize the arrears of its ironclad program.[9] The situation was not without its modern parallels. Despite the pioneering work of Reed, the opinion was quite common that Britain's navy of the time was also technologically backward. *Colburn's United Service Magazine*, a relatively friendly critic, excused Admiralty caution in applying new inventions by insisting that "we have not lost much by acting more cautiously" than France and America.[10]

The Royal Navy found it almost impossible, because of its lack of a naval intelligence department, to determine its needs and to mark its progress in relation to foreign naval powers. Even the attaché system was slighted. Unlike other great naval powers, the Admiralty did not appoint a naval attaché to each country that possessed a navy, but rather assigned one for all of Europe and one to the United States well after the Civil War.

The policy of secrecy favored by most of the Continental naval powers ensured that each attaché earned his pay. But the Royal Navy itself seemed oblivious to any need for naval security. Reed complained of the ease with which foreign naval officers and shipbuilders could visit British naval establishments.[11] At the same time, Reed and many private builders designed and constructed ironclads for nations, such as Prussia, which had naval ambitions. Some of these warships were superior to comparable British ships;

Sir William Armstrong freely shipped his guns overseas.

An example of the ad hoc "system" prevailing at the Admiralty is found in the memoirs of Lord Clarence Paget. The Admiralty, burning with curiosity about the French *Gloire*, the world's first seagoing ironclad, dispatched Paget, admiralty secretary, to see if he could learn anything about her. After hiring a shore boat at Toulon, Paget came alongside the ironclad without being seen, and mounted the side-steps. Having previously carefully measured his umbrella, he thus ascertained the height of gunports above the water-line before a French naval officer firmly removed him.[12] With such casual intelligence service, it is not surprising that the Admiralty seriously maintained that a program of sixty-three first-class and thirty-one second-class ironclads would be needed to meet France alone.[13]

Not only was the Admiralty unable to obtain a clear and complete description of foreign warship building, but it also had no systematic or definite program of its own. Apparently the only agreed-upon policy was one of a moderate but definite superiority to the French. Even this concept could be undercut, however, for the most modest building program could be reduced for reasons of economy. There seems to have been little concept on the part of the Admiralty of a two-power standard. For them, just keeping ahead of the French represented a worthy accomplishment. As Sir Frederick Grey explained in a pamphlet defending Whig naval policy of 1861–66: "The course pursued by the late Board of Admiralty has been to build those vessels only which were absolutely required to keep the Navy on an equality with other powers."[14]

There were a few calls for global naval superiority from the Commons, but the Parliamentary secretary's answer in 1864 was studiously vague. The Admiralty would build ironclads "in such numbers as would enable this country always to be in a proper position as regarded foreign powers."[15] Two unforeseen developments served to check any early moves for a two-power standard of European or global naval power. The most impressive was the sudden overwhelming of France by Prussia in 1870. The fleet of the Emperor appeared useless in staving off defeat, although it could be argued that the inability of the Prussians to mount any blockade whatsoever enabled the French to prolong the struggle by importing war supplies from Britain and America well after the disasters of Metz and Sedan. Britain's erstwhile rival, the United States, contrary to speculation, did not pounce upon Britain or Canada in a naval war immediately after Appomatox. With quiet delight the British Admiralty watched the United States dismantle its ironclad navy, selling, scrapping, and laying up its vaunted monitors, feared commerce raiders, and obsolete wooden cruisers. By the end of 1870 Lord Halifax could write to Gladstone: "I believe that we are more than equal to meet any force which can in any probable (I had almost said possible) circumstances be brought against us."[16] The Royal School of Naval Architecture's *Annual* pointed out in the following year that France had but one turret ship to defend her coasts, while the Americans possessed not one seagoing ironclad.[17] The Committee on Designs summarized this new feeling of well-being vis-à-vis foreign powers by recommending that an adequate naval construction policy for Britain would be one of building up to and beyond that of any other naval power. While the wording is ambiguous, it is obvious from the context of the Navy's building program that the committee had in mind the eclipsing of one rival power at a time, and did not consider the possibility of a hostile maritime coalition.[18]

II

It was inevitable that Britain should look upon the French Second Empire as its prime naval rival. France enjoyed a head start in the construction of seagoing ironclads dating from her 1858 program. Fear of invasion and the close proximity of France to Britain ensured that the French ironclad building scheme would be closely followed by the Admiralty, Parliament, and the press. The realization that England's superior industrial potential would enable her to surpass the French both in quantity and quality of ironclads was fairly general, and it restrained widespread panic. But the French challenge served as a standard for imitation and improvement. The second French ironclad class after the *Gloire* posed a truly formidable threat, at least on paper. No less than ten warships carrying 5.9-inch armor and five-ton guns were authorized. Comparable British broadside ironclads carried six-and-one-quarter-ton guns behind four-and-one-half-inch to five-and-one-half-inch armor plating, and were of five distinct styles. But the French program soon fell in arrears. Some ships of the *Provence* class of 1862 were not commissioned until 1867. These facts, early and accurately reported to the Duke of Somerset in May 1862, gave him confidence that the Royal Navy would be the equal of the French by the following year.[19] By the end of 1863 the Royal Navy led France by the thin margin of six to five. Yet Admiral Paris boasted that "we are so much in advance of other nations, that a marked superiority exists at present on our side." [20]

But in 1864, as the superior productive facilities of Britain's yards and her accumulated business and technological advantage took effect, the balance continued to tip appreciably in favor of England. The new iron armorclads were distinctly superior to those of the French, who still entertained doubts about the practicality of iron hulls. Admiral Robinson recognized this superiority, although he still worried about the British fleet's heterogeneity.[21] Among the new warships entering service in 1864 was the Coles-designed turret ship, *Royal Sovereign*, further evidence of technological headway. In the following year the distance between the two naval powers drew somewhat closer in the ironclad numbers race, with the British holding fourteen ironclads to the French Navy's eleven. Two of the new

British ironclads were the famous Laird coastal rams, purchased from the Birkenhead firm not only to maintain ironclad superiority in numbers but also to counter the growing French interest in coastal ironclads.[22]

That year some of the tension between the two countries was eased by an exchange of fleets. The usual fetes, banquets, and fireworks were provided at Portsmouth and Cherbourg, but officers of both navies also made good use of the opportunity to inspect rival ironclads. M Dupey de Lôme, Directeur du Matériel of the French fleet, and designer of the *Gloire*, carefully inspected the *Royal Sovereign*.[23]

By the end of 1866 Britain's lead had greatly improved. She had twenty-one ironclads to contend with France's fourteen. But this superiority did not satisfy the Admiralty. Robinson removed the two earliest ironclads, *Warrior* and *Black Prince*, from the British fleet, probably because of their lack of protection for the waterline and rudder. Yet the unarmored wooden ends of most of the French ironclads would have reduced the strength of the French fleet even more and would in fact have limited it to about four effective ironclads.[24] Robinson's attitude toward the *Warrior* class may be seen as a subtle form of special pleading; as a close associate and supporter of his chief constructor, he shared Reed's belief in the necessity for thick armor plating to cover as much of a warship's hull as possible. For these two men it was not beyond the bounds of possibility that ordnance devotees such as Sir William Armstrong could so influence the Admiralty that armor plate would be drastically reduced or eliminated altogether.

The Board of Admiralty shared Robinson's opinion that Britain was little better than the equal of France in ironclad power. Exasperated with the French program, which was subjecting them to almost intolerable pressure for corrective measures from the press and from Parliament, the board could not see any real need for France to have a great seagoing fleet of ironclads, terming such a project "a luxury and vanity" that that nation could ill afford. And this "luxury and vanity" would be able by the end of 1867, by virtue of its new heavy ordnance, to "meet our ships on fairly equal terms," according to one board official.[25]

The French challenge not only accelerated the building of Britain's ironclads, but it also exerted some influence upon their design. Alongside her seagoing fleet, a formidable squadron of coastal defensive and offensive warships was being laid down by the French. Aside from the earliest batteries designed for service in the Crimean War, and some weak armored gunboats, France's projected coastal fleet relied on the turret, either revolving or fixed, for its ordnance. Robinson feared that in case of war such vessels could either shield a French invading army or deny the coastline of France to England. Feeling that Britain was inferior in this mode of naval warfare, he urged that mastless, twin-screw coastal ironclads, armed with revolving Coles turrets, be built.[26] By the end of the decade, besides the *Royal Sovereign*, *Prince Albert*, and the Laird rams, the Admiralty had laid down seven coastal ironclads, mainly on the strength of Robinson's urging. Without his stimulus it is possible that Coles's invention would have been completely ignored in spite of public pressure.

Reed appeared to be scarcely influenced or impressed by the French ironclad fleet when he drew up plans for seagoing warships. For him the much-vaunted homogeneity of the French fleet "points to something like mediocrity."[27] This opinion marks one of the few occasions on which Reed disagreed with Robinson on a basic matter of naval design, for Robinson always envied France's unified fleet.

The Admiralty continued to worry privately about France's ironclad fleet. In January 1867 Lord Lennox, First Secretary to the Board, wrote to Disraeli: "We are as you know nearly equal with France in the number of our first-class ironclads. . . . ship for ship we are superior to the French."[28] Lennox correctly evaluated the qualitative superiority of the Royal Navy's ironclads, but he must have been served by faulty intelligence to ascribe any sort of numerical margin to the French. Two months after Lennox's letter to Disraeli, Admiral Milne echoed his first secretary's opinion by agreeing that the fleet was "somewhat inferior to [that of] France." But he went on to dismiss even the qualitative edge that England was supposed to hold securely. Provided that the ships compared were in similar categories, the actual number of ships must be the guide.[29] (In reality, the ratio between British and French ironclads at the end of 1866 gave the Royal Navy a seven-ship lead.)

Few exercises are more difficult than an evaluation of the comparative strength of the warships of different nations. But it would be instructive to see just how far the first sea lord's fears were justifiable. M Dupey de Lôme's *Belliqueuse* class can be compared with many of Reed's ironclads, for both emphasized moderate dimensions, belt-and-battery protection, and full sailing rigs.[30] The *Belliqueuse* was constructed on a wooden hull protected at the waterline and gun battery by six-inch armor, and armed with four seven-and-three-quarter and four five-ton guns in the main battery. The engines were of 1,227 indicated horsepower, driving the ship at a speed of 11.78 knots over the measured mile. This ironclad was in course of construction from 1865 to 1869.

Reed's *Bellerophon*, laid down in 1863 and completed in 1866, carried five-to-six-inch armor on an iron hull of revolutionary "bracket-frame" construction. It carried ten twelve-ton guns and was powered by engines of 6,520 indicated horsepower at a speed of well over fourteen-and-one-half knots, The comparison becomes even more favorable to Reed's ship when we note that the *Bellerophon* was commissioned and operating with the Channel Fleet by April 1866.

It may be protested that the comparison is inexact, for the *Bellerophon* was laid down a full year before the *Belliqueuse* class. But it must suffice, since no British armorclad was laid down in 1862, with the exception of three turret ships for coastal work.

A closer comparison is possible, however, if both ships

are timber-built. The *Lord Clyde*, a Reed-designed wooden ironclad built as such from the keel up, carrying four-and-one-half to five-and-one-half-inch plates, enjoyed no advantage in armor over the *Belliqueuse*. But it boasted no less than twenty-four seven-inch muzzle-loading rifles, and engines of 6,700 indicated horsepower giving a speed of thirteen-and-one-half knots; and while the French armorclad was four years in building, the British took less than three, being laid down in September 1863 and completed in June 1866. The comparison indicates decisively that Britain enjoyed a distinct qualitative advantage over the French, not the least of which was the ability of British yards, in spite of the novelty of the work, to complete ironclads with more rapidity than could the French yards.

In December 1867 additions to the French fleet of first-class ironclads narrowed the British numerical lead to three ships. But the French surge was partially achieved by the purchase of two old federal ironclads of dubious value, the monitor *Onandaga* and the broadside *Dunderburg*, renamed *Rochambeau*. Yet First Lord H. L. Corry insisted in a confidential memorandum that France and Britain were barely equals in first-class warships. By counting floating ironclad batteries of strictly problematical power, Corry was able to state that France had afloat thirty-five ironclads. He was at least consistent in his computation, for he assessed the ironclad strength of the Royal Navy at the astronomical figure of thirty-one armored ships afloat; presumably he counted the now-useless Kinburn batteries and small armored gunboats.[31] Whatever the relative numerical position of both fleets—examination shows that Britain held a close lead averaging four ironclads after 1864—the qualitative superiority of the British ironclads is marked. As already noted, this ship-for-ship superiority was given far less credit, except by Reed, than it deserved, although Disraeli, who treated naval affairs with a studied contempt, nevertheless recognized this situation:

As for the Admiralty view of the present condition of the French Navy, I believe it is marked by the usual exaggeration and false colouring which always accompanies their estimates. Five of the French ironclads mentioned only mount the old weak armament, while we have only one labouring under that grave disability.[32]

The wearying business of comparing the number of ironclads in both countries continued well into 1870, even though England maintained her lead of a handful of first-class ironclads and steadily widened her qualitative margin.[33] But the preoccupation of the Admiralty and the press with the dangers of the French ironclad programs cannot be dismissed as the workings of overwrought imaginations in a time of rapid and exciting technological change. The French were first with seagoing armorclads, and their individual warships did not appear obviously inferior to Britain's. Yet time was on the side of England, both in her technical resources and experience, and in the looming threat of Prussia, which was to bring a catastrophic end to France's single-handed challenge to Britain.[34] Henceforth, France would seek naval power in alliance, and in response Britain would assert her two-power standard.

III

The American naval challenge to Britain emerged suddenly in 1862 when the federal monitors were constructed and put into battle for the first ironclad clashes in history. When the news of Hampton Roads finally reached Britain in those pre–Atlantic-cable days, the Yankee monitors were transformed from peculiar novelties into something of a public craze.[35] Were the humiliations of 1812 to be repeated? American braggadocio did little to calm public fears. The *New York Herald*, which symbolized for many conservative Britons the vulgarity and ignorance of the ultra-Republican North, crowed: "The United States suddenly takes the first place in naval warfare . . . and now the sceptre passes out of their [British] hands and 'westward the course of empire takes its way.'"[36] Charles Francis Adams, U. S. Minister to the Court of St. James, wrote

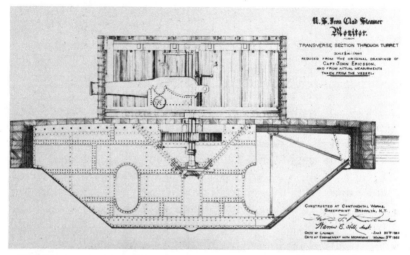

U.S.S. *Monitor*. Engraving from the original plans of Ericsson.
OFFICIAL U.S. NAVY PHOTOGRAPH.

U.S.S. *Monitor* today. On the bottom off Cape Hatteras, North
Carolina. Arrow indicates turret under hull. Photographic mosaic.
OFFICIAL U.S. NAVY PHOTOGRAPH.

to his son that the *Monitor* had become the "main talk of the town." [37] A calmer assessment prevailed in Whitehall. Admiral Robinson, while praising the energy and ingenuity of the monitor builders, still considered the new ironclads to be "mere rafts," well adapted for river and harbor work but posing no oceanic threat.[38]

The main result of the entry of the United States into ironclad building was a temporary change in British naval strategy. Previously, Britain's few and precious ironclads had been husbanded for the Channel Squadron. Now some would have to guard Britain's interests in the Western hemisphere against American designs. That the Yankees in their impregnable monitors would turn upon the Royal Navy to avenge Britain's recognition of Confederate belligerency appeared to be no remote contingency. Adm. Sir James Hope, Commander in Chief of the North American and West Indies Squadron, wrote to the Duke of Somerset that he had been informed by the New York Consul "that the feeling is very prevalent that when they have terminated their Civil War they might have one with us to avenge their imagined wrongs." Admiral Hope concluded that "the moment will be a critical one . . . and one for which we ought to be prepared, but the more quietly the better." [39] Palmerston, convinced of just such a contingency, advocated the construction of light vessels that carried heavy guns for the St. Lawrence. They would sail across the Atlantic without their guns, which would be supplied later. How such unarmored gunboats were to deal with the monitors remained unexplained.[40] With the ending of the Civil War in America, fear of imminent naval hostilities with the United States increased. Halifax, Nova Scotia, was reduced to a state of near-hysteria by the report that the United States ironclads were on their way, presumably to avenge the *Alabama* depredations.[41] A few months later Lord Henry Lennox, Admiralty First Secretary, warned Disraeli that war with the United States must be considered "the most dangerous of all contingencies." [42]

U.S.S. *Catskill* and *Saugus*. Monitors in their element, coastal and riverine waters. OFFICIAL U.S. NAVY PHOTOGRAPH.

As will be explained in chapter 7, the Admiralty soon realized that it had little to fear from the American monitors as warships fit to meet the Royal Navy on the high seas. Although the American secretary of the navy could boast that his monitors were "more than a match for the monstrous and expensive ironclad structures of Europe," he was compelled to admit that they were never designed for ocean cruising "but for harbour defence and operations upon our coast."[43] The transatlantic voyages of the American monitor *Miantonomah* that same year, however, cast some doubt upon this comforting assumption. The *Times*, bemused by the ironclad's appearance ("something between a ship and a diving bell"), asserted that the *Miantonomah* was but the precursor of a fleet of seagoing monitors.[44] This feeling that the larger monitors, at least, could safely cross oceans was reinforced by the successful voyage from the east coast of the United States to the west coast via Cape Horn, by the sister monitor, *Monadnock*. The Admiralty, however, did not rely upon the press for all of its information, and had had the foresight to assign a Captain Bythsea aboard the *Miantonomah* for the transatlantic voyage. Captain Bythsea noted the monitor's areas of superiority over the high-freeboard British ships, particularly the former's great steadiness as a gun platform. But he pointed out that any ironclad that required towing across the Atlantic, as had the *Miantonomah*, could hardly be considered a seagoing threat.[45] By the end of 1866 the foreign office was able to inform the Admiralty that, according to its naval attachés, the United States "is without armoured vessels fitted for cruising at sea, and that they are unprepared even for their construction."[46] The failures of the "super-*Alabama*" class of unarmored commerce raiders (*Wampanoag, Idaho, Matawaska*) further relieved the controller's mind,[47] while the inevitable postwar economy measures soon had reduced the once-feared American ironclad fleet to rotting hulks along the estuaries of the east coast of the United States. Disraeli was obviously relieved that the monitor threat could no longer be waved in his face as justification for increased ironclad expenditures. "We successfully resisted the appeal and it now turns out that the Americans have no navy, and not an ironclad except for coast defence." But the admirals would give him no peace. "Now it is the old bugbear of the French Navy," he complained.[48] Lord John Russell, nonetheless, continued to worry about the American commerce raider threat. He wrote to Hugh Childers, who was busily reorganizing the Admiralty in the new Liberal administration, that he had been confident that Lincoln and Seward would have kept the peace, but he added: "I am by no means confident that Grant may not throw down his glove." Childers was more in touch with the realities of naval power, and to Russell's "immense relief" he insisted that the Americans possessed nothing in armored ships with which they could think of crossing the Atlantic. He later expressed the identical sentiment in the House of Commons.[49]

The confidential reports (1870–71) of the British naval attaché stationed in Washington yielded graphic evidence

U.S.S. *Canonicus*. Sister to ill-fated monitor *Tecumseh*. OFFICIAL U.S. NAVY PHOTOGRAPH.

of a once-powerful navy rotting away, its ironclads hastily laid up, and its administration riddled with graft and inefficiency in the worst style of the Age of Grant. The *Miantonomah* and *Monadnock* still existed in fair condition, but the progress of naval architecture had left them behind in every way. Their fifteen-inch smooth-bore ordnance might have been used to some effect in a close-in action, but before this could have been achieved, their armor, which was composed of fifteen laminated strips of one-inch thickness could have been pierced by the rifled artillery carried by all British ironclads of the time. Although the dread *Dictator*, Ericcson's supposed seagoing monitor, had finally been completed, her planned speed of sixteen knots had been reduced to twelve, and her coal capacity and boiler power were cut in half. Now the *Dictator* was little more than a coast defense ironclad. A host of second- and third-class monitors existed in varying stages of repair or decay (many had been built on wooden hulls). Of the second-class monitors, only three were actually in service. One was labeled "a failure" and attached to the Naval Academy. Of the third class of forty-one ironclads, only three were fit for service. The attaché, Captain Ward, demonstrated that this state of affairs was not the result of technological backwardness. On the contrary, it reflected a common peace-time attitude on the part of the American people, who always begrudged military spending, and who were lured away from the sea by "high outside wages, an elastic and responsive internal commerce, new fields of industry and labour in the West, the innate desire of every American-born citizen to be his own master, and speculate on his own account." [50] This was no temporary decline; ten years later the United States could not boast of one seagoing ironclad, and renaissance did not come until the "New Navy" program of the 1880s. With the end of the Civil War, America not only sank into insignificance as a naval power, but forfeited any claims to originality in naval architecture that it may once have proffered.[51]

IV

Britain may well be considered the mother of ironclad navies. Only France and the United States refrained from either building their warships in British yards, or buying plans for such warships.[52] The Admiralty could see nothing amiss in the building up of foreign ironclad fleets via British yards, for these orders would hold such fleets in something like dependency on the United Kingdom, and certainly the private yards where this building took place were most anxious to continue the system. Britain's unrivaled experience in iron shipbuilding made her private yards a magnet for foreign missions anxious to add to the power and prestige of their naval forces. While the minor naval powers that looked to Britain for their ironclad impetus were never considered rivals to England's naval supremacy, they did possess more than nuisance value, for they compelled the Admiralty, as did the American monitors, to station armored warships in many areas where the navy had hoped to make do with unarmored ones. The fear was also present that, given the close balance in number of ironclads between Britain and France, the alliance of a minor ironclad power with France would tip the balance against England.

In the eyes of the Admiralty, the most important of the second-rate naval powers was Russia. An early starter in the armored warship race, Russia had contracted in British yards for the building of her first armorplated warship, a broadside battery launched in May 1863. Almost simultaneously upon receiving news of the battle of Hampton Roads, however, two wooden frigates under construction at Cronstadt were ordered converted into ironclads, which were almost equal in ordnance, armor, and speed to British ironclads of the time. By the following year, the Russian Admiralty was constructing its own ironclads from the keel up.

Fearful that European complications would arise from the Polish insurrection of 1863, the Russian Admiralty turned its attention to the protection of its coasts. It dispatched officers to Britain, France, and America to study the new methods of ironclad shipbuilding. The reports of those officers sent to the United States must have made the most profound impression, for the Russian government practically adopted the monitor as its own. With but few exceptions, the Russian Navy built no additional seagoing ironclads until well after the Russo-Turkish War of 1877.[53] Their earliest monitors were constructed according to the Ericcson plan, with eleven one-inch laminated plates forming the armor, and nine-inch rifles or fifteen-inch smooth-bores forming the armament, and were launched simultaneously for the protection of Russian interests in the Baltic. The Coles turret system, however, finally prevailed over Ericcson's and after 1864 all Russian turret ships were of the English pattern. In fact, the Russians duplicated in detail each of the steps taken by the British Admiralty in the evolution of the mastless turret ironclad: *Admiral Spiridoff* (*Wyvern*), *Admiral Lazareff* (*Prince Albert*); *Minin* (*Monarch*); *Peter the Great* (*Devastation*).[54]

The British Admiralty very reasonably worried about these Russian monitors, for in alliance with France the Russians could tip the ironclad balance against England; if the Royal Navy were occupied with the French fleet in the Channel and in the Mediterranean, Russian monitors could perhaps debouch from the Baltic, slip into the North Sea, and bombard English east coast ports and towns.[55] But such a contingency proved entirely theoretical, for it soon became apparent, to the Admiralty, at least, that the Russian turret fleet posed no more of a threat than did that of the United States. The Russian monitors, according to a report by a Captain Thompson based on his personal observations, were mere floating batteries, incapable of ocean navigation or any sort of cruising in foul weather.[56] Captain James Graham Goodenough confirmed this judgment three years later when he reported: "There is now no turret vessel fit to leave the Baltic." He further insisted that the broadside vessels of the Russian Navy were inferior to the *Warrior* and *Defence*.[57]

An effort to bring the Russian fleet more into line with modern requirements was represented by the construction of a mastless, seagoing, turret ironclad (*Peter the Great*) on the lines of the *Devastation*. E. J. Reed, now out of office as chief constructor, considered the *Peter the Great* more than a match for the *Devastation*. Reed's praise of this ship is understandable considering the agonizing slowness of construction of his *Devastation* and *Thunderer*, and the popular distrust of the basic design. However, the threat posed by the *Peter the Great* was mitigated by the ship's poor workmanship, a result of the casual attitude prevailing in Russian yards.[58]

A far more original Russian design was to be found in a pair of coast defense batteries that were actually circular in their hull shape. They carried eleven-inch to one-foot-six-inch armor and guns of twenty-eight to forty tons in weight. They were based on the carrying out of Reed's ideas of reduction of displacement and length, and of increase in breadth and armor to their logical (or illogical) end. Only a circular form could carry such armament and armor on the draught of only the four-and-one-half feet necessary for operations in the Black Sea.[59] Reed highly lauded these saucer-ironclads also, and he apparently wished to see improved *Popoffkas* designed for oceanic cruising. But he had clearly allowed theory to run away with him here. Despite his insistence that the circular ironclads were all that could be asked for as seaboats—Reed claimed to have cruised hundreds of miles in the *Admiral Popoff*—when exposed to any sort of current, they began to spin helplessly on their axes, reducing their crews to dizzy impotence.[60] It is most significant that at the outbreak of the Russo-Turkish War in 1877, the new *Popoffkas* remained completely inactive, and this at a time when Russia possessed no other ironclads of value on the Black Sea. Seen in this light, the efforts of E. J. Reed to publicize the new Russian ironclads resemble propaganda for his own design theories. A far more accurate report, by Captain Goodenough, not only predicted complete failure but also shed some light on the means whereby such a project could be permitted. According to Captain Goodenough, the *Popoff* represented the "favourite project" of the third member of the section of Naval Construction Technical Committee (Admiral Popoff), who had "complete control of all the ships now building or altering without any of the labour of the Constructor's Department." [61] The circumstances parallel those of the British Admiralty's relations with Captain Coles under the Childers regime, and it is ironic to see E. J. Reed as one of Admiral Popoff's more vigorous supporters. The *Popoffkas* proved an expensive, though fortunately not a disastrous, failure.

The remaining Russian ironclads posed no greater threat to Britain. In 1872 the controller received a report that estimated that of Russia's twenty-nine ironclads (of which

Russia's *Popoff*. Reed principles carried to an absurd conclusion.
NATIONAL MARITIME MUSEUM, LONDON.

no less than twenty carried only four-and-one-half-inch armor) only nine were available for sea service: four turret ships and five broadside armored frigates. But even these nine ironclads were "with very few exceptions, suited only for service in the Baltic." [62]

The only Russian armorclads that can be considered impressive were the armored cruisers, the first of their kind. Armor was confined generally to a waterline belt, with patches to protect the guns. Although not capital ships, these warships launched in the early 1870s are of interest as pioneers of this class. British attempts to construct armored cruisers resulted in nothing better than second-class battleships that served no useful purpose, since their armor and, most important, their speed, were sadly deficient.

Nevertheless, the Russian threat never measured up to its paper pretensions. Crippled by a centralized autocracy that smothered local initiative, so necessary in a country of such vast distances, and plagued by slovenly workmanship and a lack of interest in the navy, the Russian fleet was powerful only in coast defense. Outside the Baltic, its chief service was the loosening of British Parliamentary purse strings.

<h1 style="text-align:center">V</h1>

Of the minor ironclad powers—Italy, Austria, Spain, and Prussia—in the first half of the decade of the 1860s, Italy provoked the most uneasiness in Parliament and in the Admiralty by its ironclad building and buying program. There were no fears of invasion or of bombardment from Italy; the question was one of how Britain was to project her interests in the Mediterranean when she could spare only two armorclads to face Italy's entire fleet. The situation was not eased by Sir John Hay's lurid insistence that the Italians could muster the fantastic total of eighteen ironclads, which "could go and collar the British Admiral in the Mediterranean and turn him out of the Gut of Gibraltar, just as a policeman would turn a drunken man out of a public house."[63] But a more sober assessment by the Duke of Somerset put the Italian fleet at no more than five ironclads afloat and nine building.[64] Even ten years later, after a vigorous program to eradicate the shameful deficiencies revealed at Lissa, the Italian Navy could claim only sixteen ironclads fit for action.[65] Earlier, the ubiquitous Captain Hore could report that an extensive inspection of the covering ships and facilities of the Italian Navy had led him to conclude that it had not improved its estate since the disaster of 1866.[66] Individually, Italian ironclads had little to offer in the way of novelty, and indeed, many of the earlier warships had been constructed in Britain.[67]

The Austrian Navy could be accounted a threat only in alliance with another power. The ironclads were dependent upon British industry for their iron plates and heavy forgings, and they did not display any particular originality. The Battle of Lissa encouraged some dreams of Austrian naval expansion, but a far more cautious policy was officially followed, in which most Austrian ironclads were carefully preserved in ordinary.[68] Of eight first-class ironclads completed by 1872, one was in commission. The preference for timber building in the Austrian yards may account for the Austrians' policy of keeping the ships in ordinary, obviously designed to preserve the hulls as long as possible.

The German Navy was a comparatively late starter in the ironclad contest. It purchased two armorclads from English builders in 1864 and had launched two more in Germany by early 1867.[69] The German Naval Law of 1867 had envisaged sixteen first-class ironclads, but only four had been completed before the Franco-Prussian War put a stop to armored ship building. After the war, construction progressed on a powerful trio of masted twin-turret ironclads patterned after the *Monarch* but surpassing her in ordnance. The influence of E. J. Reed was strengthened when the German Admiralty called upon him for the design of two more ironclads according to his classic broadside and belt pattern. However, the naval power of Germany, definitely subordinated to the demands of the army, posed more of a future threat than a present menace. The national attributes of application, industry, and organization commanded respect among British naval observers, and three decades later, under the stimulus of a new Kaiser, would return to present the Admiralty its greatest challenge since Trafalgar.[70]

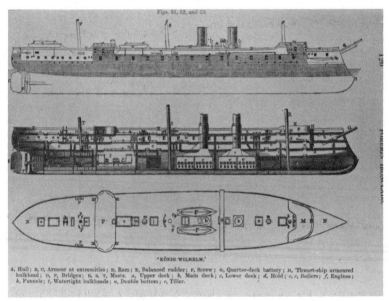

A, Hull; B, C, Armour at extremities; D, Ram; E, Balanced rudder; F, Screw; G, Quarter-deck battery; H, Thwart-ship armoured bulkhead; O, P, Bridges; R, S, T, Masts. a, Upper deck; b, Main deck; c, Lower deck; d, Hold; e, e, Boilers; f, Engines; h, Funnels; i, Watertight bulkheads; u, Double bottom; r, Tiller.

Internal economy of Prussian broadside and box-battery masted ironclad, showing strong Reed influence. T. Brassey, *The British Navy*.

The period under analysis cannot be compared with that of the naval race of the late nineteenth and early twentieth centuries. For the element of bitter national rivalry was, for the most part, mercifully lacking. Hard feelings were not wanting, of course, particularly since each major naval power could for a time reasonably hope to achieve ironclad equality; the French by their head start in ironclad construction, the British by their superior industrial plant, and the Americans by their impregnable monitors and vast, relatively untapped potential. But the safety of each nation did not appear to be bound up with its armored fleet, as it was to be before World War I. For the early ironclads were primarily a home defense weapon, and in fact they may have exerted a moderating influence by protecting each country from invasion, while ruling out the possibility of any aggressive adventures. Whereas local British merchants could be kept awake by the vision of a Yankee monitor or of a French ironclad leveling waterfront business property, the Admiralty and the government apparently shared few such fears, although they did worry about colonial defense and commerce raiding. As the fear of French invasion faded and, after 1870, evaporated, and as America revealed no sign of strength beyond its coasts, the Royal Navy could boast a naval supremacy all the more remarkable because it rested on the individual superiority of no fewer than forty ironclad warships.

3

Propulsion

If the Admiralty was certain of anything during the period of profound technical change that characterized the decade of the 1860s, it was that the sailing warship was a doomed anachronism. The last sailing ship to see action was H.M.S. *Arethusa*, fifty guns, which engaged the Russian batteries at Odessa in 1854. Six years later all ships of the Channel and Mediterranean squadrons had been fitted with screw steam engines and full-sail rig, and in 1865 H.M.S. *Edgar* had sailed out of Portsmouth Harbour on the last voyage of a sailing ship-of-the-line. Three years later the first lord of the Admiralty formally inaugurated construction of H.M.S. *Devastation*, the first mastless, seagoing ironclad, and by 1877 all of the sailing warships of the Royal Navy had been reduced to drill ships or to similar noncombatant status.[1]

Although sail power no longer completely controlled the movements of ships of the Royal Navy, it was not banished by the Admiralty. Board policy was one of combining steam and sail, a process that generally resulted in the perpetuation of the worst features of both systems of propulsion. The Service and Admiralty arguments in favor of this policy were that sail was of itself a powerful builder of the British seaman's traditional physique and character, that steam engines were expensive and unreliable in operation, and that sails provided a reserve source of propulsion for emergencies.

As late as 1869–70 the detached squadron sailed around the world on a cruise conducted entirely under sail, with the purpose of instructing officers and men in "seamanship"— the use of sails.[2] "Seamanship," smartness, and the impeccable performance of naval ceremony were deemed by many to be a far superior route to higher rank than was the intimate knowledge of the technological revolution now profoundly altering the entire navy. Admiral Hornby, who commanded the detached squadron on its global cruise, exemplified this attitude:

> We arrived here last night, coming in under sail, with a bit of a splash that has pleased all on board with themselves, and which they believe to have been the admiration of all on shore. All I can say is "more's the pity that it should be so rare a thing to see a ship come into harbour under sail."[3]

The *Times* considered sail's alleged character-building powers as the most important of its benefits. "Lounging through the watches of a steamer or acting as firemen or coalheavers" would not produce seamen that could defeat England's maritime foes.[4] C. F. Henwood, a well-known naval architect and propagandist for Captain Coles's turret ships, went even further and asserted that Britain actually owed her naval preeminence to sail, and that "character [is] acquired not in the stoke hole, but on the top-sail yard."[5]

A consideration that must have carried more weight with the Admiralty was that of economy. This is apparent in the rigid instruction given to Admiral Hornby at the outset of the detached squadron's global cruise, that even coal for water distillation was to be rigidly rationed.[6] But this argument was valid only in the narrowest interpretation of the cost of coal versus wind. Marine engines improved in efficiency during the 1860s, with coal consumption dropping from four-and-one-half pounds per indicated horsepower to only two-and-one-half to three pounds.[7] At the same time, there was no corresponding improvement in the sailing efficiency of warships. H.M.S. *Bellero-phon* required no less than two hundred of its 556-man crew for service aloft.[8] The great weight of masts and yards could never be omitted from any naval architect's calculations of displacement, nor could all the necessary apparatus for servicing, storing, and maintaining a full-sail rig. In one Reed-designed ironclad, P. H. Colomb estimated the actual saving of coal by the use of sails as no more than 7 percent of the bunkerage. If the wind resistance caused by the masts and yards while under steam were considered, an actual loss resulted. Admiral Robinson fully agreed with Colomb's calculations, and added that trials had been carried out upon masted and mastless warships, and that mastless ships had averaged well over a 5 percent increase in speed over those masted. This meant, that masts and yards caused a loss of coal, expended in laboring against the wind resistance of a sailing rig.[9] Furthermore, since these illuminating experiments were carried out while Admiral Robinson was in a very influential and powerful position within the Admiralty, it appears likely that the demand for full provision of sail for ironclads came from economy-minded political leaders as much as from the Admiralty.

Naturally the limited steaming radius of the early ironclads encouraged the continuance of sail. Because of their sluggishness under sail, the ironclad fleet was for the most part a home guard. Admiral Warden emphasized this by asserting that "there can be little doubt, in the event of war, our ironclad squadron, in consequence of their small stowage of fuel, will have to seek distant destinations in tow of each other."[10] Until the laying down of H.M.S. *Devastation*, only in the *Warrior* did the Admiralty Board even contemplate providing bunkerage for oceanic steaming. On an average, the first-class ironclads designed by Reed could steam 1,825 miles at economical cruising speed, on a bunkerage of six hundred tons of coal. By contrast, the *Devastation* could steam 4,700 miles at several knots above previous economical speeds on a bunkerage of eighteen hundred tons of coal.

The Admiralty was well aware of the imperfections of early marine engineering. All of the ironclads of the 1860s, fitted with horizontal engines that kept the machinery below the waterline, were reciprocating, and the heavy weights of the sliding parts constantly wore down surfaces. With rectangular fire-tube boilers working at thirty pounds of pressure or less, no more than two cylinders, and no compound use of steam, the maximum running of the screw was rarely above sixty revolutions per minute. A new ship with fresh and enthusiastic engine-room crews could steam from twelve to fifteen knots on the measured mile. In practice, however, few of the shorter ships of Reed's design could exceed nine knots, while the average cruising speed was closer to five or six knots in ordinary weather.[11]

Two basic types of engines were installed. Maudslay's "return connecting-rod" and the "trunk" engine and its variants were all attempts to achieve maximum power in the cramped engine space below the waterline to which the horizontal engine was then confined. Surface condensers, introduced about 1860, permitted the boiler to be supplied almost entirely with fresh feed water, inhibiting boiler encrustation, and permitting higher pressures.[12] However, mechanical breakdowns were frequent. In the words of Admiral Elliot: "Scarcely forty-eight hours passed without some mis-hap occurring to the machinery of one of the vessels."[13]

The Board of Admiralty attempted to hold a middle course between steam and sails. It divided the fleet into the three categories of coastal, European, and oceanic ironclads. For the coastal ships, sails would prove a mere encumbrance. (Even so, perfectly useless fore and aft rigs were fitted to the turret coastal rams, *Hotspur* and *Rupert*, and as late as 1877 two purchased broadside rams also carried such tackle.) For the European class a reduced rig was possible, but for the oceanic ironclads the Board required a large wind trap.[14] This policy was not carried out with thoroughness and, particularly in the first half of the decade of the 1860s, the European ironclads, which formed the overwhelming bulk of the ironclads, carried almost complete sailing rigs. But both E. J. Reed and Admiral Robinson agreed that this division would provide the best balance of sail and steam ironclad propulsion.[15]

Reed justified this retention of full-sail power in some classes of his ironclads by pointing out that the *Monarch* was an entirely different vessel from the *Devastation* in their strategic roles. The full-masted *Monarch* was designed from the keel up as a sailing ironclad for oceanic cruising, although her great offensive powers encouraged the Admiralty to keep her in European waters. As a sailing warship 42 percent of her weight went into her hull, leaving 58 percent for carrying power. Taking out the sails would make little difference, Reed asserted. But if the ironclad were designed *ab initio* as a mastless ship, he admitted that only 28 percent of her weight would need to go into the hull, and no less than 72 percent would be left for carrying guns, armor, and coal. Yet Reed did not follow his reasoning to its obvious conclusion, for he failed to recognize his overwhelming case for mastless ironclads for all of the Royal Navy's work, and asserted that "they would be utterly unfit to follow into distant waters squadrons of rigged ironclads proceeding from the Baltic or Mediterranean, while ships like the [masted] *Sultan* and the *Superb* would be in every respect capable of performing this service."[16]

Under canvas the ironclads were not, of course, so fleet as their wooden sailing predecessors. This was particularly true for those ironclads with reduced rigs designed for European waters. Although Reed attributed much of the dull sailing of the ironclads to the "excessive length"[17] of the earlier armored ships, Nathaniel Barnaby was able to lay before the Committee on Designs a more plausible explanation. He demonstrated that the area of sail to one ton of displacement in a sailing ship-of-the-line varied between

6.15 and 13.9 square feet. In the *Hercules*, a representative Reed ironclad, the sail area was only 3.26 square feet per ton because of the great weights of armor, guns, engines, and coal. The sail area of the *Hercules* would have had to have been doubled to give the ironclad a performance equal to that of a sailing ship-of-the-line. Such a proposal was out of the question, for the *Hercules* would not have had the room for the extra sail gear and men to work it.[18] The Admiralty was certainly prepared to sacrifice some of the sail power even of its oceanic ironclads in order to make the warship a more efficient fighting machine,[19] but the abolition of masts and sails seemed too radical to most of their lordships of the various Boards of Admiralty.

In order to retain the imagined benefits of sail in its masted ironclads the Admiralty adopted two expedients: the hoisting, and the disconnected or revolving screw. The former was a mechanical arrangement whereby the screw was bodily hoisted into a wall let into the ironclad's counter, or stern overhang. Under sail the ironclad would then enjoy a free flow of water around the stern. But the hoisting screw was expensive to install, weakened the stern, and could be rendered inoperative by barnacles in the connections. A far simpler, but obviously less effective, device was the disconnected, revolving screw, whereby the propeller simply rotated in the ship's wake. Thus, screw drag under sail was diminished but not eliminated.[20]

Probably the only Service officer holding high office who advocated the complete abolition of masts and sails in the 1860s was Admiral Sir Sidney Dacres. While First Sea Lord (1868–72), he persistently urged the monitor design for British ironclads. Dacres objected equally to the *Captain* and the *Monarch* because their lofty masts and rigging violated the basic principle of the monitor—a low-lying hull carrying a maximum of armor and the heaviest ordnance possible, and relying exclusively upon engines for propulsion. Masts would seriously interfere with the sweep of the monitor-type ironclad's turret guns, and falling rigging could foul the screw in battle. At any rate, the sailing performance of the ironclads was so mediocre that relatively little was gained by fitting masts and sails. Such reasoning led Admiral Dacres to encourage the *Devastation* class.[21]

Admiral Robinson came closer to Admiral Dacres's position than did any other Admiralty authority. As early as April 1865 he wrote:

> So many officers, whose judgment is of great weight, consider large sail power so essential to a sea-going man-of-war, that it is with diffidence that I state my deliberate conviction that all the essential qualities of a steamship of war, especially for an ironclad, are jeopardized by a large system of sail power.[22]

The important phrase here is *large system of sail power*. Robinson did not advocate then or later the total abolition of sail for ironclads. Before the Committee on Designs, Robinson reported that his ideal fleet would consist of mastless turret ships for European waters and moderately masted broadside ironclads for oceanic service. He looked into the future, however, and predicted the emergence of a mastless, totally armored warship discharging underwater torpedoes rather than shells.[23]

Considering such divided counsel on the part of those officials whose duty it was to guide the material development of the fleet, it cannot be said that the retention of masts and sails throughout the 1860s constituted a conspiracy of obstruction on the part of the Admiralty. At that time such authorities as Dr. Joseph Wooley, a founder of modern naval architecture, Captain Hood, Director of Naval Ordnance, and Admiral Steward, a future Controller of the Navy, asserted their professional opinion as members of the Committee on Designs that "it will *always* be necessary this country should possess very powerful ironclad ships with a sufficient amount of sail power to enable them to economize coal in proceeding to distant stations" (italics added.)[24] That same year an anonymous contributor to the *Annual* of the Royal School of Naval Architecture remarked that "to enlarge upon the necessity of sail power in cruisers is quite superfluous."[25] But it is the hindsight of a century that gives us perhaps a clearer view of the technical imperatives demanding the eventual total abolition of sails.

While sail continued to find its partisans, particularly among those who believed it essential for oceanic cruising, technological developments were making even that strategic concept obsolete. The first and most important of these was the turret. Masts and turrets proved an almost impossible combination. Masts and rigging obviously interfered with the sweep of the turret's guns and, combined with a low freeboard, could be positively dangerous. The Royal Navy's first masted turret ironclads, H.M.S. *Scorpion* and *Wyvern*, were useless away from protected waters,[26] while the first seagoing turret ironclad, H.M.S. *Monarch*, took no less than one-and-one-half hours to clear away the paraphernalia of rigging to prepare for action.[27] The second seagoing turret ship, H.M.S. *Captain*, ended her career in a catastrophe in which her full rig played a crucial role. The egregious faults of the last masted turret ship of the Royal Navy, H.M.S. *Neptune* (1877), probably the worst British ironclad ever built, can in large measure be attributed to the insistence of the Brazilian purchasing mission upon full-sail power.[28]

By 1869 it was obvious that masts and sails seriously interfered with the efficiency of the navy's two seagoing turret ships, *Monarch* and *Captain*.[29] The following year Admiral Dacres could rely upon the support of Reed and Robinson when he told the Committee on Designs: "I do not think that any turret ship ought to have a mast."[30] The first sea lord's opinions were subsequently followed in the turret ships of the *Devastation* class and all subsequent turret ironclads, with the exception of the *Inflexible* and the unhappy *Neptune* purchased by the Admiralty during the Russian war panic of 1877.

The second technical development that signaled the approaching end of sail was the twin screw. The hoisting and revolving propeller arrangements had alleviated the problems attendant upon the combination of masts and steam. But these devices were impractical if applied to twin screws. The mechanical problems involved in hoisting two massive bronze propellers into two wells ensured that only one ironclad was ever fitted with such an arrangement. Allowing the screws to revolve freely under sail was less complicated, but the propellers and their shafting still prevented a smooth flow of water and materially affected speed.[31]

The advantages of twin screws had been mooted as early as 1865 when H.M.S. *Penelope* was so equipped. Four years later H.M.S. *Captain* was fitted with twin screws by her designer. But both of these ironclads, the former utilizing the hoisting method of removing drag, the latter revolving screws, suffered from poor sailing performances. But twin screws and twin engines gave undeniable advantages in maneuverability and safety; an ironclad could now almost pivot upon her axis, while if one engine were disabled, the other could keep the ship under weigh. The question was becoming one of a choice between sail and one screw, or no sail and twin screws.[32] Reed, for one, preferred sail and the single screw for most ironclads, deviating from this policy only in the *Penelope,* and the *Audacious* and *Devastation* classes. But given the board's attachment to sail, it would be difficult to suggest a viable alternative for the time.

Finally, developments in the marine engine itself doomed sail. This period from 1863 to 1870 is one of steady improvement, rather than of startling advances. The success of surface condensers made possible higher steam pressures, and by 1870 the compound or double-expansion engine had been developed. In this type of engine the steam expanded in two stages, from a small to a larger cylinder. The stresses on framing, shafting, and bearings, so obvious in older, horizontal engines, was reduced, as was engine weight and cost. But the main benefits brought by the compound engine were increased regularity of turning movement, more economical use of steam, and a pressure of sixty pounds. Of prime interest to any Board of Admiralty was the saving of coal made possible by the new engines. Consumption was cut from about three pounds per indicated horsepower to two pounds.[33] The Committee on Designs strongly recommended the installation of compound engines in all future warships, and even, where possible, in existing ships.[34] The *Devastation* and *Thunderer* had been designed for simple trunk engines, and work had progressed too far for the change to compound engines, but the third ship of the class, H.M.S. *Dreadnought*, became the pioneer first-class warship to be fitted with compound engines.

It is worthy of note that H.M.S. *Devastation* had the simple Penn trunk engines. Even with this equipment it was possible for Reed to design a successful mastless oceanic turret ironclad. The Board of Admiralty could thus hardly plead technological hindrances to the abolition of masts and sails. But even after the *Devastation* class had been laid down, the Board commenced building two broadside, fully rigged ironclads, and not until 1874 was the last ship of this type designed for service. Masts and sails did not die out immediately even in turret ships, for the *Inflexible*, completed in 1881, carried an absurd peacetime brig rig that could be jettisoned in battle. This ironclad was the last British-designed turret warship that attempted the incompatible union of sail and turret, while the *Imperieuse* and *Warspite*, completed as late as 1886, were the last British armored warships to carry a square sail rig.

Sail was retained in the older ironclads of the navy, and as late as 1887 seventeen armored warships were equipped with it. At that date a representative audience at a lecture given in the Royal United Service Institution agreed that masts should be taken out of all warships—ironclads, cruisers, and corvettes.[35] This opinion may have had some effect, for as the older ironclads came into the dockyards for refits their sailing rigs were removed. Within a few years only the *Swiftsure* and *Triumph* (aside from training ships) carried on their lofty masts the traditions of the age of fighting sail.

The requirements for the modern capital ship were incompatible with masts and sails, for turret and twin screws could not be efficiently combined with even a moderate sailing rig. Until approximately 1868 the Admiralty had some reason for resisting any call for a mastless, seagoing ironclad; engines were still expensive and somewhat unreliable, and the superiority of the turret and twin screws had yet to be established. After the loss of H.M.S. *Captain*, the success of H.M.S. *Devastation*, and the introduction of the compound engine and twin screws, justification for such a conservative policy became almost impossible.

4
Weapons

I

The phenomenal growth of ordnance and the efforts of naval designers to cope with a situation that changed radically from year to year during the 1860s help to explain the emergence of the modern battleship. The competition between guns and armor severely taxed the inventive resources of the Admiralty constructor's department, for the "impervious" armor of the previous year often proved to be the riddled and shattered plate of the present. The constructor's and the controller's tasks were immensely complicated by the fact that the Board of Admiralty had no proper ordnance staff that could give advice when drawing up specifications for a new ironclad. Here was one area, and a most important one, that the controller did not always control. The invention, procurement, and design of ordnance were entirely out of his hands. For just prior to the gun and shell revolution that had ushered in the ironclad era, the Navy Bureau of Ordnance had been abolished and its functions taken over by the War Office, which supplied the Royal Navy's guns from then on. While this arrangement may have been an early exercise in Service unification, its consequences were disastrous for the navy. As a result, naval ordnance proved the most unsatisfactory part of the technological and popular ferment that characterized the early ironclad years. In fact, the situation was little changed until the appointment of John A. Fisher as Director of Naval Ordnance.[1]

At least five authorities could be considered responsible for ordnance development: the Royal Gun Factory, the Royal Carriage Department, the Royal Laboratory Department (all of Woolwich Arsenal), the Ordnance Select Committee (in which naval representation was a minority), and H.M.S. *Excellent*, the naval gunnery school. It was the duty of the captain of H.M.S. *Excellent* to examine and test the various ordnance pieces presented to him by the above authorities, plus those of a host of inventors, the most pertinacious being Sir William Armstrong.[2] The Admiralty was thus in reality not responsible for the navy's right arm—its guns. The first lord of the Admiralty admitted before the Ordnance Select Committee that "all the Admiralty can do is to send to the War Department and say what guns they want; but in the case of any new gun, they must rest entirely on the War Department for opinions with regard to that gun."[3]

More than any other single factor, ordnance determined the design of warships of this time. Concentration of armor, questions of freeboard, the turret controversy, armor plating, and ships' dimensions all led ultimately to the ordnance question. Yet the first lord was forced to admit that his board exercised only an indirect responsibility over the navy's guns. The price paid for this curious arrangement was a stultifying of ordnance development, slow procurement, and an ultimately unsatisfactory state of gunnery. Capt. John Fisher, who was later to command the *Excellent* and become Director of Ordnance and Torpedoes, denounced in 1871 "the studied and deliberate manner in which the Navy is ignored at all these places, especially at Woolwich . . . and it takes its origin from the Admiralty being subordinate to and dependent on the War Office for almost any specimen of war-like stores, from a thirty-five ton gun down to a boarding pike and a common shovel." [4]

It was customary for the Admiralty in November of each year to furnish the War Office with a list of ships intended to be commissioned in the ensuing financial year, which included details of guns needed. According to at least one authority, however, these estimates were then "criticized, manipulated, and reduced by the War Office." Furthermore, the Admiralty was kept in ignorance of the amount of rounds and other ordnance stores that the War Office had in stock. Finally, no distinction was drawn between expenditure for naval or army ordnance, and it was obviously to the War Office's advantage to bolster its own ordnance stores at the expense of the Admiralty.[5] This confused situation did not escape public notice. The *Times* termed it a "monstrous anomaly," while the *Naval and Military Gazette*, hardly the voice of progress, demanded: "Why should confusion worse confounded hamper the Navy by harnessing it to the War Office?"[6] It was not surprising that naval guns so often failed in practice; Admiral Robinson was driven to remark on the formidable difficulties inherent in such a system in "constructing such guns as can be relied on."[7] This statement gains force when it is realized that Robinson was writing in 1869, by which time the early vicissitudes of ordnance, of rifled versus smoothbore and of breech versus muzzle-loading, had been fairly settled.

With such materiel and with so faulty an organization the actual use of the gun proved indeed inefficient. Fire control was practically nonexistent until approximately 1868, when simultaneous electrical firing equipment was installed in some ironclads.[8] The rapid growth of the gun from the sixty-eight-pound smoothbores that formed the bulk of the armament of H.M.S. *Warrior*, to the thirty-five-ton rifled muzzle-loaders of the *Devastation*, had surpassed any improvements in gun handling and aiming. One knowledgeable foreign observer was driven to assert that "all idea of firing at sea in iron-cased ships at long range had been banished. The opinion of the most competent naval officers in England, with regard to the range with which fire can be opened at sea does not differ very much. The extreme limits lie between four hundred and at most one thousand yards, under favourable conditions."[9]

These "favourable conditions" were utilized to the full

in naval gunnery tests in 1870 and served to confirm Admiralty neglect of gunnery. The tests, practically the only ones of their kind, utilized a large rock off Vigo, Portugal, for a target. Superficially, the practice made by the ironclads involved—*Monarch*, *Hercules*, and *Captain*—appears respectable. Each ship discharged its guns within a space of five minutes at the target one thousand yards away. The *Monarch* scored nine hits on the rock out of twelve fired, the *Hercules* ten out of seventeen, and the *Captain* four out of eleven. But the target was twice as long as any ironclad and four times its height, and conditions of sea and wind were eminently favorable.[10]

Two years later, when ironclad fired at ironclad under even more favorable circumstances, British naval gunnery proved even less effective. On a summer day with a flat, calm sea at Portsmouth, H.M.S. *Hotspur* and *Glatton* were drawn up at a range of a mere two hundred yards. Elaborate precautions were taken to ensure accuracy of shooting. A new twenty-five-ton gun on the *Hotspur* was to fire at the *Glatton's* turret, conveniently marked by a bull's-eye. An hour's interval between each shot ensured careful aiming. First, four trial shots were discharged. The fifth round, intended for the *Glatton's* turret, missed altogether; the sixth and seventh hit the structure, but both were eighteen inches wide of the target. Neither shot caused serious damage; the turret and guns of the *Glatton* worked freely and the gun crew would have survived these blows with but few casualties. This minor damage was all that could be effected by the most proficient marksman of the *Excellent* and by a crack gun crew firing at almost point-blank range on a clear, calm day.[11]

In most of the ordnance experiments described, the shells were heard to "gobble" or "puff" as they passed overhead, a sure sign of imperfect rotation. Thus the shells were behaving erratically in flight. The fault was generally attributed to the clumsy "Woolwich" system of rifling, which depended on two soft metal studs on the projectile to im-part rotation from the gun barrel; the bore was cut by deep, broad grooves arranged with an increasing twist toward the muzzle. In practice the system was not a success, for shells tended to shear off their studs and to jam or wobble in the bore, causing unstable flight.[12] Accuracy with this method of rifling proved impossible at almost any range. Yet the fiction of long-distance firing was maintained by the Admiralty. Tables of ranges of up to four thousand yards were carried in the gunnery manual of 1868. At that extreme distance, even assuming that aim and projectile flight were efficient, an enemy could almost maneuver out of the way, since the shot took over thirteen seconds to travel that distance and must have been quite visible as it puffed and tumbled its way to the general vicinity of the target.[13]

The action of the Peruvian monitor *Huascar* with the British cruiser *Shah* in Latin American waters illustrates further the unreliable nature of the early muzzle-loading rifled ordnance. The *Huascar,* completed by Messrs. Laird in 1866, carried armament similar to that issued to the Royal Navy, two ten-inch muzzle-loading rifles of twelve tons mounted in one Coles turret. Eleven years after her completion, the *Huascar* fell into the hands of rebels who proceeded to bombard and levy tribute along the Peruvian coast. The British admiral in command of the Pacific Station ordered H.M.S. *Shah* to put an end to these depredations. The *Shah* was one of the large Reed-designed unarmored cruisers similar to the *Inconstant,* carrying two nine-inch-twelve-ton, and sixteen seven-inch-six-and-one-half-ton muzzle-loading rifles, the former capable of penetrating nine-and-one-half inches of armor at one thousand yards, and the latter seven-and-one-half-inch plate at the same distance. But in battle at sea the case proved quite different. From fifteen hundred to twenty-five hundred yards the *Shah* and her small consort *Amethyst* (armed with useless sixty-four-pounder rifles) could register only sixty or seventy shots on the Peruvian ironclad. A total of 280 rounds had been discharged by the *Shah* in two-and-one-quarter hours of firing, with the result that one nine-inch shell had penetrated the *Huascar's* thin hull armor and killed one man; a seven-inch shell merely dented the five-and-one-half-inch armor protecting the turret. Admittedly the two British warships labored under great difficulties since they were compelled to maneuver rapidly to compensate for their total lack of armor protection, and at the same time had to avoid dropping shells into a coastal town before which the *Huascar* had inconveniently drawn up. But the following day the rebels surrendered the turret ship to the Peruvian fleet. Hardly a glorious passage of arms, the *Shah-Huascar* action is significant in its revelation of the state of gunnery of the day.

Just two years later the *Huascar* was embroiled in a far more sanguinary naval battle with two Chilean broadside-battery ironclads designed by E. J. Reed. They each mounted six nine-inch-twelve-ton rifles. The range in this battle was practically point-blank, close enough for rifles and Gatlings to reap a bloody harvest. Yet the *Huascar* was hit only about twenty-seven times by the seventy-six heavy rounds fired by the Chilean ironclads. From her turret guns the *Huascar* could score but three hits, none of which penetrated the armor of her enemies. After losing sixty-four of her crew, the *Huascar* was surrendered to the Chileans. She remained structurally sound and was taken into the Chilean Navy, where she survives to this day as a national memorial. Perhaps British naval gunnery would have made better practice (although one English authority called the Chilean shooting "excellent"), but the disparity between the number of guns involved and the close ranges, and the lack of decisive results nonetheless indicate that gunnery, as distinct from technical improvements in the guns themselves, remained inefficient.[14]

When in 1882 the British fleet bombarded the Egyptian forts at Alexandria at a range of a few hundred to thirty-eight hundred yards, damage wreaked by the guns was slight. Although ships' commanders reported their shooting

Huascar. Peruvian-Chilean turret ironclad in the 1860s. NATIONAL MARITIME MUSEUM, LONDON.

Huascar today. EMBASSY OF CHILE.

vaguely in terms of "good" or "very fair," later minute examinations showed that the opposite was the case.[15] Only the *Inflexible* and *Téméraire*, equipped with hydraulic gun handling gear, shot at all effectively. The United States Navy Commander who carefully examined all the forts after bombardment noted that "a successful hit meant either good luck or phenomenally good shooting."[16] His evidence is confirmed by Capt. Percy Scott, who was assigned the task of collecting the unexploded British shells, of which there were many. According to Scott, only ten of the forty-two Egyptian fortress guns were wrecked by gunfire,[17] although the armored British fleet had fired over 1,617 projectiles of seven inches and over on a calm, enclosed body of water.

The official Admiralty ordnance manuals share much of the blame for gunnery backwardness. The manuals of both 1868 and 1873 devoted no more than a page to the aiming of heavy naval guns.[18] Rather, the overwhelming bulk of these volumes is given to what an anonymous writer in *Naval Science* referred to with acerbity as "gymnastics," the manhandling guns, drill for gun crews, and firing of ordnance.[19] Gunnery targets sometimes consisted of nothing more than a cask with a flag attached, thrown out by each ship to fire upon even when in fleet formation.[20] Evidently, therefore, gunnery efficiency played a minor part in a ship's life; it was not until 1903 that Admiralty ship inspection included an appraisal of ordnance efficiency. In the eyes of many officers, a warship was primarily a floating gymnasium whereon seamen could exercise aloft in the maze of masts and rigging and develop those virtues of fearlessness and pluck firmly believed to be the naval contribution toward improving the breed. In the succinct words of Admiral Scott, who almost single-handedly revolutionized naval gunnery in the early twentieth century, "gunnery did not matter."[21] The Royal Naval College had no professor of naval gunnery, there were no men or officers particularly trained as gun layers, sights were ill adapted for changing distances, and means were totally lacking to measure such varying ranges.[22] As a result, a contemporary wrote: "We have certainly known of comparisons made between the interest felt by commanding officers and others in exercise aloft, or in washing decks, etc. to that evinced by them in carrying out the gunnery exercises—but it is hardly to be wondered at if some officers are found who prefer to bestow their energies in a direction which leads to certain results." [23] With gunnery in such a moribund state, the ram naturally held a powerful attraction for sensible officers.

Perhaps another reason for the lack of efficient gunnery lay in an assessment of the guns and armor of any probable opponent that the Royal Navy might have had to face. The guns and armor of the French ironclad fleet could hardly be used as a bogey by the Admiralty. Even when their ships' external armor plating was of the same or greater thickness as that of contemporary British armorclads, their wooden construction rendered them far weaker and more vulnerable, for no inner skin of thin iron was carried to absorb splinters and flying nuts. In consequence, the Ordnance Select Committee was informed that on the basis of experiments carried out by the Special Committee on Iron, in which a hull section of the French ironclad frigate *Flandre* was constructed and fired at, almost twice as much force (measured in foot-tons) was required to pierce the *Warrior* as was needed for the French target.[24] Trials of American laminated armor at Shoeburyness testing ground conclusively proved its inferiority to British plate; the *Warrior's* four-and-one-half inches of solid armor gave the same protection as six inches of laminated plates.[25]

As for foreign ordnance, the American threat was definitely considered the weakest. The vaunted Federal fifteen-inch smoothbore, firing a spherical steel shot of 480 pounds with a charge of fifty pounds of powder, could penetrate the *Warrior* at any distance up to five hundred yards. The British seven-inch muzzle-loading rifled guns, firing a solid shot of one hundred pounds with a charge of twenty-five pounds, were capable of piercing the *Warrior* at a distance of up to six hundred yards. As for the argument that American guns would be irresistible at close quarters, experiments indicated that the fifteen-inch smoothbore could not penetrate the *Lord Warden's* thicker armor and backing even if the muzzle of the gun were touching its armor plates.[26] As for the French threat, Reed asserted that their twenty-one-and-three-quarter-ton breech-loader was only the equivalent of the British eighteen-ton muzzle-loader, their thirteen-and-three-quarter-ton the equal of the British twelve ton, and so on.[27]

The main reason for the astronomical increase in gun size and power, therefore, was not the result of any objective study of foreign advances in ordnance or armor, nor, certainly, of the combat experience of Britain, France, or America. Rather, one reason was an appreciation that armor, from the time of Hampton Roads through Lissa and even to the bombardment of Alexandria in 1882, clearly enjoyed (in battle) an ascendancy over the gun. The mutual invulnerability of the *Monitor* and the *Virginia* was well known, and throughout the Civil War no monitor was ever penetrated by ordnance while at the battle of Lissa, no armor plate on either the Italian or Austrian side was pierced.[28] At the bombardment of Alexandria, not a British plate was penetrated by Egyptian shot, some of which were fired from modern nine- and ten-inch Armstrong muzzle-loading rifles. The *Huascar's* immunity has already been noted.

Still, the invulnerability of armor in such actions would not alone justify the Admiralty in continually increasing ordnance power and armor protection. Rather, the opposite course of resting upon the navy's armored supremacy might be expected. A further explanation for the Admiralty's policy is found in the artificial conditions of the Shoeburyness testing ground, and in confused but strong claims of various inventors and manufacturers, plus the demands of the popular press. In the words of the biographer of Captain Key of the *Excellent*: "The real condition was that

there was a crowd of inventors, designers, and manufacturers all let loose with their inventive and constructive
powers in the highest state of activity, each of them intent
on his own point and none of them under such control as
could harmonize their work with that of the others."[29] The
most sweeping claims were made by gun manufacturers to
guarantee to pierce any thickness of armor with their latest
weapon, while armor makers asserted just as vigorously
that no gun could penetrate their newest plates. It took the
strong hands of Reed and Robinson to prevent ironclads
from being designed as mere gun platforms, with little or
no armor protection, or as floaing impenetrable forts with
no means of offense. Inventors, manufacturers, and publicists almost invariably proved themselves completely ig-
norant of such questions as the qualities of seaworthiness,
stability, and economy of ironclads. Certainly, the defective
organization of those departments concerned with naval
artillery made it even more difficult for the Admiralty to
evaluate correctly conflicting claims and assertions. As for
Shoeburyness, a comparison of the results on the proving
ground there and those of actual battle would show a wide
disparity through which the gun's powers could be greatly
exaggerated.[30]

II

Prior to 1863 the Admiralty had ushered in the ironclad
era with a serious and costly mistake in ordnance—the
Armstrong seven-inch, 110-pound rifled breech-loading gun.
Although great results were expected from the weapon, it
had to be withdrawn by 1863 because of mechanical difficulties, particularly with the breech.[31] Armstrong's gun was
simply too advanced for the technology of the time. Its
method of manufacture, however, remained long after the
gun itself was withdrawn. Built up in sections so that each
part was in mutual tension around the bore, the Armstrong

gun was a pioneer. But it was useless against ironclads, and the Admiralty wrote off its losses and reverted to the old sixty-eight pounder smoothbore of four-and-three-quarter tons which, if equipped with steel shot, could penetrate four-and-one-half-inch armor at close range (approximately two hundred yards).[32] There seemed no reason why the Admiralty could not rest content with the sixty-eight pounder and perhaps improve its performance by the substitution of gun cotton and steel shot for gun powder and cast-iron shot.[33] But Sir William Armstrong, naturally eager to retrieve his reputation after the breech-loader fiasco, requested the *Excellent* in 1863 to evaluate his new system of rifling, known as the "shunt" method of studs and grooves. The main advantages of rifling were increased accuracy and range, and retention of velocity at considerable distance. But the Admiralty, with good reason, was not particularly interested in long-range accuracy. Both tradition and the primitive state of ordnance ruled out long-range gunnery duels between ironclads.[34] In fact, the overwhelming majority of experiments of armor versus guns was carried on at a mere two hundred yards.

But Armstrong had evolved a principle of construction for heavy guns that promised an almost unlimited increase in their size and power, and that remained in use almost until the end of the century. He was made chief engineer for rifled ordnance at the Royal Gun Factories (Woolwich), where he was able to adopt the construction methods first utilized in his unfortunate breech-loaders. A bored cut-steel block formed the bore of the gun, over which an iron breech piece was shrunk at the base, the fibers running lengthwise to the bore. Coiled tubes of wrought iron were then shrunk in descending thickness over the rest of the barrel. This system, greatly modified and cheapened by a Woolwich employee in 1865, came to be termed the Armstrong-Woolwich method of construction. Sir William found the Admiralty willing to utilize his method for the heavy gun program soon to be adopted. One major objection to the gun so constructed was its extremely short life. It had to be inspected or repaired after a little more than one hundred rounds. But a far more serious drawback was the notorious inaccuracy of the projectiles, referred to above, but this appeared of little moment when one thousand yards was the maximum distance for a naval battle.[35]

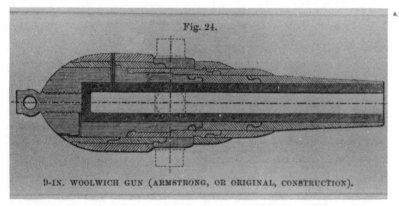

Fig. 24.

9-IN. WOOLWICH GUN (ARMSTRONG, OR ORIGINAL, CONSTRUCTION).

Armstrong-Woolwich rifled gun. T. Brassey, *The British Navy.*

The Armstrong-Woolwich method gave the navy a gun far in excess of its present needs, which needs could have been as well served, according to Captain Key, by a one-hundred-pounder smoothbore of six-and-one-half tons. He felt that rifling was also unnecessary at any distance of under fifteen hundred yards.[36] Key's opinion on the value of the smoothbore might have carried more weight with the Board of Admiralty if it had not been for the continued progress of shells, which relied upon rifling to achieve penetration of a warship's armor prior to exploding inside. Solid round shot was inferior to the new pointed Palliser shells in accuracy and penetration, and was useful only for close-in engagements.[37] Early in 1863 Admiral Robinson warned that all British ironclads could be penetrated by shells at eight hundred yards.[38] This observation meant in effect that a foreign ironclad, armed with rifled shell guns, could penetrate an English armored ship with impunity if the latter carried only smoothbores. Robinson obviously included the *Minotaur* class of five-and-one-half-inch armor, which the solid-steel shot thrown by the sixty-eight-pounder smoothbore had failed to penetrate.[39] Since French ships had similar protection, a change to rifled, shell-throwing guns seemed imperative. Before the year ended, the Duke of Somerset could write with satisfaction to the Prime Minister that smoothbore, solid shot guns were to be withdrawn.[40]

By May 1864 Key was compelled to admit that the Armstrong seven-inch muzzle-loading rifled gun of six-and-one-half tons was superior to larger smoothbores, but he could still see little necessity for its adoption by all ironclads.[41] Nevertheless, the Admiralty brushed aside Key's doubts, and in 1865 finally ordered the new Armstrong seven-inch rifled guns for the timber ironclads.[42] The new gun, at Shoeburyness, easily proved its mastery of a target representing the *Warrior*'s flank.[43] The guns were also ordered for the giant *Minotaur* class and for Reed's new first-class ironclads. Some of the smaller armored vessels were still armed with the smoothbore "Somerset" gun favored by Captain Key. However, at this time pressure for ever-increasing gun size mounted so rapidly that a ship's armament might be changed two or three times from design to completion, and until approximately 1864 most ironclads carried a mixed armament of seven-inch breech-loading rifles, nine-inch muzzle-loading smoothbores, and the reliable sixty-eight-pounder muzzle-loading smoothbore.

While the new muzzle-loading seven-inch rifle could easily penetrate protection of the *Warrior* class, it was mastered by five-and-one-half-inch plates at two hundred yards by 1864, as had been the sixty-eight pounder.[44] Since this had been the protection of both the *Minotaur* and *Lord Clyde* classes, and because Reed was planning heavier armor for even the converted wooden ironclads, the Admiralty ordered testing of the Armstrong nine-inch twelve-ton rifle. In tests held in 1864 the new gun penetrated the five-and-one-half-inch *Lord Clyde* target, using Palliser shell.[45] This gun was first mounted in the *Prince Albert* and *Bellerophon* (1866). With this new rifle, the process of concentration of armor and armament becomes far more obvious. In contrast to the *Minotaur*'s armament of thirty-one heavy guns or to the *Royal Oak*'s thirty-five pieces, the *Bellerophon* required only fifteen heavy guns to throw a far more effective broadside. Such reduction permitted a saving in gun crews and a simplification of the internal economy of the ironclad. Fewer guns and reduced armored surfaces also made it possible for Reed to carry out his concepts of shorter, beamier, and maneuverable warships. With the passing of the many proud ports of the frigates, both wooden and armored, one further step was taken toward the modern capital ship.

Yet the growth of heavy ordnance was no process of steady evolution. Captain Key certainly had some reservations about the new Armstrong ordnance. In fact, while the *Bellerophon* was still on the stocks, the Admiralty itself on several occasions expressed an aversion to larger ordnance. Lord Clarence Paget declared to the Commons in February 1864 that the seven-inch rifle was the largest that could be worked at sea, except, presumably, in turret ships.[46] The Duke of Somerset assured Lord Russell that no French seagoing ironclad could resist the British seven-inch rifle, and that he considered the nine-inch-twelve-ton gun "inconveniently heavy" for shipboard use.[47] Three days later, writing this time to Palmerston, he was prepared to accept the nine-inch piece on board the *Bellerophon*, but he still wished to replace the old sixty-eight pounder with nothing larger than the seven-inch rifle.[48]

When pressure from Reed and probably from Sir William Armstrong forced the Admiralty into adopting the nine-inch rifled gun, the Ordnance Select Committee also called for a halt in the growth of naval ordnance. It seemed folly to throw away the experience, so expensive and difficult to acquire, of the seven- and nine-inch guns.[49] In fact, by September 1866 only the turret ship *Prince Albert* and the new *Bellerophon* were even partially armed with the new guns.[50]

Such considerations, however, paled before the reports from the Shoeburyness testing ground, which showed that in the same year (1866), the nine-inch rifled gun that had been approved for general service the year before had been resisted by the nine-inch armor target representing Reed's new *Hercules*.[51] The Shoeburyness authorities were definitely anticipating matters here, for the *Hercules* did not enter service until the end of 1868. Captain Key again advised a more cautious ordnance policy, pointing out that the *Hercules'* nine-inch armor protected only the battery; other sections of the hull were covered by six- to eight-inch armor, while some portions had no protection whatsoever.[52] But Krupp at Essen was turning out more powerful guns, while a British manufacturer was performing a similar service for the Russian Navy. However, the Ordnance Select Committee was so impressed by the resistance of the *Hercules'* target that it questioned whether the nine-inch plating was not excessive and whether the ship would not prove equally invulnerable with eight inches.[53] This suggestion, coupled with the recommendation of the committee in the previous year that the nine-inch gun remain the limit of ordnance size, could have led to an equilibrium between gun and armor, and it is not inconceivable that attention and energy previously directed to piercing plates at Shoeburyness could have been diverted to correcting the obvious deficiencies in gun control, aiming, and rifling. But the committee then reversed its earlier attitude, declaring that "the progress made by foreign governments and by British manufacturers who work for them in producing still heavier pieces, call for similar British progress."[54] Accordingly, while still issuing improved marks of the seven-, eight-, and nine-inch rifles to second-class ironclads, the Admiralty ordered the ten-inch, eighteen-ton muzzle-loading piece for the more powerful of the box-battery warships coming into service after 1867.[55]

However, the development of the turret ship had permitted the mounting of considerably heavier ordnance in ships of war. When Captain Coles's indefatigable efforts finally resulted in the building of two seagoing turret ironclads, both the *Captain* and the *Monarch* carried the heaviest ordnance afloat in the British Navy: twelve-inch-twenty-five ton muzzle-loading rifles capable on paper of piercing at one thousand feet more than thirteen inches of armor, far more protection than any ironclad of that day enjoyed. Such heavy guns had been tested in prototype form as long ago as December 1863. Two years later, at a range of six hundred yards, they roughly handled the *Hercules'* target that had defeated the nine-inch gun at two hundred yards.[56] The nine- and twelve-inch guns were tested almost simultaneously, but the lighter was chosen because of the supposed difficulty of working at sea a twelve-inch gun weighing twenty-five tons. No such problem existed if the gun were securely mounted in a revolving turret. Reed, however, firmly believed that the heaviest ordnance could be worked from a box-battery ironclad if only improved gun carriages could be developed, and throughout the 1860s he spurred the search for a mechanical gun carriage.

III

When the decade had opened and for several years afterward, the standard gun carriage remained the old wooden "rear-chock" carriage of a pattern more than a century old. Development of heavy ordnance mountings had been retarded by the requirement that guns be enabled to move from port to port. For the days of sail this dictum was sensible, but steam's gift of unlimited maneuverability rendered the requirement a stultifying anachronism, for it would now be quicker to turn the ship than to move the guns. Captain Key, ever on the side of caution, used the primitive nature of the timber gun carriages to bolster his case for not plunging into a giant gun program. Early in 1864 he asserted that the six-and-one-half-ton gun was the largest that could be efficiently worked on the broadside at sea. But he did conclude that iron would have to replace wood in the carriages, and that there was no longer any necessity to transport the guns. Later that year Key evaluated Comdr. R. A. E. Scott's wrought-iron mountings, which relied on powerful compressors and permanent rollers instead of rope tackle to control the heavy guns.[57] Admiral Robinson showed himself far more willing to adopt Scott's carriage than did the conservative Key, who had far less justification in this case than when he had called for a cautious approach to ordnance.[58] When Sir William Armstrong improved Scott's carriages by the addition of automatic compressors, which eventually made it possible for guns of almost unlimited size to be mounted on the broadside, Key reluctantly recommended the new carriages for service use, although as a conservative old seaman he still repudiated machinery, which was liable to derangement in action.[59] Key's caution must have been reinforced by the action of the Royal Carriage Department, completely bypassing him and the Admiralty, in independently introducing modifications and so-called improvements in service gun carriages.[60]

A year later Key finally admitted that the Scott carriage would enable the twelve-ton gun to be worked under any circumstances likely to occur in naval warfare.[61] In 1866 the Committee on Carriages for Twelve-Ton Guns approved, with reservations, the Scott carriage. After exhaustive trials the Committee reported that this mounting answered every possible requirement for naval service, but complained of its complicated machinery. Armstrong's carriages came next in order of preference, while those mountings supplied by the Royal Carriage Department were excoriated for their weakness and slovenly workmanship. The committee concluded by recommending that Scott's running-in-and-out gear be combined with Armstrong's carriage and compressors.[62] Nonetheless, full credit was always given to Captain Scott as the originator of the basic system of mechanical carriages.[63]

Although the recommendation was carried, the Scott-Armstrong carriage, much to Admiral Robinson's and E. J. Reed's disgust, was not adopted throughout the fleet until the autumn of 1868.[64] Until then a motley assortment of composite carriages served the navy's heavy guns: the mountings of Scott, Armstrong, and others; "improvements" from the Royal Carriage Factory; and carriages still worked by rope tackles. Considering the primitive state of gunnery and the enormous difficulties in working heavy naval ordnance on the broadside, it seems extraordinary that Scott's system was not adopted in its entirety. In 1865 the Captain of H.M.S. *Hector* testified that, using the old carriage, the six-and-one-half-ton "Somerset" smoothbore required twenty-two men to work it with the ironclad heeling only six degrees. Yet a month later, Captain Scott with his carriage was able to work the same model gun in a roll of seven degrees with a mere nine men. Early the next year Scott asserted that experiments had proved that his mountings enabled the gun to save from three to five minutes in gunnery practice over the Armstrong and Woolwich models, respectively. Equally important, the Scott carriages required only nine men, whereas the Arsenal and Armstrong mountings needed nineteen men to man them.[65]

Captain Key of the *Excellent* was probably the greatest obstacle to progress in ordnance mountings, although he was ably assisted by the confusion and antagonism arising from the divided authority between War Office and Admiralty over these matters. Captain Key's biographer, in describing the reason for his reluctance to plunge into technological adventures, gives a picture that could be expanded to cover many Admiralty and Service individuals who were castigated by the forces of "progress" as vicious reactionaries. Key held to "ideas which [were] generally sound from the administrative point of view, where doing the best under the conditions was the object, but which do not pursue the subject to any further point." [66]

With the final application of the Scott mountings, naval ordnance could increase at an even more rapid pace. Coupled with this technical advance was the creation of the office of Director-General of Naval Ordnance. Whether this step was an advance is problematical, however, since the first director-general was the now Rear Admiral Key. He now had no objection to the ten-inch-eighteen-ton guns that were coming to supplement the standard, nine-inch-twelve-ton rifles, but continued averse to those pieces to be carried by the *Monarch* and her rival, the *Captain*. Key still envisaged naval battles as close-action affairs and could see little reason for the turret ships' twenty-five-ton guns. Admiral Key was struggling against what his biographer vaguely termed "outside forces" (probably the turret ship advocates), and Reed. And in 1869, the year he left office, his discomfiture was complete when the *Devastation* with her twenty-five- (later thirty-five-) ton guns was laid down.[67]

Just before leaving the position of Director-General of Naval Ordnance, Key was able to make his influence felt in one further area of naval ordnance when he negated the recommendation of the Ordnance Select Committee for a further investigation of the value of the breech-loader. Key drew up a memorandum in which he dwelt on the unfortunate Armstrong breech-loading rifles and on the serious accidents that had plagued the Krupp and French breech-loaders. But his most telling point, at least in the eyes of the board, was his assertion that if the navy changed over to breech-loaders when it had barely mastered the problems of the first revolution of rifled, muzzle-loading ordnance, the fleet would be defenseless, and this time foreign naval powers would not be in a similar state. Finally the Admiralty would be compelled to repeat the weary sorting out of the claims of rival inventors and would have to hold a universal competition to allay suspicious public opinion that it had played favorites. "The cost of such a measure puts it out of the question," concluded Key. Most obvious here is the lack of detailed technical argument; the question was skillfully made one of high public policy and, as such, carried the full board with it.[68]

The technical advantages—primarily accuracy and penetration at long range—were all with the breech-loaders. But the Admiralty and Key were as one in the belief that future naval battles would be fought at close range, and so the transition to breech-loading rifles was viewed as an expensive, unnecessary, and dangerous luxury. It could well have been argued that aside from the expense and confusion of rearming the navy, breech-loading ordnance would ensure that the fleet could cope with any variety of naval clash at either long or short bowls, for the breech-loader's advantages were hardly negated in close-in fighting. By clinging to the inaccurate muzzle-loader, the Admiralty ensured that the ordnance of the fleet would prove effective only at short range.

In the meantime, the size of muzzle-loading artillery continued to grow. Admiral Key must have been appalled at the progression in gun weights from the twenty-five-ton guns that he had disapproved in the *Captain*, through the *Devastation's* thirty-five tons, to the *Inflexible's* eighty-ton rifles, the largest and slowest-working British naval guns ever built on the muzzle-loading pattern. Even before the *Inflexible* was completed in 1881, however, technological developments had rendered the muzzle-loader an anachronism. Slow-burning powder made it possible to increase gun power by merely lengthening the barrel rather than by increasing the bore and weight of the gun. But long barrels were incompatible with muzzle-loading. Furthermore, the clumsy machinery necessary to load an eighty-ton gun through the muzzle, coupled with a dreadful explosion aboard H.M.S. *Thunderer* (when two charges were inadvertently fired from one gun—something practically impossible with breech-loading), compelled the Admiralty and the War Office, after much delay and confusion, to stipulate breech-loading for the *Colossus* and *Edinburgh*, which were launched in 1882. By clinging to the muzzle-loader long after it had been discarded on the Continent, the Royal Navy probably slipped behind other European naval powers in naval ordnance by the 1870s.[69] Captain Key's arguments against the breech-loader in the 1860s could hardly be expected to hold true a decade later. The simplicity and ruggedness of the muzzle-loader appeared sufficient for the job of close-in action envisaged for it. European and American gun manufacturing was still in its infancy and British guns, in the words of Reed, were superior to any possessed by the French and Americans." [70] The situation was actually to deteriorate vis-à-vis the European naval powers until the ordnance reforms of John Fisher as Director General of Naval Ordnance in 1886 and Capt. Percy Scott's gunnery improvements at the turn of the century.

IV

A study of the plans of early ironclads reveals a significant cycle of armor protection. The earliest concept of iron-armor defense envisaged protection of only the gun crews from the new shell guns. Thus, H.M.S. *Warrior* was protected (to below the waterline) only in most of her gun battery; the rest of the hull would have had to take its chances in battle.[71] With the *Hector* and *Valiant* (laid down in 1861) armor was extended throughout the length of the gun deck, but stopped short at the lower deck thirty feet from bow and stern. With the *Achilles*, also laid down in 1861 the standard pattern of broadside protection emerged—a waterline belt from stem to stern extending up to the gun battery amidships. This extension of armor was made possible by an increase in beam that gave added buoyancy, and by improved methods of iron construction.

The only exceptions among the broadside fleet to this "belt and battery" protection were the converted timber ironclads, which were given complete armor plating above the water because of their obvious inflammability. Wooden construction, furthermore, meant that it would be impossible to install watertight bulkheads, therefore the liability of damage had to be reduced. The earlier Coles turret ships also enjoyed complete protection. Since they were not intended for sea duty, the fullest armoring could be given without fear of overloading the warship. With their low-lying hulls, presenting so little target for an enemy's gunners, the necessary armor could be thicker than that required for lofty broadside ironclads.[72]

E. J. Reed, upon assuming the chief constructor's post, continued the belt-and-battery method of protection, but the rapid ordnance revolution forced him to modify this system severely, for heavier guns meant that the "old" standards of protection would have to be changed; to plate a warship on the scale of the *Achilles* with the thicker protection needed to keep out the shells of the new rifled muzzle-loaders would have destroyed the buoyancy of the ship in a seaway. Reed realized, however, that larger ordnance meant fewer guns, and consequently a less extensive gun battery to protect. Thus, the smaller battery could be protected by thicker plates. Up to the beginning of Reed's career, four-and-one-half inches had been the standard of protection, exceeded only by the giant *Minotaur* class and by Coles's turret ship, the *Royal Sovereign*, the former made possible because of its inordinate length, the latter because of the great beam of the converted wooden hull. On Reed's initial first-class iron armorclad, H.M.S. *Bellerophon*, the ten nine-inch rifles concentrated amidships were protected by six-inch plates, and a six-inch waterline belt encircled the hull. The *Achilles*, considered the best of the pre-Reed ironclads, protected her mixed bag of four sixty-eight pounders and sixteen six-and-on-half-ton "Somerset" smoothbores with four-and-one-half-inch plates. Reed continued his process of concentration of armor and armament in H.M.S. *Hercules*, which boasted of no less than nine inches of plate to protect a main battery of a mere eight ten-inch-eighteen-ton guns. When the target based on this ironclad foiled the standard nine-inch guns of the day, the *Times* asserted that "the ships have for the present gained the day over guns." [73] Soon after the *Hercules* was laid down, Reed declared that only an ironclad with her protection would "be fit to encounter the larger vessels of the American Navy." [74] But in reality, the *Hercules'* protection was years ahead of current requirements, since American artillery appeared to English experimenters to be distinctly inferior to British naval ordnance in its power to penetrate even the five-and-one-half-inch protection of the timber-hulled *Lord Warden*.

The *Hercules* represents the classic Reed system of protection, probably the most efficient that could be devised for the box-battery ironclad. While the first seagoing mastless turret ships were afforded almost overall protection because of their low freeboard, the continuing increase in gun power soon compelled once again a reduction in protected area and a corresponding increase in armor thickness. The aptly named *Inflexible* again serves as the extreme example: a midships protection of the astounding thickness of two feet. The remainder of the hull, with the exception of the turrets (sixteen inches of plate) and a three-inch armored deck, was to be "protected" by coal bunkers, cork, and minute subdivision.

Throughout the 1860s and early 1870s French armorclad protection varied little from that of the British Navy, either in thickness or in extent. The same principle of the belt-and-battery system was applied as ordnance grew in size. But soon the French were in difficulties, for their wooden hulls meant that any unprotected area left the ironclad vulnerable to destruction by fire.

The Admiralty felt that it had even less to fear from the armor carried by the American monitors. Although boasting the respectable figure of six inches of hull armor (with twelve to fifteen inches on the turrets), the plates themselves

were merely one-inch thick, "laminated" or sandwiched together. This system was utilized because of the inability of
the American iron industry to roll heavy plates, and only
publicists for Ericsson, such as Mr. John Bourne, ever saw
it as anything more than a necessary evil.[75] The iron industry
of Britain assured that the Royal Navy's first-class ironclads
would be constructed in iron, and that their armor would be
of superior quality.

From the days of the first ironclads, each improvement
in gun power had provoked assertions that armor was
useless in resisting shot and shell from modern ordnance.
Certainly the Shoeburyness testing indicated that, no matter
how thick the plate, a gun could eventually be found to
pierce it. Theorists contended that anything less than impenetrable armament was therefore worse than useless, for
thin armor would trigger off a shell and would confine its
blast, with destructive effect, below decks. If the practicable
limit of armor thickness had been reached, it would be far
better to design a warship "which lets the shot out just as
fast as it comes in." [76] However, the Committee on Designs
again saw the question more realistically and, against the
claims of Sir William Armstrong for a radical diminution
of armor protection, pointed out that in combat the armored
ship could pierce the side of the unarmored with impunity
if it chose its range well.[77]

Armor continued to increase in thickness but to decrease
in extent, until advances in metallurgy made possible a
tougher yet thinner plating. Protection remained a vital and
permanent feature of British capital ships.

V

The imperviousness of armor-plated ships in battle stimulated the search for underwater attack, while the successes
of the Confederates in the American Civil War in sinking
a number of federal ironclads indicated the feasiblity of the

concept. From that war, three methods of underwater attack emerged as practical weapons—the submarine, the torpedo, and the mine. The blowing up of the federal monitor *Tecumseh* by a mine at Mobile Bay was the first case of the instantaneous destruction of a major warship in battle, and a preview of a disaster that would prove all too familiar within the next half century and beyond.

The Royal Navy waited a full decade before it began to take the mine and torpedo at all seriously. In 1866 a Committee on Floating Obstructions devoted its entire attention to harbor booms, explaining that more active forms of underwater weapons were "still under consideration." [78] Yet in that same year the Austrians made good use of floating mines to ward off the Italian fleet.[79]

The Royal Navy expressed some interest in explosive charges fastened to the booms of small torpedo boats. In 1866 Robinson termed such a project.a "subject of the utmost importance," [80] and the following year the *Excellent* carried out a spar torpedo attack that damaged a target hull.[81] By 1868 the official *Manual of Gunnery* outlined a method of converting ships' boats into spar torpedo carriers.[82] Yet such amateurish and suicidal makeshifts were already obsolete, for in 1866 Robert Whitehead had developed the basic concept of the automobile torpedo—the compressed-air motor.[83] By 1868 he had perfected the essential balance chamber, which assured that the torpedo remained under water. Two more years were to pass while the Austrian naval authorities experimented with Whitehead's apparatus before the British Admiralty took notice of this vital weapon. The Admiralty then struck a financial bargain extremely advantageous to Whitehead and began a series of tests in 1870. The first impressive achievement of the Whitehead automobile torpedo was its destruction of a hulk from a distance of 136 yards. This achievement, illustrated by what must be among the first action photographs of military experiments ever taken, led the Committee on Whitehead's Torpedo to recommend the installation of the weapon on every man-of-war where possible.[84]

Confederate "David" torpedo boat. Photographed at the U.S. Naval Academy, Annapolis, Maryland, after the Civil War. OFFICIAL U.S. NAVY PHOTOGRAPH.

In the ensuing four years the Royal Arsenal improved the torpedo's accuracy and method of construction. Yet progress was slow, and much time and energy were diverted by the "divergent" torpedo of Commander Harvey, a towed weapon that presumably "deviated" from a towing warship and nestled under the keel of the enemy.[85] Aside from its cumbersome apparatus, the realization that the contraption might well foul the screw and travel back to the attacker determined that Harvey's towing torpedo would enjoy a relatively brief service life.

E. J. Reed in his position as chief constructor was fully aware of the potential threat of mines or torpedoes (the terms were used interchangeably). Although he may have expressed doubt as to their practicability at sea,[86] Reed built increasingly elaborate subdivision into the hulls of his ships, particularly in the *Glatton* and in the *Devastation* class.

In 1868 Comdr. (later Lord) John A. Fisher published his *A Treatise on Electricity*,[87] the foundation of the subsequent mine progress. By 1877 the first *Torpedo Manual* contained sections on the Whitehead and Harvey torpedoes, electrical and mechanical mines, minesweeping and the protection of ironclads from torpedo attacks.[88] However, in the 1860s the development of torpedoes and mines was greatly hindered by lack of funds. Only the successful defense of the German littoral in 1870–71 made the Admiralty amenable to more substantial experiments in mine and torpedo warfare, and hastened the purchase of the Whitehead torpedo.[89] Until then the standard Admiralty mine was a floating apparatus electrically detonated from the shore upon a warning signal from a circuit-closer mounted on the mine itself.[90] At this early date, however, even the charge of explosive theoretically necessary to sink an ironclad had not yet been ascertained.[91]

Submarine warships were not unknown at this time, for throughout the first half of the century experimental underwater craft had been projected and, in some instances, built. The American Civil War proved the possibility of undersea warfare. But the first practical submersible warship, designed in France before the commencement of the Civil War in America, made her first successful underwater trials in 1863. But as the British naval attaché had predicted, *Le Plongeur* was not a successful ship of war.[92] Her underwater control was erratic and her time of submergence limited. The development of the submarine menace had to wait another three to four decades until it could be united with the automobile torpedo and the internal combustion and electrical motors. Certainly the Admiralty in the 1860s and 1870s revealed little or no fear of the submarine.

The new underwater weapons of mine, torpedo, and submarine remained in embryo during the 1860s as well as in the following decade, and these armaments had little effect, if any, upon the design of ironclads. Watertight subdivisions had been perfected by Reed as much for protection against the ram and for accidental holing as against mine or torpedo.[93] As late as 1877 the only defenses of the ironclad against torpedo attacks were extempore wire nets and picket boats. Yet in mock warfare the *Monarch* had been easily "torpedoed" by both the Harvey and Whitehead weapons.[94] The only protection at the time against submarine mines was countermining and sweeping.[95] Naval architects had no battle experience upon which to draw, for the mines torpedoes, and submarines of the American Civil War were indeed too crude to hold any profound lesson.[96] They were considered a mere hint of things to come, far more valuable for their psychological effect than for any destructive powers.[97] Thus the design of British and European ironclads was not influenced by these new weapons. Only in the early 1880s did ironclads begin to enter service equipped with torpedo tubes and quick-firing secondary guns to repel torpedo-boat attacks.

But in the mind of the navy and of naval architects the gun—and the ram[98]—were the prime weapons, and around them the ironclads were built.

5

Tactics and the Ram

I

In the steam-powered ironclad, the mid-Victorian Royal Navy was presented with an impressive weapon of unprecedented power and maneuverability. Naval and popular writers could well wax enthusiastic over the new ironclad fleet, while apprehensively noting France's progress under the technologically minded emperor. Every new development, every refinement, every improvement was earnestly debated in Parliament and in the press. Even the suspicion that the Admiralty was not fully abreast of the fast-moving times would bring down instant thunderbolts of virulent public condemnation.

But the study of the tactical use of the ironclad, both singly and in fleets, was strangely neglected. By its very magnificence and bulk, the armored warship drew attention to itself, its construction, armament, and power. The building of an ironclad provided a brilliant spectacle of showering sparks, infernal heat and noise, and a very tangible reaffimation of the ability of the nineteenth-century master builder to overcome all technological problems.[1] By contrast, the theoretical use of the ironclad in an imagined naval battle was an almost academic speculation. No British ironclad fleet was to engage in naval battle until 1914.

It fell to foreign powers to first "blood" the ironclad in action, beginning with the well-known battles of Hampton Roads, Mobile Bay, and Charleston. The effect of the

118

American Civil War upon British naval architecture will be explained below. Royal Naval observers considered that conflict barren of tactical lessons since its naval actions took place in coastal and inland waters. It appeared rather a question of the technology of the North versus the courage and ingenuity of the South. A number of minor actions in Latin America fought with surplus American and contracted British equipment offered little information for fleet actions.[2] Only the battle of Lissa yielded any tangible guide for the effective employment of ironclads in action.

Such neglect of tactical studies did not escape some notice even at the time. Comdr. (later Adm.) Philip H. Colomb remarked succinctly at a professional meeting: "I envy no naval officer who thinks the science of tactics is rightly placed in the shade to which our navy has tacitly condemned it." [3] Commenting on the cruise of the Combined Fleet in 1869, the influential *Army and Navy Gazette* remarked that

> the public are made to believe that the only contest of capability—the only tests of strength—have been sailings on a wind, off a wind, staying, wearing, striking topmasts, making sail, and all the hundred other devices and amusements of the good old days, are steam was, ere John Brown of Sheffield was born, and before the names of Armstrong and Whitworth had been heard in the land.[4]

Official tactical publications from the Admiralty—what few there were—allotted only a few pages to the conduct of a fleet in the face of an enemy, and devoted reams of paper to complex and confusing "evolutions" of sail and steam.[5] Comdr. Sir Cyprian Bridge, a dominant naval figure of the late nineteenth century, lamented of tactics: "In the British Navy especially it has not been so much neglected as despised." This contempt he ascribed to the traditional opinion that a British admiral need hope only for "plenty of searoom and a willing enemy."[6] Yet Nelson and Rodney were only two of the more prominent officers of the old sailing navy who indeed had studied tactics and had achieved startling success. Bridge also denounced useless evolutions carried out "for no other reason, apparently, than because they are to be found in the signal book."[7] Service neglect of tactics was no more than a reflection of apathy by a public far more interested in mock military maneuvers of almost opéra-bouffe quality at Salisbury than in the tedious evolutions of far-off ironclads.[8]

One of the earliest writers to appreciate that steam had introduced a completely new dimension of maneuver to naval tactics was Sir Howard Douglas, who at the age of eighty-five threw off much of the deadweight of tradition and produced the first significant British work on steam warfare at sea. Douglas rejoiced that steam had eliminated the element of chance from naval warfare. Henceforth fleets could be maneuvered with the same precision as armies on a plain. The old broadside-to-broadside fight would be a thing of the past, for steam enabled a fleet to concentrate on any part of the enemy squadron where bow and stern fire would deliver the telling blows. For these actions, oblique formation in which a ship's bow and stern would be unmasked, would be preferable to the traditional line-ahead formation. The palm of victory would go to the admiral most skilled in naval maneuvers. Douglas's mistake was to overestimate the amount of precision and control that steam gave to a fleet, but his book marks a definite break with traditional sailing ship tactics.[9]

Four years after Sir Howard Douglas's pioneer study, a Royal Navy lieutenant, Duncan Stewart, privately printed some of his early observations on steam. Unlike Douglas, he realized that steam had now accentuated the differences in speed among ships, that it would be more difficult to estimate an enemy's speed or to keep station in fleets composed of ships powered by engines in different stages of obsolescence and repair. But steam had given the warship a new flexibility and invulnerability in battle, since fitful breezes and calms meant little or nothing now. Engines, if situated below the waterline, were far less vulnerable than lofty masts and rigging. Yet, Lieutenant Stewart complained, ships utilized this priceless boon of steam only when absolutely necessary. His final observations on the value of exercising at General Quarters and of meaningful gun practice, rather than mere firing at a cask from a stationary ship, remained pertinent for years to come.[10]

The coming of iron spelled as profound a change in naval tactics as had the arrival of steam. Iron armor coupled with steam made the ram a seemingly invincible weapon, while iron construction permitted vastly increased tonnage for warships removing restrictions on gun size and machinery. The unsatisfactory marriage of wooden hull to heavy machinery and ordnance could now be dissolved.

One of the original writers to deal with the tactics necessary for the new ironclad was Comdr. Philip H. Colomb, who from 1865 until his death in 1899 exercised a profound influence over tactical thought in the Royal Navy.[11] Colomb's maiden essay, "Modern Naval Tactics," which was delivered before the Royal United Service Institution in 1865, outlined the basic principles of tactics he would hold for the rest of his life. Calling for an end to complicated, artificial evaluations that would never be of any value on the day of battle, he laid down uniformity of speed and clear, terse signaling as the basic requirements for fleet tactics. But the whole essay was constructed around the new weapon that Colomb was certain would literally sweep everything before it. The ram, used with ghastly effect at Hampton Roads, was to be the ultimate weapon for the future. Armor had decreased the effectiveness of artillery and only the submarine slash of a well-handled ram could break the deadlock between guns and armor. For this new weapon, new tactics would be necessary. Line-ahead formation was useless because it masked the ram and exposed the vulnerable broadside. Colomb was uncertain whether angular formation, double echelons, identical columns, or line-abreast was preferable. But most important, the turning radius of each ship must be known in advance, and the ram given full priority.[12]

Colomb's disdain for the traditional line-ahead formation was nothing unique to him. In fact, most of his ideas had previously been published or privately broached. A Lt. A. H. Alston and Adm. W. Fanshawe Martin, Commander in Chief, Mediterranean, both called for line-abreast or angular ironclad arrangements that would permit unobstructed bow fire. Writing several years before Colomb, neither seems to have considered the new formations as an aid to ramming, but they could obviosly be adapted for that peculiar form of naval warfare, and it is not unlikely that Colomb found these tactical studies useful.

Lieutenant Alston's unpublished work is a useful exercise in tactical common sense, a quality greatly to be desired in those days when theoretical exercises had to make do for battle experience. Writing of the naval maneuvers of his time, Alston asserted: "It is plain that you will not make tacticians of your officers by providing them with a book of instructions for the manoeuvring of fleets which they command which contains only mechanical directions for throwing the ships into geometrical figures of squares, oblongs, angular formations, lines, and so forth." Practice and individual initiative would be of far greater importance than such sterile exercises, Alston felt, for at the moment of battle, signaling and flagship control would be almost impossible. Alston preferred angular formations, giving a squadron mutual defense with flank support for all ships. But his chief contribution was to attempt to bring a sense of realism into the study of naval tactics.[13]

Admiral Martin divided his fleet, in theory, into several angular or close line-abreast formations, thus ensuring unobstructed bow fire and mutual support.[14] His *Observations on the Scheme for Screw Ship Evolutions* helped to strengthen the prejudice against what Sir Howard Douglas had termed the "vicious practice"[15] of line-ahead formation, and cleared the way for total acceptance of the ram.

The Admiralty, however, continued to provide for the line-ahead formation in its tactical manuals, but it also outlined the newer tactics based on the ram and bow fire. No single formation was favored, and in 1872 Admiral Bridge complained that no new arrangement had yet been agreed upon that would replace the line-ahead, "now so completely passed away." [16] But lacking "hard" information of the type that can be gained only through battle, the Admiralty cannot be criticized for not adopting some form of oblique line-ahead formation to the exclusion of all others. Not only the confusion brought about by the new technology, but also the powerful attraction of the old ways inhibited any abrupt break with the past on the part of the Admiralty. Even ramming could be welcomed simply as an extension of the old broadside and boarding form of battle.

Comdr. John A. Fisher, the future First Sea Lord, in unmistakable terms rejected the complicated formations favored by the Admiralty and so many tactical writers and, along with Lieutenant Alston, called for more simplified fleet tactics, pleading that no one could quickly master the multitudinous signals that covered every conceivable maneuvre. In any event, at the time of battle all signaling would be worse than useless. Line-ahead and line-abreast formations, the only ones that should be required when facing any enemy fleet, could safely be assumed if each captain went directly to his place, obeying the rules of the road rather than going through complex evolutions that only consumed valuable time and coal. In the battle itself, Fisher thought close-in fighting would still be the rule. Since warships were no longer tied to the wind, each captain could pick his opposite number and lay alongside. The four modes of attack for the modern fleet—bow-gun approach, ramming, torpedo, and the broadside—should be carried out Fisher suggested, in the following manner: "I. Give him the bowgun. II. Ram him, if possible. III. One electric[ally fired] broadside, or you just graze him. IV. One of the torpedoes should now catch him. V. Hard a-starboard (or port) and give him the other electric broadside. VI. Finally, the torpedo on the opposite quarter may strike him." Here is the familiar Fisher touch, the right combination of conviction and lucidity.[17] If Fisher exaggerated the power of the ram and the efficacy of close-in action, he was right in calling for an end to the complex and artificial evolutions that cluttered the signal books and distracted so much from the business of fighting. His penchant for dismissing deadwood in materiel and in the mind was an early characteristic.

But the development of the ironclad had been too rapid to enable all the tradition and prejudices of the sailing ship to be modified or superseded in the light of the new technology. This almost insuperable barrier and the lack of battle experience seemed to block any attempt to do away with the traditional close broadside-to-broadside action. That new and heavier guns mounted on iron hulls would annihilate any warship attempting to fight by laying alongside was incomprehensible. In fact, even boarding occupied an honorable place. Admiral Martin advised Captain Key that the good gunner should also be "perfect in rifle, cutlass, pistol and company drill."[18] Key, who needed little encouragement for his conservative proclivities, lauded sail for providing brawny *"topmen* worth double the number of any other class for boarding, cutting-out expeditions."[19] Even the turret controversy was further confused by the question of whether a turret ship would be more or less liable to be taken by boarders.[20] While the military correspondent of The *Times* took some pains to point out that the speed and maneuverability of steam warships made boarding a virtual impossibility,[21] *Colburn's United Service Magazine* could insist:

> We are inclined to the belief that the principles which Lord Nelson laid down in 1805 when wooden ships were in their glory, are equally applicable when iron-clad and armour-plated monsters take the lead—and that victory will favour those who are enabled to lay their ships most advantageously along-side those of the enemy.[22]

Soon after Colomb's first paper, an unsigned Admiralty

memorandum illustrated the combination of tradition and the fascination with ramming that characterized tactical thought in the early ironclad era. The memorandum considered artillery to be subordinate to the ram, handiness of primary value for ramming, and called for twin screws to be installed in all future ironclads. The memorandum urged high freeboard and lighter armor, as well as a smaller, and thus cheaper, ship. Coal should be carried only for short bursts of speed, and therefore a nearly complete sailing rig would be needed. The captain would direct this craft from the tops, thus giving the rig some further justification. Although no such warship was ever built, this memorandum gives some indication of the thinking of these members of the board, who were more or less completely converted to the use of the ram, yet who retained traditional tactical opinions.[23]

The mixture of the new and the traditional was further evident in the first official Admiralty manual to deal with ironclad warfare, issued in 1867. It recognized line-abreast, quarter-line, and two-quarter-line (a triangular arrangement) formations. A fleet, divided into from one to four divisions depending on its size and the circumstances, was to be arranged into two subdivisions. Maneuvering and steam and sail evolutions were detailed, but action with the enemy was confined to two pages. When facing the enemy, captains were to remember to remove all unnecessary top hamper and to fall into station quickly with full steam power. At the commencement of battle, captains were to take care not to fire over friendly vessels, nor to chase fleeing enemy warships alone, to help disabled friendly ships, and to keep station, no matter how hard pressed or disabled. But individual judgment was not to be subordinated to signals from the admiral, and captains were to use their initiative if signaling were impossible or if orders were inapplicable. These directions were quite sound, and in them may be seen the hand of Colomb, but the devotion of a mere two pages out of one hundred and seventeen to the

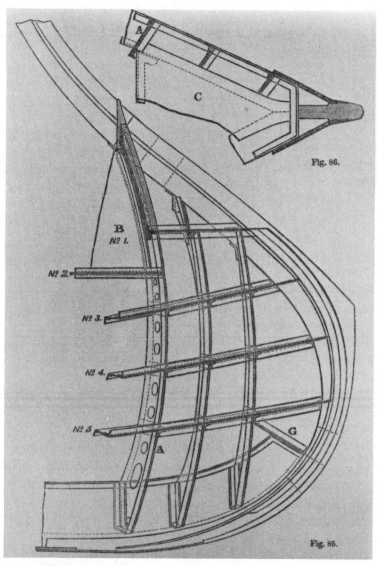

Construction detail of ram bow for ironclad of Reed era. T. Brassey, *The British Navy.*

primary purpose of the whole book, the day of battle, is some indication of just how theoretical and tentative was the tactical thought of the day.[24]

That some of the more rationally indefensible battle traditions were still in evidence well after the Admiralty had concerned itself with ironclad warfare is revealed in a paper presented in 1868 by Capt. E. A. Inglefield before the Royal United Service Institution. Captain Inglefield pointed out that the traditional policy of allocating ships a place in formation on the basis of a captain's seniority (!) was still a very present evil, and called for the obvious solution of arranging warships according to their speed, gun power and, of course, ramming ability.[25]

By the end of the 1860s the French peloton formation was gaining in popularity. This arrangement arranged groups of three ironclads in the form of a triangle. Concentration of fire, ease of movement, an ability to meet the enemy from any point of the compass, and a clear field for bow fire were claimed as the advantages of the peloton system by its advocates, the most prominent being Adm. A. P. Ryder and Adm. Sir Cyprian Bridge.

Admiral Ryder, Second in Command, Channel Squadron, was attracted to the peloton by his belief in bow fire, whereby large guns mounted behind adequate armor in the bow would enable an attacking ironclad to keep up a heavy fire with impunity, bearing down upon its adversary with the ultimate weapon—the ram. The bow itself, small and sloping, would present a most difficult target.[26]

Commander Bridge, then at the beginning of his career as naval tactician and strategist, preferred the peloton formation for basically the same reasons as did Admiral Ryder. Bridge, however, was able to go beyond the mere maneuvering of ironclads to a detailed analysis of the problems of tactics for armored warships. Taking the Admiralty signal book, Bridge divided its complicated maneuvers into the *evolutionary* for training, and the *tactical* for battle. This was a somewhat artificial division (reminiscent of that utilized by the unfortunate Persano at Lissa), although Bridge did feel that the evolutionary signals, constituting by far the greater bulk of the manual, would be useful for maneuvering the disparate ironclads into battle quickly and in order. Of greater significance was Bridge's insistence upon realistic tactical maneuvering under simulated battle conditions.

The following year, Bridge essayed the naval battle of the future. During the approach to battle, at a speed of about eight knots, all ships would attempt to keep their bows toward the enemy, laying down fire from bow guns. Soon the bow fire would cease, since its smoke and confusion would detract from the main purpose of a sea fight —to ram and sink the enemy. While this maneuver took place, a sharp watch had to be maintained for enemy-towed (Harvey) torpedoes. Up to this point in the battle, Bridge expected little serious loss to either side. But now: "Voici le beau moment pour la cavalerie." The admiral who had yet an intact reserve fleet of rams could swoop down on the confused and exhausted enemy, and with broadside and ram, and possibly even Mr. Whitehead's locomotive torpedo, could gain the day.[27]

Another writer who favored the peloton formation published his work in *Naval Science*, the short-lived journal founded by E. J. Reed. The author (who may have been Reed himself) agreed with Lieutenant Stewart that the speed and maneuverability of any fleet is limited by the warship possessing the least of these qualities. In this period, when most British ironclads were mere samples of different ideas in design, such limitations could nearly cripple a fleet. The writer recommended the end-on position for attack in order to use the ram. He discounted the dubious possibility of laying down artillery fire from the bow because of the difficulty in aiming during the rapid approach to battle and because of the sloping target presented by the enemy's bow.

The author envisaged the naval battle of the future in two different ways. The first, a general melee, although much favored by the French, was one in which "as of old the stalwart Englishman may show his peculiar prowess." He preferred fleets divided into three or four relatively independent groups (pelotons), each waiting to attack the enemy fleet at any weak point and leading again to the melee. Bows were to be used for ramming alone; if the enemy avoided the snout, broadsides could then be discharged at close quarters while passing through the enemy line. Warships would be arranged on a narrow front of great depth in order to best use the ram and broadside. These conjectures were never put to the test of battle, for all subsequent naval engagements were determined by the gun. But the author at least was on firm ground in pointing out the amount of practice and experiment needed to determine just what form future naval conflicts might take.[28]

Unfortunately, coal consumption was so prodigious in warship engines of this time that Commander Colomb had to admit that "evolutionary drill of a large steam fleet is so expensive a matter that no nation can practice it to any great extent in time of peace."[29] This consideration of economy, plus the lack of battle experience, led Commander Bridge to lament: "The rapid advance of construction had altogether outrun the progress of tactical knowledge, and naval officers found themselves in the perplexing situation of commanding ships for which no adequate evolutionary or tactical rules had been laid down."[30]

II

Study of mid-nineteenth-century naval tactics clearly indicates that such tactical thought and experiment as there was centered around the resurrected "always-loaded" weapon, the ram. Steam permitted the new ironclad fleets unprecedented maneuverability, while iron gave them new strength. Thus the ram became feasible once again. H.M.S. *Warrior* concealed her ram beneath a traditional frigate bow, but after her, and until the laying down of Fisher's *Dreadnought*, almost all battleships boasted a ram bow in more or less exaggerated form, giving the warships of the day a strangely Greco-Roman appearance. Even when the power of ordnance had been developed to the point where any ship attempting to ram would have been blown out of the water, this device was stubbornly retained. After the sinking of the *Vanguard* (1874) and the strange and ghastly *Camperdown-Victoria* collision (1893), the ram finally came to be associated almost exclusively with disaster. But when it came dramatically into its own on the bows of the C.S.S. *Virginia* at Hampton Roads, these Service tragedies lay far in the future. Four years after Hampton Roads the Austrian victory over the Italo-Sardinian fleet was ascribed almost exclusively to the ram. In fact, it seemed no coincidence that at Hampton Roads and at the battle of Lissa, the first sea fight between ironclad fleets, the ram gave the victory.

The ancient ram had disappeared when sail superseded galleys. The modern ram's antecedents, like the turrets, are shrouded in uncertainty and conflicting assertion.[31] Adm. George Rose Sartorius, a veteran of Trafalgar and generally considered the "father of the ram," claimed full credit for its reintroduction in Britain, which, according to him, took place during the Crimean war. In that conflict, which also stimulated Captain Coles's inventive powers, the sight of the first British ironclads, the Kinburn batteries, led the Admiral to speculate on the value of a small, handy, iron steam ram for clearing coasts and roadsteads of enemy craft. He then proposed a double-ended shot-proof ram of moderate dimensions (2,500 tons), with great speed and maneuverability, to be used against the cumbersome screw ships-of-the-line. Apparently he envisaged cutting down one of these doomed leviathans for his rams. "Reduce her weight one-half, strengthen her internally, put in her forty heavy guns, firing molten-iron-loaded shells, case her with shot-proof iron, and then let all the actual navies of the earth try to pass up our channels without our permission."[32]

But Sartorius's claim to have first proposed the steam ram was disputed by a Douglas Campbell, who claimed to have first proposed a low-lying, streamline ram-vessel in November 1852, well before the Crimean War. Campbell's ram was to be much smaller, carrying a reduced crew, and to be used exclusively in home waters, free from the top hamper of masts and sails—in effect, as he wrote, "a hollow iron bolt." In 1870 Campbell also claimed credit for the whole concept of the ram bow, although he objected to its being fitted to seagoing ironclads.[33]

Another pioneer of this old-new method of sea warfare was the Russian Admiral, Gegorie Boutakov, the first naval officer to put the ram concept into practice. In the late 1850s Boutakov "stumbled upon the very simple idea that all maneuvers of steam vessels unavoidably had for their base two geometrical lines, the circle and the tangent to the circle." He claimed that every ship could be made to follow prescribed circles if the ship's turning capability were known beforehand. Boutakov worked out over a period of years elaborate mathematical formulas and principles for determining a ship's turning power, but his work held little permanent value because he ignored, as did so many tactical theorists, the influence of wind, seas, wakes, and the rates of acceleration and deceleration of ships of varying displacements.[34] One reason for the Admiral's discounting of the natural factors that could interfere with his scheme was undoubtedly the fact that his maneuvers were carried out in the sheltered water of the Baltic and Black seas, on which the Russian Navy regularly exercised low-lying American and the Coles type of monitors.

In 1868 Admiral Boutakov carried his experiments beyond the realm of naval evolution and mathematical theory. He staged an actual demonstration of his ships' abilities to ram and to avoid the ram. Two gunboats at a time were fitted with protective fenders all around, and lashed together bow to stern. The other ships of Boutakov's evolutionary squadron were drawn up around them as spectators. At a signal, the two cast off and attempted to ram each other, presumably to the accompanying cheers and groans of partisan supporters. The loser of each contest lost his command, apparently only temporarily. In each case, ramming was effected, but usually at smaller angles. The results seemingly satisfied the advocates of ramming, even though it could have been pointed out that naval battles rarely commence with two warships lashed together, and rarer still would be any clash in which guns were prohibited.[35]

Admiral Boutakov had at least provided protection for the ships in his rather dangerous experiments. Admiral Sartorius would have dispensed with armor altogether. Reversing his earlier position, he likened it by 1870 to the protection worn by the medieval knight, and considered it now just as useless and detrimental to the wearer. According to Sartorius, the trials of modern heavy guns had shown "beyond doubt" that no thickness of armor plating could resist the penetrative power of the new rifled artillery. Yet to carry the armor that naval architects in their lamentable ignorance supposed would stop projectiles, larger and larger ships were being built, and the Admiral complained that the situation was so out of control that "although opposed to all that practice and experience had taught, even vessels of ten thousand tons were spoken of."

According to Admiral Sartorius, the ram's attack would be irresistible. Cruising at night on a conveniently dark sea, masts lowered, hull barely visible above the surface, the ram could approach to within a few hundred yards unseen. Weaving and bobbing, safe from enemy shot because of her high speed and small target, she would drive for the iron-clad behemoth. The blow could be delivered with impunity since the ironclad would prove too huge and clumsy to out-maneuver the ram, which could then escape into the night.[36] Sartorius did not explain how a ram vessel of such limited tonnage was to navigate the tumultuous waters of the North Sea and the Channel. He laid great stress upon the ram's necessity for high speed. But how could a tiny ram develop speed superior to that of a warship of five or ten times its displacement? And how could such a small vessel penetrate a heavy ironclad? For in that day of heavy reciprocating steam engines, speed could be attained only by a multiplication of boilers and increased engine size. Nor did he ever mention the necessity for large seaworthy ships to guard Britain's commercial and strategic interests in the colonies and on the high seas. That such a farrago of near-nonsense could be presented to the eminently sober and professional Institution of Naval Architects indicates the untried ground on which naval tacticians and designers found themselves. Sartorius's fellows at the institution criticized only details of his paper. Chairman John Scott Russell, constructor of the *Great Eastern*, mildly defended the large ironclads of the *Warrior* class, which he had helped to design and build, while Admiral Edward Belcher proposed an improvement on the ram, namely, a hammer on a trolley mounted on the keel of a warship, arranged to fly forward and strike a hole in the enemy side.[37]

III

The only ironclad fleet action of this period, the Battle of Lissa, gave substance to these assumptions about the power of the ram, and influenced warship design for several decades. The naval battles of the American Civil War had indeed involved ramming on almost every occasion. But with the exception of the Battle of Hampton Roads, ramming attempts had been generally unsuccessful. The Battle of Lissa yielded apparently incontrovertible proof of the awful power of the ram.

Upon the commencement of hostilities between Italy and Austria, 1866, the chief commands of the Austrian and Italian fleets were given to two quite dissimilar officers, Wilhelm von Tegetthof and Count Carlo Persano.[38] Tegetthof, immediately upon declaration of war, headed for the Italian port of Ancona, and upon arrival challenged the Italian fleet to battle. For various unsatisfactory reasons, Persano's fleet would not come out. The moral effect of this failure is credited by most later authorities with having contributed in large part to the results of the battle of Lissa. Persano had taken command reluctantly. He lacked any clear tactical thought, hoping only to win by a preponderance of materiel. In this alone he was superior to Tegetthof, for he boasted of nine ironclads, soon to be increased to ten. In every material respect, his fleet outclassed that of Tegetthof's which numbered seven inferior ironclads.[39]

For six weeks after the fiasco at Ancona, Persano's fleet idled, while exasperated telegrams flew among the Court and the Ministry of Marine, and Persano. The Italian Admiral had to be forced by official pressure out of Ancona harbour, where he was awaiting the arrival of the turret ram *Affondatore* ("sinker") from her British builders. Completely ignoring the principle that the first object of any naval action is the destruction of the enemy's fleet, the political and naval authorities decided that Persano should first capture the relatively unimportant island of Lissa. The most charitable explanation of this inane decision would be that it was designed to draw Tegetthof out. Actually, the problem was one of drawing Persano out into battle with his weaker enemy. An inconclusive campaign against Lissa followed, but not before the Austrian garrison had telegraphed the presence of the Italian fleet to Tegetthof. Persano had neglected to cut the telegraph lines. The Austrian Commander was almost positive that the attack on Lissa was a feint, but the flood of telegraph messages finally convinced him that Persano was indeed using up his powder, shell, and coal, in the face of the undefeated Austrian fleet. The unstable Persano had now swung from the depths of indecision and inactivity to extreme rashness. He still had not received the *Affondatore*, and his projected fleet of thirty-five vessels amounted in reality to twenty-four.

Persano obviously should have compensated for this lack by intensive drilling of his fleet in realistic combat maneuvers and gunnery, by perfecting his signaling, and by generally gaining the confidence of officers and seamen. Tegetthof did all these things, hoping to overcome his inferiority in ironclads and guns by well-trained and enthusiastic personnel. Persano, on the other hand, chose only to bombard Lissa and to complain that the odds were still not sufficiently in his favor. He had drawn up a plan of fleet maneuvering that envisaged no less than three formations: one for administrative purposes, one for evolutions, and one for battle. The first divided the fleet between armored and unarmored ships, the second was a formation of three groups of four ships each, and the last, which was never achieved at the time of battle, consisted of two groups of four ironclads, a reserve of three, and the *Affondatore's* ram, hovering outside the line of battle to strike when needed.

Tegetthof had one formation for both cruising and battle. Thus no confusion would prevail when the Italians were sighted. His formation was disposed in oblique line-abreast, in a series of wedges, with the Admiral leading an ironclad spearhead to, in Tegetthof's succinct words, "charge the enemy and sink him." Tegetthof's formation was admirable in that it arranged his stronger ships to receive the enemy's heavier fire, protected the unarmored warships, masked no ships broadside, and concentrated the greatest power in the smallest area. He could rely on his captains to follow him through the enemy's line because of the trust and confidence he had inspired in them.

When elements of Tegetthof's fleet appeared out of a rainstorm off Lissa, the effect upon the exhausted, demoralized Italian fleet was immediate. Persano, his ships battered by the bootless bombardment of Lissa and his men worn, inflicted a multitude of conflicting signals upon his hapless captains. He then realized that his fleet, originally in line-abreast, faced in the wrong direction. Slowly and with great confusion, the Italian fleet assembled in the traditional line-ahead formation. Chaos was compounded when Persano suddenly decided that his place would best be found in the newly arrived *Affondatore*, an ironclad more heavily protected, incidentally, than the Admiral's usual flagship, the *Re d'Italia*. The transfer opened great gaps in the line. The battle was joined as several Austrian ironclads steamed through a gap, discharging broadsides. The Italian fleet was now cut in two. The *Affondatore* raced up and down the broken line displaying signals, but since all the ships were wrapped in flags, banners, and pennants, and since the captains were not at all sure where the Admiral was, the signals were ignored. The Italian fleet, confused and disorganized, engaged a fleet that was inferior in guns, armor, and numbers, but that fought as a disciplined, enthusiastic unit.

The Austrian ironclads divided, wheeling to port and starboard to attack the two segments of the Italian line. A point-blank melee ensued. Ironclads and wooden warships rammed each other indiscriminately and bravely, with the rammer generally receiving the worst of each encounter. Persano, ensconced behind the five-inch plates of the *Affondatore*, attempted several times to ram, but at the last minute each time he turned his exaggerated ram bow aside. The wooden ships suffered in this melee, but the ironclads endured surprisingly light casualties. The supposed Italian flagship, *Re d'Italia*, her helm disabled, became the gruesome exception. Tegetthof, noting the *Re d'Italia*'s condition, immediately made for her with the intention of ramming. The Italian captain appeared to share the palsied irresolution of his Admiral and, while deciding whether to go ahead or astern, received Tegetthof's blow full amidships. A hole three hundred square feet in area was opened; heeled over to starboard by the shock of impact, the ship rolled back to port and plunged beneath the surface. For decades, the fate of the *Re d'Italia* was to serve as an example of the awful power of the ram.

A confused ramming and counter-ramming continued, but this time, because all ships were under way, although in complete confusion, no serious damage resulted. The Italian wooden ships, plus the ironclad *Terribile,* remained passive spectators throughout the entire battle, completely unlike the Austrian unarmored ships, which were to be found in the thick of the action. With the loss of the *Re d'Italia* and the withdrawal of the burning *Palestro,* which later blew up with almost all hands, the Italian fleet was reduced to eight ironclads. Also notably absent was the misnamed *Terribile.*

After an hour and a half of fighting, the fleets began to draw apart, each in line-ahead formation. Tegetthof, now between the Italian fleet and Lissa, had no wish to continue the battle, while Persano, with the odds increasing in Tegetthof's favor, was even less inclined to fight. From the *Affondatore* the wretched Admiral signaled to inquire the whereabouts of the *Re d'Italia.* With exquisite irony the answer returned, *"affondato"* (sunk).

The "Sinker" sinking. Italian ironclad turret ram *Affondatore* foundering after the battle of Lissa. NATIONAL MARITIME MUSEUM, LONDON.

Perhaps the most striking finding of the battle was the imperviousness of armor to guns. Tegetthof's ironclads were almost unscathed. Only the Austrian wooden line-of-battleship *Kaiser* suffered appreciable damage. Much of this good fortune can be attributed to wild Italian gunnery. Whole broadsides were discharged minus shot, which was sometimes rammed in before powder, and aiming was practically nonexistent. Nonetheless, even those shot which by some miracle were correctly loaded, aimed, and fired, failed in every case to penetrate the Austrian ironclads.

Obviously, the Italian fleet had suffered far more. Two ironclads had disappeared, and, to some extent, all but the dilatory *Terribile* had suffered some damage, caused in most cases by shells entering through the unarmored portions of the hull. But no ship was lost or even severely damaged by ordnance alone. Again, it must be remembered that Tegetthof possessed only one hundred twenty-one rifled guns, the only ordnance of any value against armor, to Persano's two hundred seventy-six.

Tegetthof's victory was seen by its partisans as a wonderful affirmation of the ram. The one successful ramming was vividly remembered; the score of unsuccessful attempts, both at Lissa and in the American Civil War, were ignored. The fact that no further ironclad fleet actions took place for almost three decades after Lissa served to perpetuate this opinion about the ram. Naval tacticians of the time may be said to have made the same mistake as Persano, that of overestimating the value of materiel.

IV

One of the first reactions to the battle of Lissa, a Foreign Office report passed on to the Admiralty, correctly attributed the Italian disaster to "the inability and indecision of the supreme command." The officers were dispirited although they were composed "of the best families in the country." [40]

Not many months had passed, however, before contemporary opinion had seized upon the ram as the major "lesson from Lissa." *Colburn's United Service Magazine* opined that Lissa had demonstrated the ineffectiveness of naval ordnance, and thought that "it would be well worth considering whether it would not be advisable to build ironclads for the express purpose of ramming, and instead of arming them with guns, putting the metal on their sides so as to render them entirely impregnable to shot." [41]

But the most influential analysis of the battle was drawn up by Commander Colomb. Obviously delighted to find the opinion he had expressed in 1865 apparently so triumphantly vindicated, Colomb was little disposed to criticize Persano. Therefore he concentrated on the tactics and formations of the two commanders. For Colomb, Lissa had proved the value of close-in fighting, which was "more consistent with our English character, and more suited to it than fighting at range." The gun had reached its apogee; only decline was left for it. The utilization of the gun, particularly in broadside, was ineffectual. To use its guns, a warship had to expose its flanks to some extent, and such exposure would be the ram's opportunity. For the rammer, only the bow would be revealed. The ram could thus press its attack with near impunity. Colomb carried out elaborate calculations to prove that the gun was practically incapable of stopping an attacking warship, especially a low-lying ram, because of the smoke and rapidly changing distances in battle. The notoriously inefficient Italian gunnery served only to confirm Colomb's deprecation of ordnance. The results of Tegetthof's gunnery were not so readily ascertainable since two Italian ships had been lost during the battle, and the *Affondatore* foundered after Lissa, possibly because of battle damage.

According to Colomb, the fleet of the future, trusting to its rams instead of to its powder, would arrange itself in a line-abreast formation with a very wide front, thus ensuring mobility, and keeping the enemy in a state of perplexity as to where the dreaded ram would strike. To his critics who pointed out that the ram might be disabled by well-directed gunfire, Colomb replied that the number of misses due to improper elevation far exceeded those due to error of direction. Therefore, to hit a target at a distance altering at a rate of three hundred yards per minute, with ordnance firing less than one round in a minute and a half, would be almost impossible. And the psychological effect of a broad line of ironclads, each equipped with a deadly underwater snout and rushing irresistibly upon the enemy, would be as disabling as any material damage. For Colomb, the ram was the ultimate weapon, but like so many advocates of such sweeping concepts, he neglected countermeasures. Colomb's observations, presented in May 1867, again before the Royal United Service Institute, were opposed by gunnery officers, and were generally coolly received.[42]

But when Comdr. Pownell Pellew's paper was presented the following month before the Royal United Service Institution, Colomb found a ready ally. Pellew's naval battle would be of short duration; a half hour would see the demolition of one or the other of the opposing fleets. And Pellew warned that such a disaster could well befall the British Navy unless, among other considerations, emphasis were not given to the ram, "the arm of naval warfare to which I attach the chief importance." Pellew apparently envisaged the use of rams only in coastal waters, even though he thought that "the aim of all manoeuvring and preliminary practice with the guns should be to get a fair opportunity for letting slip the rams." These craft should be "low, unsinkable, quick-turners, and of great speed.[43]

During the discussion on Pellew's paper, the old-school supporters of grappling hooks and boarders, still quoting Nelson, were much in evidence. Generally, the assembled officers agreed that tactics and fleet evolutions were in a most unscientific state. But again the emphasis was upon the perfecting of the movements of fleets and ships, and very little was said about the day of battle. Commander Colomb did take the opportunity to "clarify" his previous thesis:

"I do not mean to say that the ram will do the most destructive work; but I believe that it will become the governing weapon of fleets, and that fleets will have to fight more with reference to avoiding the stroke of a ram than getting their guns to bear."[44]

The cruises of the Channel Fleet in 1867 and 1868 presented a further opportunity for naval officers to give their opinions on naval tactics and the ram. Adm. A. P. Ryder evaluated the ships of his fleet almost entirely according to their ability to ram. He had no doubt that the new, shorter warships designed by E. J. Reed were better suited for the task than were the previous lengthy ironclads of the *Warrior* and *Minotaur* classes. Since both the older and the newer classes possessed speed and weight enough for effective ramming, preference must be given to the warship most easily handled, able to ram another moving ironclad at any desired point or at any angle. Such a warship should also have greater ability to avoid a ram because of moderate dimensions. Admiral Ryder reflected that recent French works on tactics evidently entrusted their warships' fate almost entirely to ramming. The peloton formation, in particular, seemed intentionally designed for this purpose.[45]

Adm. Lord Clarence Paget, Commander of the Mediterranean Squadron, wrote in the same year that "Lissa seems to prove that the offensive and defensive qualities of the *sides* of vessels of war [that is, ordnance and armour] are wholly secondary to those of their bows."[46]

The Battle of Lissa and the writings of advocates of the ram had their repercussions in the Whitehall precincts of the Admiralty. Capt. John D. Hay, a member of the Board of Admiralty, apparently became a complete convert to the ram. He noted in an Admiralty paper: "I quite agree with the remark made by Admiral Tegetthof that the stem will decide future naval battles. I believe that our attention should be directed to powerful, swift, handy steam rams."[47]

The chief constructor, who had asserted three years before Lissa that "the wholesale destruction of ships by ramming them will never be a favourite system of warfare among European navies," by 1869 had come to believe that even increased gun power would not remove the ram from its position as an important auxiliary weapon. Reed also praised his own ships for their handiness, which he attributed to moderate dimensions, and was convinced that his form of ram bow, a gracefully curving spur reaching well below the waterline and an enemy's side-armor, would prove to be the only correct design.[48] A year later, however, Reed seemed far more convinced of the ram's efficacy, proclaiming, "it is the ram—and with it the 'sea torpedo'— that will henceforth work the greatest destruction in a naval action."[49] Reed's faith in his underwater ram bow was to be justified, but tragically, when several British and foreign ironclads so equipped later were rammed and sunk accidentally by their own consorts in time of peace.

A balanced view of the power of the ram and of artillery was maintained by Admiral Robinson. In his opinion, "Modern naval warfare shows that there are two distinct powers of destruction in fleets or ships, the power of artillery and the power of impact; the latter abundantly difficult to use but fearfully efficacious, the former easier to handle, but not so instantaneous in its effects."[50] Robinson, the year previous, had quickly scouted the idea of small steam rams. He agreed with the chief constructor upon the impossibility of combining a small and a fast warship. The impact from such a small ram would be negligible, particularly against an armored ship's flank, and low speed would accentuate this lack of offensive power. But Robinson, thinking that rams of moderate tonnage could slip in during battle to deliver a few blows surreptitiously, strongly defended the policy of equipping all ironclads with the ram bow, although he still held to the view that guns and armor, not mere speed and impact, would give the victory.[51]

In 1868 an Admiralty publication issued to naval captains gave the first detailed instructions for ramming. Upper yards were to be cleared away and the bowsprit run in, ports and scuttles closed, anchors and davits turned inwards, and ladders, boats, and booms secured. The warship was to be fully cleared for action, with guns shotted and run out, and watertight doors closed. Just before the awful moment of impact, the crew was to throw itself on deck and the engines were to be stopped. After the blow, engines would be reversed to withdraw the prow from the rammed enemy, taking care to avoid wrenching the ram. But this Admiralty paper considered the ram as an auxiliary to ordnance, and not the ultimate weapon.[52] Admiralty thought on the subject found tangible expression the same year with the laying down of the first of a trio of British rams that combined ramming with coastal defense duties. (cf. chap. 6).

The ram continued to acquire its advocates. Captain Inglefield agreed with Robinson's conception of ramming, asserting that the ram would make its greatest impact after the first shock of battle by striking down disabled ironclads, "in a perfectly cool, almost cold-blooded manner." [53] In the discussion that followed Captain Inglefield's paper, Commander Colomb expressed his gratification at the number of naval officers devoting their attention to the ram since he had first publicly broached its use in 1865. For Colomb, the popularity of the ram was "a sign of the times" pointing the way to "the weapon of the future for naval attack and defence." Colomb disagreed with Inglefield's proposition that the ram would be most effective after the first stages of a naval battle. He believed that the ram should be unleashed first, because the moral effect—the "nerve-disturbance" of the enemy—would give the attacking fleet the mastery. If the ram were held back, the confusion of battle would make it difficult to distinguish between friend and foe.[54]

John Scott Russell, designer of the *Warrior*, continued this theme in a lecture before the Institution of Naval Architects. He agreed that naval battle would revolve almost entirely around the ram. "It is no longer guns, turrets, or broadsides that end the fray. It is the stem that wins or sinks. 'Give her the stem' is the order of battle." Russell concluded: "Think of an engagement between two fleet ships of modern speed. They are two miles apart and in four minutes one is stem-on in the other—perhaps they strike—perhaps they miss? If they miss they are off at full speed to come on again; that is a sea fight." [55]

However, Commander Colomb and the advocates of the ram did not enjoy unanimous support, nor did everyone ascribe the Austrian success at Lissa exclusively to the ram. The *Naval and Military Gazette* objected to the ram bow, which by then was fitted to all ironclads, because of the extra weight at the extremity, the destruction of fine sailing lines by the ungainly underwater protuberance, the consequent bow-wave, increased resistance, and lack of maneuverability. The journal also pointed to the difficulty of ramming an alert opponent and the danger of the rammer's bow being forced under and broken off. In fact, the damage to the rammer might very well be as great as that to its supposed victim. [56]

Capt. Houston Stewart, later Controller of the Navy, also doubted the possibility of ramming a ship that was under weigh, especially if both warships were of almost equal size and speed. He pointed to the American Civil War for proof. In actions fought almost exclusively in inland waters and in harbors, no ship under weigh, whether ironclad or wooden, was successfully rammed. When ironclad rammed ironclad, the damage had proved negligible. [57]

Officers with conservative tactical concepts regarded the ram with suspicion. Adm. Sir Edward Belcher extolled "the glory of the old tar-boarding" and professed himself extremely dubious about the entire concept of ramming because it jeopardized "the very essence of the gallant seaman's aim, *getting alongside his adversary*" (Belcher's italics). However, Belcher rightly emphasized that an enemy warship must suffer from incompetent handling and loss of speed before it could be rammed effectively. [58]

The Battle of Lissa itself was more accurately interpreted

by some observers. *Colburn's United Service Magazine* asserted: "In fact nothing further is taught by this battle than that no improvements or inventions in either guns or naval construction can make up for badly-trained sailors." [59] The astute Disraeli also attributed the Italian defeat more to lack of training than to the Austrian ram: "I can only say that in that instance [Lissa], the Italian guns and gunnery were notoriously deficient." [60]

With the coming of the Franco-Prussian War, the apostle of the ram, Admiral Sartorius, burst into a flurry of letter writing to The *Times*, demanding the full utilization of rams. Peering into the near future, he predicted that to the side "with the strongest nerve, guiding the handiest and quickest ram, and trusting the least to guns" would go the victory. He also asserted that for ocean service, the ram should be stripped of all guns and armor. If England were to be dragged into the Continental struggle, the gallant Admiral would offer to volunteer for service on any ram that the Admiralty might fit out on his principle. A fortnight later Sartorius's patriotic gore had somewhat subsided, and he set out detailed instructions dealing with the strategy of battle by ramming. He was on firm ground when he pointed out the extreme difficulty at that time of hitting any target with the methods of gunnery then in use, the primitive sighting, and the slow rate of fire. Thus rams, by virtue of their small target area, handiness and speed, could cripple a fleet of lumbering ironclads. The rams would approach from different directions, forcing the ironclads to divide their fire. The latter, paralyzed by indecision and fear of hitting their fellows with gunfire, would fall easy victim to the fast-moving rams. If the ironclads attempted to outmaneuver the rams, they would soon find themselves with empty coal bunkers.

Sartorius divided his rams into coastal-defense, European, and high-seas classes. In the first class he had the satisfaction of seeing some of his ideas put into effect, because the Admiralty had already laid down a number of coastal-defense turret rams. The coastal class of ram was to be armed and armored, but to be stripped of masts and sails; the second class was to be partially plated and armed, with fore and aft sails; and the last, a seagoing ram, was to be a very fast (eighteen–nineteen knots) warship, bereft of guns and armor, equipped with masts that could be lowered in combat and a hull that could admit water to sink it almost out of an enemy's sight.[61]

Few authorities of the time went to such lengths as did John Scott Russell or Admiral Sartorius in advocating the abolition of large ironclads and guns and armor and in pressing for the exclusive use of the ram. But a consensus of official opinion appeared to be that the large conventional ironclad, broadside or turret, would be able to use its ram to greater advantage than its guns. For example, Admiral Ryder gave a great deal of attention to the technique of ramming. In his memorandum to the Admiralty, he called attention to the angle of impact in ramming, pointing out the danger of the ram's being wrenched off if the attack were made at right angles to the victim's course. The rammer should approach parallel to his intended victim's course, then put over his helm hard and attempt to ram. Breaking free after the blow would then be a mere matter of reversing engines, unless the rammer wished to board the rammed. But Admiral Ryder said nothing of rams superseding guns, or of rendering armor obsolete.[62]

These theories of the ram and its use could not be put to the test during the Franco-Prussian War. The Prussian ironclad fleet was effectively blockaded in the Jade until the signing of the armistice, and no battles have been recorded between ironclads in that war. Only in the West Indies was the conflict carried to sea. Since both the French *Bouvet* and the Prussian *Meteor* were wooden unarmored warships, little in the way of tactical lessons could be learned from their clash. It was precisely this lack of battle testing of the ram that permitted the most fantastic claims for its superiority to be so little questioned by informed opinion.

The Committee on Designs, whose recommendations

were to influence naval architecture for the next two decades, turned its attention briefly to naval tactics, concentrating its deliberations and recommendations almost exclusively upon the ram. It reported: "The importance of ramming in future naval warfare is likely to be so great, that in designing armour-clad ships particular attention should, and we doubt not, will be paid to the best means of resisting it." The committee was one of the first authorities to consider the question of defense against ramming. Previous writers had merely stressed maneuverability and handiness as a defense against an enemy's prow. The Committee on Designs recommended the "cellular or raft system of construction" that could absorb and dissipate the blow from an underwater ram, mine, or torpedo without affecting the integrity of the entire warship.[63]

As important as the recommendation of the committee was the testimony of representative witnesses upon whom the committee relied. Admiral Robinson asserted that all future naval engagements would be dominated at the outset by ahead-fire, both for closing with the enemy and for ramming, which he now believed "will decide most naval actions." [64] E. J. Reed (no longer chief constructor), asserted that the gun was now secondary to the ram, and that all warships should be designed as efficient rams.[65] The current Chief Constructor, Nathaniel Barnaby, had nothing to say on the subject of naval tactics. Admiral Symonds reinforced Admiral Ryder's preference for ramming on an enemy's quarter rather than beam-on, but pointed out that "it is a difficult thing to ram a ship." [66] Captain Sherard Osborne, Captain Coles's intimate associate, was equally cautious about the power of the ram. It could decide naval actions only after the enemy was disabled. If the commander of the enemy ship were a "lubber," ramming might destroy him. But if the enemy warship were efficiently handled, gunfire would be needed to pound him into submission. Nevertheless, all ironclads should be fitted as rams.[67]

Neither in its report nor in its witness's testimony did the

Committee on Designs dwell at any length on the broader question of naval tactics. This was left to the minority report of Admirals Elliot and Ryder who entirely dissented from the conclusions of the majority of the committee. Ryder and Elliot were firmly convinced that "as regards sea-going vessels, the most destructive means of attack will be found in the *ram* and the torpedo. . . ." End-on artillery fire was to be an important auxiliary weapon to the ram. Elliot and Ryder called for ramming experiments after the example of the Russian Admiral Boutakov. Since hull armor was useless because of the increasing power of artillery, subdivision and the cellular raft-body would take its place. In battle, "rapid movement and close quarters will be the rule of fighting, and depressed fire at close quarters the most deadly practice, because it will search the vitals." The dissenting report called for end-on formation in battle, based on the French peloton, "the system *par excellence* for end-on attack and ramming." Finally, the authors preferred moderate tonnage for handiness in ramming and torpedo warfare.[68]

The Committee on Designs, in both its official and dissentient reports, was undoubtedly influenced by the writings of Capt. J. C. R. Colomb, particularly those works dating from 1870 and 1872. Colomb felt that his belief in the supremacy of the ram had been more than proved in the years since his first articles on naval tactics appeared in 1865 and 1867. He argued that, since the Battle of Lissa, the gun had declined to the point where it was now five times as inferior to armor as it had been in 1867: "This seems to me a very startling conclusion to arrive at, and one which lies at the root of all construction and armament." Because of increases in thickness of armor and the demonstrated difficulty of moving ships to hit targets at any appreciable distance, ordnance was powerless except at short range. At the time of Lissa the *Bellerophon* could fire four rounds per gun in six minutes. But the later *Monarch*, according to Colomb, could now fire only one round per piece in three minutes, because of the increased size of her guns. At distances beyond one thousand yards, inefficient aiming would serve to complete the invulnerability of an ironclad. Colomb was thus forced by the logic of his complex arguments to accept the ram as the only weapon capable of delivering a decisive blow in a naval battle. He asserted: "Dating from the first utterance of our gallant Admiral of the Fleet, Sir George Rose Sartorius, the ram has carried all navies by storm"—all except Britain's. He lamented that the Royal Navy had failed to heed the lessons of Lissa, and had persisted in constructing huge, heavily gunned warships (although they were armed with ram bows). But compared to Russia's ramming jousts and to France's belief "that the ram, and the ram only, need be feared at sea," Admiralty efforts seemed only halfhearted tokens of interest in the ram.

Colomb carried on the detailed work of Admiral Boutakov by carefully ascertaining the best method for ramming and for avoiding the ram. On each side of a vessel he predicted an imaginary circle based on a ship's turning power. Another ship within this circle could with impunity ram the first vessel, unable to turn within its own circles. Outside the circle neither ship could ram. Colomb asserted: "It seems to me that the whole art and mystery of ramming will be found to consist in this endeavor to get your adversary outside your own circle while you remain inside his." He now condemned the end-on approach to ramming, since one ship or the other must give way and present her bow-quarters in so doing. Otherwise, two adversaries would press on and ram bow to bow—an unthinkable proposition. Bow fire would also be useless since it merely served to blind the gunners. Broadsides could be used to good effect if they were reserved until passing by the enemy after a ramming attempt. Colomb saw little likelihood of elaborate maneuvering in battle; the opposing fleets should be in formation before the clash and should maintain that formation as much as possible throughout. The fleets would advance in good order and charge through each other, discharging broadsides, but rarely bow guns. For all his continued advocacy of the ram Colomb had now come to favor the old line-ahead formation. He saw no value in an extended-front arrangement, for by 1872 he had come to feel that the ram would be useless for fleet action, although still decisive in single-ship combats. But since he had demonstrated, to his own satisfaction at least, that the gun had practically reached the limit of its usefulness, Colomb's fleet battles had to rely on the dubious prospect of close-in broadside firing to gain the day.[69]

Following Colomb's lead, Staff Comdr. Philip Going called for the same practice of ramming as was utilized in gunnery. The human eye, personal judgment, and courage were not enough. A captain attempting to ram should be fully informed of his warship's exact speed at various revolutions of the screw, its backing power, and the time required for turning quarter, half, and full circles. By utilizing a series of geometric segments drawn up in accordance with this information, a ship intent upon ramming would find such work not only immensely simplified, but also emancipated from human error. These scientific maneuverings would be invaluable also for artillery fire and torpedo warfare. But if mathematics failed, then recourse could be taken to boarding, "that well-practised physical force, always a favourite means adopted by our predecessors for bringing the contest to a successful issue, (*and has it ever failed?*)." [70]

Although controversy raged around the question of the relative value of the ram and the gun, few critics ever dared to question the entire concept of ramming. Perhaps the only writer of this time who actually did so was Comdr. Wallace B. Hardy, who in 1873 asserted the heresy that "Lissa, itself, which is so often quoted by the advocates of the ram as an instance of its success, is, on the contrary, the best illustration of its possible failure." He pointed to the fact that Tegetthof's efficient fleet could manage to sink only one disabled Italian ironclad, although both sides made continual, desperate attempts to ram: "Is this, we ask, the mode of attack which offers to the British Navy the surest guarantee of success, the largest scope for our national characteristics of undaunted courage and coolness?" He explained that if speed and handiness were equal, avoiding a ram's blow would be simple. The vessel attacked could alter its speed or course at any time, forcing the potential rammer to change completely the path of collision. Hardy also delivered some trenchant criticisms of current naval gunnery, and deplored the Royal Navy's serious experiments with the Whitehead torpedo. As a gunnery officer, he felt that the torpedo and ram were good examples of the Royal Navy's "blind confidence in untried weapons." Although Commander Hardy's denunciation of the navy's impulsive adoption of any new invention sounded strange then, as now, his arguments against the ram were based on sound reasoning, and his was a more accurate interpretation of Lissa than that of any of his contemporaries.[71]

But Commander Hardy's doubts carried no great influence within the Royal Navy. The prize essay of the Junior Naval Professional Association for 1874 was won by a paper that insisted that all naval powers must have ramming warships, that all warships ought to be rams, and that all officers should be skilled in ramming.[72]

Another competitor for the Junior Naval Professional Association's prize, John K. Laughton, later professor of Modern History at King's College, London, approached the ram from a more scientific viewpoint. He studied the numerous collisions between merchant ships and the battle experiences of the American Civil War and Lissa, and from these was able to estimate striking-forces and angles of impacts for warships. Laughton urged that this information be calculated and distributed to all warships. But, withal, the knowledge of the ram would be better acquired by practice allied to practical skill, cool judgment, a quick eye, and "a sound digestion." [73]

The ram continued to receive the highest encomiums for

H.M.S. *Hotspur*. Royal Navy ram ironclad. Circular structure forward is encased turntable mounting one gun, but the main armament was the underwater ram. Note total absence of stern protection. NATIONAL MARITIME MUSEUM, LONDON.

the next two decades. For example, Lord Brassey, one of the most respected authorities on the Royal Navy, wrote in 1882: "It was proved at the Battle of Lissa that the ram is a most formidable offensive weapon of naval warfare, destined perhaps to take the first place in future engagements." [74] And as late as 1904, one year before the laying down of the first British battleship without a ram, H.M.S. *Dreadnought*, Nathaniel Barnaby could discourse on the most efficient forms of the ram bow.[75]

Although the ram persisted until the twentieth century, as a serious weapon it was given its deathblow, literally, by a series of accidental collisions that were sometimes attended with serious loss of life. These disasters were compiled and precisely analyzed by William Laird Clowes, an influential naval writer and Fellow of King's College, London. He demonstrated that, of the seventy-four cases in which the ram was essayed in action between 1861 and 1879, thirty-six resulted in no damage whatsoever, eighteen caused slight damage, and only twenty ended in serious injury to either rammer or rammed. Clowes reached the "remarkable" but not original conclusion that ramming on the open sea was impossible unless the enemy were disabled. Pointing to the recent *Victoria-Camperdown* disaster, Clowes concluded that the ram had proved to be more dangerous to friend than to foe.[76] His arguments seem overwhelmingly convincing today, but they did not pass unchallenged at the time. Only the continued development of large and small breechloading ordnance, the torpedo, and marine engines finally convinced the Royal Navy that ramming as a mode of warfare was not only worthless, but also dangerous.

In summary, the conclusion seems inescapable that the study and practice of tactics filled a distinctly subordinate role to design and construction in the Royal Navy in the 1860s and early 1870s. In fact, Admiral Bridge, looking back over this period, noted that "the word 'tactics' was rarely heard, and when it was heard it applied to the practical evolutions or drill of a fleet."[77] Official manuals of fleet evolutions would allot only a few pages to battle tactics, the rest being devoted to evolutions that at best developed the unity of a squadron, and at worst became the sole criteria for evaluating battleworthiness.

Much of this situation seems almost inevitable. Lacking battle experience, the British Navy was compelled to rely upon Lissa, the more or less accurate accounts of the American Civil War, and theory. Furthermore, coal was too costly and engines too inefficient to permit the extensive and realistic battle maneuvers necessary to test the validity of current tactical theory. Consequently, there was little agreement on the method of naval warfare for ironclads.

These reasons, plus the lack of a naval staff, go far toward explaining the great popularity of so untried a weapon as the ram. But a general apathy toward tactical thought is also evident, both in the paucity of official writing on the subject and in the chidings of those few writers who did concern themselves with tactics. This lack of interest may well have sprung from the same conservative, anti-scientific attitude that hindered the establishment of the Royal School of Naval Architecture, a Naval Intelligence Department, and a naval staff. Nevertheless, the design and development of the British capital ship was greatly affected by the prevailing tactical opinions of the day, such as they were.

Those officers who troubled to study and write about tactics never grouped themselves into schools of thought, or united in any way to press their views upon the Admiralty. The only point upon which most agreed was the supposed dreadful power of the ram. But all held differing views as to its employment, as to whether it would be best utilized in the traditional line-ahead formation, line-abreast, or a combination of the two. Their writing may be generally described as purely theoretical, for the writers all lacked ironclad battle experience and were compelled to rely upon foreign examples that were in many respects totally inapplicable to the probable demands upon the Royal Navy. Yet their work did affect Admiralty tactical thought, and official manuals allotted space to most of the prevalent tactical theories. More important for this study, tactical writing profoundly affected ironclad design.

The emphasis upon the ram is most obvious, with the sweeping cleaver bow dominating the prow of most armored warships of the 1860s. The consequent demand for maneuverability and handiness for delivering and avoiding the ram accounts in large measure for Reed's emphasis upon stubby hulls, and later led to the introduction of twin screws. The development of the turret ship, on the other hand, was postponed by the consideration that such a vessel would be seriously deficient in ahead-fire, particularly if fitted with masts, when compared to a box-battery vessel, which could bring four heavy guns to bear in axial fire to clear the way for a ramming attack. (cf. chap. 7). The widespread belief (reinforced by the battle of Lissa) that future naval battles would be close-action melees meant that the unsatisfactory state of gunnery continued with only a muted chorus of protest. This primitive concept of battle further delayed the acceptance of the turret, for the Coles-Ericsson invention was primarily an aid to the efficient handling of heavy, long-range ordnance. In summary, the general effect of tactical thinking of the 1860s and 1870s was to inhibit the development of the modern capital ship.

6

Deployment

I

Strategy may well be considered another major area of neglect in the early ironclad era. Such negligence is hardly surprising at a time when a conscientious naval officer or Admiralty administrator had all he could do to keep abreast of the rapid and complex technological changes so drastically transforming the materiel of the fleet. It was as yet too early to assess the total role of the new steam navy and the purpose of its component ironclads; three decades were to pass before Admiral Mahan would magisterially outline the principles of seapower. As L. G. Carr Laughton reminisced: "The men in this country who knew, before the publication of Mahan's first volume, what [sea power] is and what it can do might have been numbered on a man's fingers, perhaps on those of one hand." [1] As a result, the Royal Navy reversed its traditional strategy of relegating the home waters to last-ditch defense, and now elevated them to the United Kingdom's primary moat defensive.

At the beginning of this period, the Admiralty rather fondly hoped that the deployment of its armored warships would be of the most simple nature, with the valuable ironclads remaining in port for most of the time, embarking on an occasional cruise. [2] As long as France remained the only other ironclad power, this policy had some justification, especially that of economy. But the Admiralty had failed to reckon with the laissez-faire propensities of private United Kingdom shipbuilders, who soon provided Russia, Prussia,

Spain, Italy, and Austria with ironclad fleets of their own. And, of course, the phenomenal emergence of America to pretensions of ironclad power enormously complicated the deployment of British ironclads. Other naval powers soon began to develop something of a defensive invulnerability, for, to a greater extent than Great Britain, they could concentrate on the armor and ordnance of their ironclads and slight their sea-keeping abilities. Great Britain and, to a much lesser extent, France, had to consider questions of colonial defense, commerce, and communications, and to attempt to strike a balance between the Channel and Mediterranean fleets and the overseas demands for ironclads. The Admiralty and the government found themselves in an uncomfortable dilemma: a home fleet was essential to survival as a nation, and as a shield against invasion, but Great Britain's commerce and colonial power were of almost equal importance. But the great cost and length of building-time required for each ironclad rendered impossible a policy of satisfying both demands. The course adopted was one of constant strengthening of the Channel and Mediterranean fleets, with the older or weaker ironclads sent overseas. At the same time, the unarmored fleet was kept busily engaged in the familiar tasks of showing the flag, anti-slaver patrol, protection of colonial interests, and support of minor military operations.

The major ironclad units of the fleet, such as the *Warrior*, *Bellerophon*, and *Monarch* could be considered as a home guard, with the ability to proceed under sail to distant waters. All such first-class armorclads were assigned to the Channel or Mediterranean fleets. Here they could deal with the ironclad fleets of Britain's European rivals. In the words of Admiral Robinson, "If we have to contend for great national purposes with either France or Russia, the contest must be in European waters; the Channel, the Mediterranean, or the Baltic will be the scenes of strifes [*sic*] fearful to contemplate." [3] Commerce protection and colonial defense, then, were considered subordinate to the "great national purposes" that could be settled only by first-class ironclads (possibly aided by the more powerful coastal armorclads) contending in European waters. Nonetheless, and somewhat paradoxically, all first-class warships, until the laying down of the *Devastation*, carried square sail rig to enable them to take up duties anywhere in the world.

Early in 1863 Admiral Robinson submitted a memorandum on Admiralty construction principles that crystallized strategic policy for the coming decade. For Robinson, the sending of first-class ironclads on distant oceanic cruising or on commerce protection duties would seriously weaken the Home Fleet, leaving it on a bare equality with France. Therefore, the aim should be to station at home turret ships in which seaworthiness was subordinated to guns and armor, and to dispatch partially belted cruisers, equipped with full-sail power, to stations abroad.[4] With modification, this policy was implemented by the Admiralty. Whereas in 1863 all five of Britain's commissioned ironclads were stationed with the Channel Fleet, by late 1867 six ironclads (out of twenty-four completed) were patrolling the Channel, four were in the Mediterranean, two wooden armorclads were in the Pacific station, and two were on the North American station. Until E. J. Reed designed the *Audacious* class for distant service, the Admiralty's policy was to send wooden ironclads to far stations such as North America and China, where their inflammable construction would not prove such hostages to fortune, nor would their wooden hulls be crippled by fouling.[5] But the wooden ironclads were not particularly speedy and were thus unsatisfactory for anti-privateer or commerce-raiding work. Later, as new ironclads were accepted from the fitting-out yards, the earlier iron armorclads were also sent overseas.

II

Not until 1868 did the Admiralty feel justified in diverting facilities from ironclad construction to lay down the

Inconstant, the first unarmored iron cruiser. Depredations of the *Alabama* had indeed provided an object lesson on the vulnerability of British merchant shipping. But such delay is understandable considering the French challenge in iron-clads and the still-prevalent fear of invasion. The concept of the inviolability of private property on the high seas, of which John Bright was only the most prominent exponent, may have influenced the Admiralty to assign protection of commerce a relatively low priority.[6] But the demand for protection from commerce raiders for Britain's scattered merchant ships developed and gathered strength after the effects of the *Alabama*'s spoliations became obvious. Lord Palmerston warned that the Yankees would soon emulate the Confederates in the probable war with Britain, and that they would dispatch "a swarm of fast steamers, not armour-plated and not meant for fighting, but speedy enough to escape from our cruisers, and strong enough to capture any merchantman." The only answer to these commerce raiders would be to lay down faster, more powerful warships to "catch and make an example of such cruisers." [7] The end of the American Civil War revealed how the American merchant fleet had been driven from the seas and forced to seek shelter under foreign flags, and had suffered a blow from which it was never to recover. The fact that this blow was dealt by a mere handful of often extemporized cruisers was not lost upon the Admiralty, or on the Americans for that matter. In April 1866, Reed submitted designs for a warship "to carry a few heavy guns at a high speed without armourplating." [8] While the ship's duties were not defined either in Reed's particulars or in Admiral Robinson's covering submission, they were obviously directed toward anti-commerce raiding.

Lord Lennox briefly summarized the task of this *Inconstant* class: "They are designed to protect our commerce in case of a rupture with America." [9] But of the three cruisers proposed, only one was immediately laid down. Those who feared for the safety of Britain's mercantile marine could hardly be satisfied with one commerce protector when the Americans were boasting of a whole class of seventeen-knot, wooden-hulled commerce raiders, laid down since the Civil War. If Britain could effectively guard her merchant ships, she could dissuade the Americans from belligerent adventures. As the First Sea Lord, Admiral Dacres, noted, "nothing would tend to preserve peace between ourselves and the Americans so much as the knowledge that we could protect our own commerce and harrass theirs." [10] British cruisers would pose little threat to America's fast-dwindling merchant marine, and even less to her territory, strongly defended as it was (at least in the eyes of the Admiralty) by a swarm of powerful monitors. But Dacres hesitated to build more cruisers of the *Inconstant* type, as large and almost as expensive as a seagoing ironclad. Lord Lennox, First Secretary of the Admiralty, had written to Disraeli that "smaller vessels of immense speed and carrying heaviest guns" [11] were more needed. But Lennox was calling for the impossible, a not-uncommon trait among civilian Admiralty administrators. Two greatly reduced *Inconstants* were ordered at a much lower cost. They could mount only eighteen sixty-four-pounder rifles, and steam at a top speed of a little under fifteen knots; the *Inconstant* carried in its main battery ten twelve-ton rifles at a speed of sixteen-and-one-half knots. Reed and Robinson understandably protested against such "economy." [12]

Agitation for a cruiser squadron more in accord with the size of Britain's merchant navy continued. [13] But the Conservative government in 1866 refused to lay down any more large cruisers, concentrating instead on sloops and gunboats, all of negligible help to oceanic commerce. This policy was continued the following year. [14] In fact, attempts were even made to justify the retention of wooden warships for commerce protection. Admiral Milne gloomily asserted that "no nation has, and never will have, sufficient ironclads for the many purposes war would demand." Wooden ships would be needed to fill the breach. Old line-of-battleships and frigates should be refurbished for this purpose. Since the Americans and the Austrians were still constructing unprotected wooden cruisers, Milne felt that his recommendations were even further justified. Although Milne's memorandum circulated among the members of the Board of Admiralty, his suggestions for the rehabilitation of the rotting wooden fleet were never carried out.[15]

The following year Disraeli's first lord of the Admiralty submitted a similar proposal, adding that the American Admiral Farragut had told him that wooden ships could be a decisive factor in battle and that the Battle of Lissa had proved this point. Again these retrograde suggestions were practically ignored. Disraeli correctly saw wooden warships as a waste of money, a mere means of finding employment for officers, men, and dockyards. He pointed out that some of the smallest South American states possessed ironclads, and that wooden warships arrayed against them would perhaps find themselves in a fatal inferiority.[17]

Gradually the concept of large, fast cruisers and second-class ironclads as protectors of commercial and colonial wealth gathered support. Early in 1868 Lord Henry Lennox and Admiral Robinson called for "flying squadrons" to replace the old wooden "station" squadron composed of ships that could *"neither fight nor run away."* [18] Similarly, Lennox, in moving the new estimates for 1868, explained the government's policy of gradually withdrawing from foreign stations the wooden sloops and gunboats which, when approached by an ironclad or any warship of sufficient displacement to mount heavy ordnance, "must what is vulgarly termed 'cut and run.' " [19] Not until two years later, however, was the decision taken to complete the two remaining large, seagoing cruisers of the *Inconstant* type. And the Royal Navy lagged far behind Russia in the development of armored cruisers, contenting itself with second-class battleships of slow speed and poorly defined purpose.[20] In all, the Royal Navy, preoccupied with securing the home isles from invasion and raids, and in surpassing French ironclad programs, allotted the protection of vital maritime commerce a far lower priority than it deserved.[21]

III

Closely allied to the problem of commerce protection, and relegated to a similar low priority, was that of colonial defense. With growth and increasing prosperity, some of the colonies turned their attention to their exposed and relatively defenseless positions. Canada, in particular, realized the impossibility of repulsing any irruption of the now fully mobilized and belligerent federal states.

Early in 1862 the Duke of Somerset ruminated upon the problems of colonial defense in a memorandum to Lord Palmerston. Because it was difficult enough to extract sufficient funds from Parliament for current naval needs, Somerset concluded that it would be necessary for the colonists to contribute to their own defense, and that such defense should consist of harbor ironclad warships. Unless the colonists could be induced to contribute to their own protection, they would continually renew their calls for more aid as they prospered and expanded. Yet he understood that their contribution to their own defense could lead even to demands for independence or, at the least, to squabbles with foreign powers.[22]

Such thinking led to the Colonial Defense Act of 1865, which provided for a naval reserve and authorized the maritime colonies to put their warships under Admiralty control.[23] This act was to alleviate some of the impossible burden placed upon the resources of the Royal Navy, even in time of peace, for colonial and merchant marine protection. The old wooden corvettes and frigates would no longer suffice in the face of the ironclads now possessed by almost every power of any maritime pretensions. The colonies were in no position either to construct or to maintain a fleet of first-class ironclads, but coast and harbor defense warships should not be beyond their resources. However, only three such armorclads paid for by the colonies were ever constructed, two being stationed in India and one in Australia, where they gave economical, uneventful service until the early twentieth century. The value of such ironclads was questionable, as was the whole concept of local defense with its beguiling promise of economy, but the vessels were of interest for their design because they embodied in their mastless, turreted, twin-screw plan the pattern of future warships.

These three harbor craft could hardly be considered the answer to the problem of colonial defense, and they fell far short of the twenty-six estimated by Capt. J. C. R. Colomb to be necessary for the protection of the more strategic colonies.[24] Yet Admiralty policy remained one of affording protection to all colonies. The second secretary of the Admiralty expressed this resolve clearly in a memorandum to the First Lord, Sir John Pakington, in September 1866: "It is certain that demands for protection will be made from all parts of the world on the first alarm of war; and England will not be satisfied to abandon any of her possessions in the hour of danger." [25]

Because the colonies failed to provide adequately for their own maritime defense, the Royal Navy was compelled to assume the task of defending all British possessions that could be directly threatened from the sea. For this task new ironclad designs would be necessary. The converted wooden ironclads with their average of four-and-one-half-inch armor and their vulnerable timber construction would be no match for the new *Belliqueuse* class of "cruising ironclads" that the French were sending to distant stations.

To meet the French ships Reed drew up plans in 1867 for what was to be called the *Audacious* class. These six box-battery ironclads were remarkable in several ways. They were the first to be designed with a strategic principle in mind, other than that of keeping the French at arm's length. They were among the few capital ships to be built as a class, an economic and efficient arrangement not to be repeated until 1882. But the procurement of the *Audacious* class followed the standard pattern; the board attempted to limit tonnage, this time to three thousand tons, in the interest of economy. On such tonnage the constructor designed an ironclad carrying eight nine-inch and two seven-inch rifles behind six-inch armor plate at a speed of twelve knots. Reed and Robinson expressed their dissatisfaction at so retrograde a step, particularly since the French *Suffren* class carried eight inches of armor, protecting four 10.5-inch rifled guns, and boasted a speed of over fourteen knots. The Admiralty only reluctantly agreed to an increase of tonnage, but insisted upon light draught and full-sail power. The constructor and the controller were willing to accept these conditions in order to obtain the increase of tonnage that would give the new design eight inches of armor plate, ten nine-inch and four six-inch muzzle-loading rifles, and thirteen knots.[26]

Reed deserves full credit for his successful *Audacious* design, which was so hampered by official attitudes. Although the Admiralty intended the ships for distant cruising, Reed envisaged them also as a reply to the turret-ship partisans, whose campaign was reaching its zenith. Unlike Coles's *Captain*, or Reed's own *Monarch*, for that matter, the *Audacious* class could lay down fire directly ahead, and for the first time twin screws were installed on a warship of heavy tonnage. Finally, the *Audacious* was the first British ironclad to float lighter than designed, a tribute to Reed's ability as a designer. The *Audacious* class, officially listed as second-rate, not only dominated the French second-rates sent to foreign stations, but also enjoyed a distinct supremacy over French first-rates.[27]

In the *Audacious* class the influence of Admiralty strategic policy upon design is clearly revealed—the provision of full-sail power for high-seas cruising, even though such provision would naturally affect the fighting efficiency, steaming, and expense of an ironclad. The reason for such a policy lay in the state of marine engineering, in the interest of economy (as noted), and in a lack of sufficient coaling stations and bases. One year after the completion of the *Audacious* class the Parliamentary Committee on Naval Designs recognized that for all its superiority to contemporary French models, the design represented a dead end. The committee undertook a heroic effort to modernize Admiralty strategic thinking. Recognizing the mastless *Devastation* as the true capital ship of the immediate future, the committee maintained that "our transmarine possessions, and other important interests in distant parts of the world, will be more efficiently protected by the establishment, where requisite, of centres of naval power, from which vessels of the *Devastation* class may operate" than by cruising masted ironclads. Since such war-engines as the *Devastation* would be too slow to catch commerce raiders, the committee proposed that protection of the merchant marine be entrusted to unarmored cruisers of the *Inconstant* class.[28]

Such a plan of imperial defense proved far too radical and expensive to be implemented, particularly at a time when colonial relations with the mother country were unsettled. Furthermore, the Admiralty still looked upon France or a Continental combination as the main threat to British sea power. Of course, such strategic planning further undermined the case for sails, for coal was more readily available in the narrow seas, and increased bunkerage could be provided to enable ironclads of the fleet to cruise under steam alone in European waters. The committee recommended that no further first-class ironclads be designed for sail power, but the Board of Admiralty also ignored this advice.

The committee did not achieve unanimity in its recommendations. The dissenting report of Admirals Elliot and Ryder pointed out just how expensive it would have been for the Admiralty to have carried out the majority recommendation that mastless turret ships should operate from global "centres of naval power." In the whole of the Pacific, east of 180° longitude, no such center existed south of Vancouver Island. In the western Atlantic there was nothing of value south of Trinidad except the Falkland Islands. In the Mediterranean, Malta was the only center. Gibraltar was considered an extremity, while in the East no center of naval power existed north of Shanghai. In Africa the ports were too widely spaced. Although the dissenting report agreed on the need for coaling ports, repair bases and docking facilities appeared out of the question at a time of peace, when it was difficult enough to obtain funds for a powerful ironclad fleet even for European waters.[29] In fact, the committee's majority recommendations found favor in almost no public quarter. Reed's magazine, *Naval Science,* denounced the proposals, pointing out that the *Devastation* class was fully two knots slower than foreign commerce-raiding cruisers.[30] The president of the Institution of Civil Engineers called for unarmored, high-speed "sea-hornets," armed with one gun, for ocean patrol work.[31] This impossible combination, which was to be coupled with high coal capacity, was practically the antithesis of the Committee on Designs' majority report. Thus, although recommendations had been made for the establishment of fortified naval bases capable of repairing and replenishing mastless ironclads and for commerce protection by large cruisers, the policy of depending solely upon steam-powered ironclads had to wait at least two decades until the mastless seagoing ironclad and imperial defense were both established realities.[32]

IV

The problems of commerce protection, colonial defense, and global warfare occupied a definitely subordinate category in the already low priority generally assigned to strategy by the Admiralty and by public opinion. This neglect was a complete repudiation of traditional British naval strategy, which had been based on bringing economic pressure, supplemented by amphibious expenditures, on an enemy. In those halcyon pre-Mahan days of the 1860s, the immediate surrounding sea was considered England's moat. Lieutenant Colonel Soady, speaking before the Royal United Service Institution, laid down as a maxim hardly necessary to be discussed that "the frontier of Britain, from its insular position [is] the coast." [33] Previously, in 1860, the Parliamentary Defense Committee had termed the Channel the "first and most obvious line of defense." [34] Gladstone, who remained a firm believer in this principle, envisaged the Royal Navy's task almost entirely in terms of coastal defense. [35] J. C. R. Colomb, who summarized British strategic thought as effectively as his brother, Philip H. Colomb, influenced naval tactics, considering the Channel as the pivot not only for defense against invasion but also for the protection of commerce and even for colonial defense. Although cruisers could render invaluable service abroad, and monitors would be useful for colonial harbor defense, J. C. R. Colomb maintained that "ships adapted for the combined action of fleets (i.e., first-class ironclads) should be kept at home or in the Mediterranean." [36] In 1866 the controller ranked invasion of Britain by a Continental power as the primary contingency for which the navy should be prepared. Colonial defense was second in priority, with protection of commerce a poor third. [37] Admiral Robinson believed that ironclad clashes on the high seas would be rare, and that British warships would do well to sacrifice the "showy" qualities of high speed and great coal capacity, to concentrate on the features of ramming, armor, and ordnance more fitted to the restricted waters surrounding the United Kingdom. [38]

These opinions from the Admiralty and Service writers may seem unimaginative and reactionary, but the limitations of the early ironclads could not be ignored. Admiral Ballard has pointed out that as late as 1870 no British battleship steaming at full speed could reach even Gibraltar. [39] H.M.S.

Hercules, a Reed broadside ship, carried enough coal in her bunkers for only two-and-one-half days' steaming at full speed.[40] Under sail, ironclads could make a passage to distant oceans but, when they arrived, there was no assurance that coal of sufficient quantity or quality would be available for naval warfare, and no one contemplated ironclads' fighting under sail. Thus it is hardly surprising that from 1863 to 1871 a mere five second-class ironclads were stationed overseas on the Pacific, North American and West Indies, and China stations. The British ironclad battle fleet was indeed a home guard.

But while the relatively primitive state of marine engine technology does much to explain the Admiralty's reluctance to station ironclads overseas, public opinion and pressure, as in so many decisions of the Admiralty at this time, influenced board policy. The merchants and manufacturers along the great estuaries of Britain felt strongly that they were defenseless from marauders. *Nautical Magazine*, which spoke for the merchant marine as well as for the Royal Navy, feared that "on a sudden outbreak of war our great ports of trade would be perfectly at the mercy of any daring fellow, who, with a good ship under him, a daredevil crew, and the prospect of 'loot,' should make a dash into any one of them; and after loading his vessel. and perhaps two or three others with booty, escape before we can summon a force to resist him."[41] Such highly imaginative speculations were repeated by the member for Leith, who demanded of the Commons in 1871: "What would be the state of Lancashire and the manufacturing districts if a gunboat were to go up the Mersey and burn up the stock of cotton in the port of Liverpool?"[42] To prevent the looting of Leith and the kindling of Liverpool's cotton stocks, commercial interests demanded light-draught gunboats, preferably on the Coles's turret plan. In this respect the Admiralty constructor and the controller were at one with public agitation. In early 1863 Admiral Robinson had noted with satisfaction that the coastal-defense turret ironclads *Prince Albert* and

Royal Sovereign were finally under construction.[43] He later termed the coastal-defense turret ram "a class of ship our Navy can never be without." [44] The Admiralty, looking back to its experiences in the Crimean War, had been impressed with the possibilities of offensive operations against an enemy's coast. For this type of warfare coastal-defense warships would be eminently suitable. Ignored, of course, was the fact that such coastal operations had rested upon a secure supply route stretching for thousands of nautical miles, and upon a seagoing Royal Navy to overawe Russia's fleet. However, public opinion was still the main force pushing a willing Admiralty into an ill-considered policy of diverting men and money from seagoing to coastal ironclads. The Admiralty was well aware that nearly two coastal-defense-offense ironclads could be built for the price of one oceangoing capital ship, and that such procedure would not only keep the estimates steady but would also swell the gross total of ironclad ships in the navy list. Merchants would be further reassured by the obvious fact that coastal-defense craft would be tied to the immediate area to be defended, ready to protect their stocks of cotton and, because of their unseaworthiness, unable to answer any call for work on the high seas to protect ships bringing that cotton. Few, if any, responsible policy makers or writers went so far as Gladstone however, to assign the navy a mere coast keeping role. Over all, the concept was one of a divided fleet, the major segment for coastal and European waters and a lesser one for the ocean.[45]

The fear of a cross-Channel invasion still provided a further rationale for coastal armorclads. "Hippophlax" in The *Times* painted a lurid picture of enemy dragons carrying off the squire's daughter and other womenfolk on the way to London, after disembarkation from a fleet that had just decoyed or destroyed the Royal Navy. As a variation on the theme of levying contributions on major ports, "Hippophlax" envisaged ruthless troopers methodically burning down London neighborhoods until an astronomical indemnity had been paid.[46] Although such imaginings rarely appeared to have intruded upon Admiralty planning, after 1870 a spate of articles decrying England's vulnerability to foreign invasion appeared. Two articles on different aspects of the same problem were published in that year by the *Journal* of the Royal United Service Institution.[47] All assumed that the navy would be defeated and that enemy troops and munitions would flow into England as a matter of course. In reply, William Vernon Harcourt, M.P., accurately summarized official views as the vast difficulties attendant upon invasion of England. Harcourt showed that a mere defeat of the fleet in a single battle would not suffice; the invaders would need command of the sea for weeks to transport corps and impedimenta to a landing area. Even if the high-seas ironclads were put out of action, the enemy would still have to contend with the navy's coastal warships.[48] Harcourt's views, which may well have been encouraged by the government as an answer to ill-conceived agitation from a public figure of known independence, appeared to have been fully shared by the Admiralty.

Invasion agitation and panic could be countered effectively by the Admiralty's strategic policy, which came more and more to add explicitly coastal-defense ships to the classes already restricted to the Channel, North Sea, and Mediterranean. As Adm. Sir Sidney Dacres, First Sea Lord in 1870, saw the navy's task, Britain's very existence depended "on our being able to bring into action such a fleet of ironclads as will keep us masters of the seas which surround our coasts. That position once lost, England is out of the roll of nations." [49] Admiral Robinson had already laid before the board the requirements for British ironclads of the near future, almost all of which were drawn up to deal with operations in coastal waters. Of first importance were the heaviest ordnance and thickest armor possible, plus handiness. After these were secured, a good turn of speed, coal capacity, and seaworthiness sufficient for Baltic, Channel, and Mediterranean cruising could be added.[50] All of these qualities, with the reduced sail rig that Robinson favored, posed no great difficulty for short-range ironclads.

One of the first results of the Admiralty emphasis upon coastal ironclads was H.M.S. *Glatton* (laid down in 1868), a turretship with the lowest freeboard coupled with the highest ratio of armor-to-displacement of any warship in the British Navy. These dubious claims to consideration as a powerful capital ship should not conceal the fact that the *Glatton* was the embodiment of the strategic thought, or lack of such thought, of the time. Reed, who designed her, termed the ironclad "a very exceptional vessel, and designed under a very peculiar stress of circumstances . . . which had to be produced in conformity to ideas which were not those of the designer." [51] Just what these "peculiar circumstances" were, Reed never explained, and Admiralty records shed little light. The Admiralty agreed that the *Glatton* was to be used for the defense of Britain's coasts and for offensive operations against the shores and ports of an enemy. But her low freeboard made even a voyage across the Channel or the North Sea in any but the finest weather highly problematical, while her deep draught ruled out any real shallow-water work. Well could Reed remark that "there is no vessel with the objects of which I am less acquainted than the *Glatton*." [52] Admiral Robinson concluded that the *Glatton* was "truly formidable" for assaults on an enemy's roadsteads, for defense of the home coasts, and for service in combination with the fleet, but he admitted that these missions could be accomplished only "where there is plenty of water," a peculiar requirement for a coastal warship. This deficiency he blamed on "the conditions laid down" to him by the board.[53]

At this nadir of strategic thought, confusion was further compounded by the addition of the fallacious and dangerous ram theory to the concept of coast defense. As a result, two ironclad rams, H.M.S. *Hotspur* and H.M.S. *Rupert*, not only practically useless but a positive menace to their consorts, were added to the fleet. Thus Britain could rely upon the supposedly irresistible power of the ram as well as the gun to keep her shores inviolate. In their design these two ships displayed the confused strategic thought of the time. Like the *Glatton* they suffered from deep draught. They were designed for maneuverability in ramming, but both were underpowered and of slow speed; the *Hotspur* could be stopped dead in the water when facing rough weather. Finally, although they were intended to remain practically within sight of land, both were fitted with fore-and-aft rigs, which added nothing but deadweight. Admiralty pressure for small dimensions must have been primarily responsible for such unsatisfactory performance.

In 1870 Hugh C. E. Childers, Admiralty First Lord, decided "to push forward rather less than had been intended" the completion of the great ironclads [*Devastation* class], and to concentrate on coast defence warships, gunboats, and "anti-Alabamas." This decision was neither unexpected nor opposed by members of the Board.[54] In fact, Robinson agreed that instead of another *Monarch* or *Devastation*, preference should be given to further coast defenders of the *Hydra* class, diminutive editions of the *Devastation*. "We should get four ships instead of two," he wrote to Admiral Dacres.[55]

The four vessels, *Hydra, Gorgon, Hecate, Cyclops*, laid down in 1870, were described by one authority as "the most unsatisfactory group of ironclads ever to fly the White Ensign." [56] Reed, who had resigned from office just prior to their commencement, later termed the class "far less terrible vessels than their formidable names would suggest." [57] Hastily ordered in the wake of the Franco-Prussian War, they were completed leisurely over a period ranging from four to seven years, when the fear of England's embroilment had passed. Although the basic design of the *Hydra* class was excellent and the armor and armament equal to those of many seagoing broadside ships, the *Hydra* class suffered from an obvious lack of seaworthiness (a long-armed man could dip his hand into the sea from the upper deck). They were certainly useless as warships in the tempestuous waters surrounding the British coast. As harbor craft they eked out an existence under Service contempt until finally sold in one lot in 1903. By 1871 the coastal-defense craze had reached such a stage that proposals were seriously advanced for *reduced* versions of the *Hydra* class that could be hauled up on shore or even dismantled in time of peace, and manned by "artillerymen" or "volunteers" when war threatened. Almost the only attraction of these armored cockle-boats would have been their economy.[58]

While the Admiralty, fortunately, refrained from accepting such extreme suggestions, it did persist unabatedly in its predilection for coastal defense. The experiences of the Franco-Prussian War had reinforced those of the Crimean War, in both of which high-seas fleets had found themselves comparatively helpless in dealing with an enemy's ports and fortifications. The realization that the first ironclads were coastal craft for reducing the Kinburn fortifications during the Crimean War may help to explain the attraction of the miniature armorclad in the early ironclad era. In 1870 the powerful French fleet with its heavy oceanic capital ships had found itself singularly unable to attack the German littoral. This failure so impressed the normally thoughtful Admiral Milne that, as late as 1873, while First Sea Lord, he called for an increase in the *Hydra* class to meet a similar contingency in case of war with Russia. The reasoning here was that France's superior naval power was unable to affect Prussia because the deep draught of its capital ships precluded shore bombardment, amphibious assaults, and so on. Thus shallow-draught turret ships were needed by the Royal Navy. But such vessels were always considered for coastal defense, while the French failure was in the offense. Significantly, the considerable French fleet of coastal ironclads never went near the German littoral. But for the decade of the 1860s, the example of the American Civil War appears from a perusal of the literature of the time to have been the major determinant of the Admiralty's inclination toward coastal defense, for only in America had ironclad fought ironclad extensively, and those combatant warships were shallow-draught, low freeboard, coastal and river vessels. Again the vital difference was ignored: that the swarms of Union ironclads were specifically designed for the offensive against a "nation" lacking even the pretense of a seagoing navy.[59]

Faced with a conglomeration of coastal ironclads, the Committee on Designs could only point out the great difficulties inevitably involved in any attempt to design a first-class warship on a second-class hull. It would be impossible, the committee reasonably concluded, to combine all the requirements of heavy armor and armament and good speed with shallow draught and small dimensions. As a result, most, if not all, coastal ironclads had proved to be unsatisfactory compromises. But the committee refrained from drawing the logical conclusion that the whole concept of special coastal-defense warships was impracticable. Instead it asserted that "there is no alternative but to give the preponderance to each (speed, armor, ordnance) in its turn amongst different classes of ships which shall mutually supplement one another."[60] Again this recommendation was not followed by the Admiralty, which soon terminated its coastal-defense ironclad program. But the doctrine remained, and manifested itself for at least two decades in the provision for second-class capital ships that was made periodically by the board in the inveterate interest of economy as much as for any strategic purpose.

It is indeed strange that so little protest was raised against a strategic concept so at variance with traditional British naval practice. British warships had a free and plentiful source of locomotion, as in the days of Nelson; sail could still be used in conjunction with steam. Even granting the necessity for concentration of the ironclad fleet in home waters (and ignoring the demands of colonial defense and commerce protection), weather conditions in those seas would fully justify the employment of first-class ironclads. The fact that France, Russia, and the United States built coastal-defense ironclads was slight justification for a global naval power such as Britain to follow suit.

Perhaps the most telling criticism that can be made against coastal ironclads was that they siphoned funds that could have gone into first-class capital ships. In 1868 Reed maintained that such was not the case.[61] But in that year the *Glatton* and *Hotspur* were laid down, and Childers, as has been noted, resolved to retard work on the *Devastation* class in order to forward the coastal rams. Although the *Hotspur* was completed in thirty-seven months and the *Glatton* in forty-four, the *Thunderer* and *Dreadnought* of the *Devastation* class each took approximately seven years to complete. Thus they were robbed of much of their value by the time that they entered service.

Even in actual cost the coastal ironclads were not particularly economical. The *Rupert* cost £239,197 and would be valuable only in restricted circumstances. For £361,438 the Admiralty could call upon the services of the *Devastation* for operations anywhere in the world, in almost any weather. The three ships of the *Devastation* class would have cost less than the entire coastal ironclad program and would have given the Royal Navy an enormous and probably unchallengeable technological lead over all her possible naval rivals combined.[62]

But no thorough critique of the coastal-defense-offense theory seems to have been applied after 1862, when John Scott Russell denounced "steamships that cannot steam to India, Australia or to Canada at full speed" (!), and insisted that "money spent in guns or ships that are unfit for ocean service is so much money thrown into the sea."[63] Scott Russell, of course, was a firm believer in large ironclads, even to the extent of calling for plated *three-decked* ships-of-the-line, and he failed to see any virtue in Reed's more moderately proportioned ironclads.

Yet for all this strategic confusion, the great majority of

British ironclads were entirely capable of ocean cruising, either under sail or, had the bunkerage been increased, under steam, and were thoroughly seaworthy. H.M.S. *Monarch*, Reed's turret ship of 1866, had a radius of two thousand miles. Using both steam and sail, she proved her seaworthiness by taking the body of the American philanthropist George Peabody back to New York from Britain without incident. In fact, Admiral Robinson pointed out that Britain had a larger proportion of cruising ironclads than France or Russia, and it could not be said that Britain was falling behind in this category of warship.[64]

Nonetheless, strategic planning occupied far less time and energy at the Admiralty than did questions pertaining to the ironclads themselves. Considerations of imperial, colonial, and commercial defense were never welded into one plan that could have had any influence upon naval architecture. In despair, or sarcasm, C. W. Merrifield, principal of the School of Naval Architecture, assured his readers that such a plan was bound to exist somewhere. But if it did, he was unaware of it.[65] The Admiralty preferred the concrete to the theoretical, and thus it seriously neglected the systematic study of both tactics and strategy. For the Admiralty, specific situations called for ad hoc responses. In tactics such neglect led to the gross overestimation of the power of the ram and to the subordination of naval tactics and architecture to this unproved weapon. In strategy the emphasis upon special, and ultimately useless, coastal ironclads stunted both the design and disposition of capital ships of the Royal Navy. Unfortunately, the strategic situation did not improve during the remaining years of the nineteenth century. In 1899 George Goschen, First Lord of the Admiralty, conceded that "there is not now, nor has there ever been an established school for the study of strategy by naval officers of the higher ranks." Goschen went on to explain that the whole system of education in the navy should "lend" itself to a knowledge of strategy. This is precisely where matters stood in 1870.[66]

7

Captain Coles
and the Turret Warship

I

No study of the development of the modern capital ship could possibly be complete without an analysis of the contributions of Capt. Cowper Phipps Coles. Captain Coles was one of those extraordinarily inventive figures whose ideas seem literally to overtake his capacity for carrying them out, whose provoking sense of absolute faultlessness brooks no opposition, and, indeed, who look upon such opposition as proof of personal animosity. Coles was not unique for his times. His great antagonists, Reed and Robinson, were as violent polemicists as their official positions would permit. Other naval inventors, such as Captain Halsted and C. F. Henwood, and a host of private citizens all pertinaciously demanded official recognition of their several concepts and, with Captain Coles, marshaled truly formidable support from the press in their campaigns. The phenomenon of the "angular, cross-grained man, the almost professional exposer of 'jobs' and abuses" was common to the mid-nineteenth century.[1]

But Coles's virtual refusal to admit to any possibility of error and his single-minded pursuit of his goal of a seagoing turret ship against even informed and disinterested criticism led to disaster, in which his own life was lost. The catastrophe always associated with his H.M.S. *Captain* has

177

Captain Cowper Phipps Coles. NATIONAL MARITIME MUSEUM, LONDON.

overshadowed Coles's unique inventive gifts and has denied him his place as one of the most original naval inventors of the nineteenth century.

Captain Coles's career up to 1863 has been definitely outlined by James Phinney Baxter.[2] Briefly, Coles was born in 1819 or 1820, the third son of a Hampshire clergyman, and entered the naval service in 1831. In 1855, during the Crimean War, he conceived the idea of a low-lying raft that was equipped with a turntable upon which a gun would be mounted, protected by a cupola or turret. Coles's concept was not unique, and the controversy over its excellence between partisans of Coles and followers of John Ericsson as to priority was never settled. Captain Coles was certainly not behindhand in claiming credit and in asserting the superiority of his system over Ericsson's.[3] But he saw his main task as that of proving the overwhelming superiority of the turret to the traditional broadside arrangement of ordnance that had persisted since the day of Henry VIII.

The primary advantage of the turret lay in the fact that a warship need no longer maneuver to secure a favorable fighting position for her guns. Rather, in the words of Coles: "Turn the gun, not the ship." With a turret able to direct its fire in any quarter regardless of a ship's evolutions, evasive action could be taken while maintaining an accurate fire. Since the turret guns rested on the upper deck, gunports would no longer be swamped in heavy seas, and the entire weakening arrangement of lines of ports could be abolished. The gunports of the turret could be far fewer in number, and fitted snugly around the gun barrel, unlike the many wide ports necessary for aiming in a broadside vessel. Fire could be concentrated in salvos, rather than discharged as each gun came to bear. In a mastless turret ship, in theory, no "blind" areas would exist on which guns could not bear. Mounted on the centerline rather than at the extremities of the hull, the weight of ordnance and armor would inhibit rolling and thus improve aiming. Finally, far fewer men would be needed to man the few heavy turret guns.[4]

With such powerful arguments (viewed in the light of over a century of hindsight), it might seem little short of incredible that Coles's invention was not welcomed wholeheartedly by the Admiralty. Some of the resistance to the turret principle could be considered as mere objection to change, a worship of the past of Nelson and Blake, coupled with a more intelligent fear of a naval revolution in which British broadside supremacy might again be threatened as all powers began anew on an equal footing.

But in the departments of the controller of the navy and

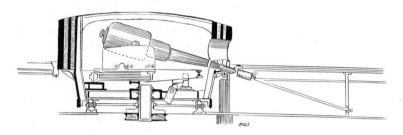

Coles's turret and mechanism, as developed by the end of the 1860s.
T. Brassey, *The British Navy.*

the chief naval constructor, more professional objections
were raised. The chief constructor pointed out that an oceangoing turret ship would not enjoy that all-around fire so
much praised as one of the prime advantages of the turret
ship and so valuable for ramming. A forecastle, and possibly
a poop, would have to be fitted to keep the decks of a low-
freeboard turret ship dry. Since masts and sails were deemed
a necessity, they would also seriously interfere with the
sweep of the guns. The great weight of armor needed for
the turrets would demand low freeboard, with its disadvantages of unhealthy living conditions and the dangers of
swamping and uncertain stability. If a shell were to penetrate a turret, half of the armament of a two-turret ship,
and the whole of the offensive power of a single-turret ironclad, would be destroyed. The turrets might also jam, im-
mobilizing the warship's power. As this study progresses,
the more technical objections to each of Captain Coles's
many designs will be explained in more detail.[5]

Reed and Admiral Robinson agreed that the benefits of
the turret ship should be confined to coastal-defense vessels,
at least for the present. In this limited capacity the turret
ship would not be greatly embarrassed by its low freeboard,
nor would its all-around sweep of fire be diminished by a
full-scale sailing rig.[6] It would also be far less dangerous

and expensive to experiment with small coastal-defense turret ships than to construct a first-class seagoing turret ironclad upon no experience whatsoever. In this course the chief constructor and controller were supported by most of the Board of Admiralty, and Coles was ordered to supervise the cutting down of a wooden ship-of-the-line and the converting of the hull into a coastal turret ship. Simultaneously, the construction of the *Prince Albert*, the first iron turret ship, was authorized.[7]

H.M.S. *Prince Albert*. First Royal Navy iron turret ship. NATIONAL MARITIME MUSEUM, LONDON.

But by the beginning of 1863, Coles was entirely dissatisfied. From the first (as shown in his published lectures), he had designed seagoing turret ships, and now he wanted them built. He denounced the two coastal-defense turret ships as "comparatively useless without masts" for cruising, and complained that his invention would be tried under the greatest disadvantages.[8] The Admiralty pointed out to Coles later in 1863 that the *Prince Albert* and the *Royal Sovereign* (the razed three-decker) were never intended for any other use than that of coastal defense.[9] Such caution in official quarters seems logical, since nowhere in the world did any seagoing turret ship exist, nor had any turret ship been put to the test of a high-seas voyage. Captain Coles, however, saw matters in a less understanding light and in February 1863 had demanded that he be given permission to submit designs for a seagoing turret ironclad.[10] To this proposal the Admiralty agreed, requesting Coles to send to them specifications and plans of what he would desire in such a ship.

H.M.S. *Royal Sovereign*. First Royal Navy turret ship to be completed, and thus the first to carry her armament outside of her hull. NATIONAL MARITIME MUSEUM, LONDON.

The Admiralty, far from blindly obstructing any idea of an oceanic turret ironclad, now laid down its own requirements for a cruising turret ship in March 1863. Admiral Robinson and Nathaniel Barnaby of the constructor's department were ordered to draw up plans based on these lines: a speed of not less than thirteen knots, to carry twelve- or twenty-ton guns and, in the all-important question of freeboard, to have not less than five feet if the ship were 120 feet in length, and an additional foot of freeboard for every additional thirty feet of length.[11] On 30 March 1863, a sketch based on these specifications was forwarded to Captain Coles for his comments.[12] But Admiral Robinson himself reported that it would be impossible to build a ship fulfilling all conditions laid down by their lordships of the Board of Admiralty. To fulfill the necessary speed and armor requirements, a larger and more expensive warship would be necessary.[13]

On 14 April, rejecting this clumsy expedient of trying to marry his ideas of a turret ship to those of the Admiralty, Coles submitted drawings and specifications for his own seagoing turret warship to carry four three-hundred-pound guns in two turrets, an arrangement that Admiral Robinson generously informed him was "in all respects a preferable proposal." [14] Nonetheless, the controller recommended that the design be "postponed" until trials of the *Royal Sovereign* and *Prince Albert* had been completed. The door was not completely closed on the inventor, and he was given permission to perfect his designs, provided that they were based on the Admiralty specifications of 6 March.[15]

This was the last to be heard from Captain Coles for some time on the subject of seagoing turret ships. But he continued to bombard the controller's department with ideas and changes of ideas for the coastal turret ships under construction. He displayed a lamentable ignorance of the shipbuilder's craft by calling the attention of the Admiralty to the nearly completed state of the *Prince Albert* and urging that a decision be made as to whether the turret ship should be masted. He apparently did not realize that a ship is designed for her masts from the keel up. In any event, the very thought of the diminutive low-freeboard *Prince Albert* putting to sea with a full spread of canvas would have been scotched by any qualified naval constructor.[16]

Reed's and Robinson's cautious attitude could hardly be considered unreasoning opposition to Captain Coles's principle. The turret, particularly when carried on a ship intended for blue-water cruising, was an unproved quantity.

Yet Coles denounced Chief Constructor Reed for "his determined opposition and condemnation of my principle." [17]

One reason for the audacity and belligerence of Captain Coles may be found in the amount of public support he enjoyed. He was a nephew of Lord Lyons, one of the dominant naval officers of the Crimea period, and a brother-in-law of Adm. Geoffrey Phipps Hornby, holder of some of the most important commands in the post-Crimea navy. But Captain Coles enjoyed more than just the accident of powerful relatives. Increasingly, The *Times* encouraged him and his invention.[18] Coles had powerful and vociferous partisans in the *Standard*, and later in the *Naval and Military Gazette* and the *United Service Gazette*. Even *Punch* felt led to dabble in naval architecture, and congratulated itself on its support of Coles.[19] As an obvious corollary, there was an inverse relationship between the support given to Coles and that given to Reed.

In Parliament Coles had his champions as well. One of the most prominent, Richard Cobden, extended his support of Coles into attacks on Chief Constructor Reed. Cobden was no mere political polemicist. On naval matters generally he adopted a strikingly progressive mood, not only promoting the Coles system, but decrying the sums wasted on the building of coastal forts during invasion panics and the retention of useless piles of timber for wooden shipbuilding. In his journal he confides that a tour of the Downs fortifications and the dockyards in the company of Captain Coles had led him to the conviction "that we are now wasting our money on iron-clad vessels with broadsides, whilst a new invention is in the field which will entirely supersede them."[20]

In still more august quarters, Captain Coles had gained the patronage of the Prince Consort, who had strongly encouraged him.[21] And it was only natural that the widowed Queen Victoria, vowing to continue everything exactly as Prince Albert would have wished, should take an interest in Coles's work. In the summer of 1864, for example, she visited the newly completed *Royal Sovereign* (Captain Coles

was aboard at her express wish) and informed him publicly
of how she hoped for every success for his invention, about
which Albert had been so concerned. Later that year she
presented him with a bronze statuette of Albert.[22] Through
the Queen's influence, the other coastal turret ship, the
Prince Albert, was held in service long after it had ceased
to retain any military significance whatsoever.[23]

While in Britain the merits of the turret were argued, in
North America the monitor turret warship had already been
put to the test of battle. One of the first detailed descriptions of the federal monitors and their possibilities to reach
the Admiralty came from a Captain Vansittart, who concluded that the ships were "not well adapted for sea voyages," although they could menace Halifax and cause
enormous damage among the ironclads of Britain if they
could ever cross the Atlantic.[24] Reports on the monitors
began to stream in by the spring of 1863, but they were
almost uniformly uncomplimentary to Ericsson's new weapon. Donald McKay, the clipper-ship builder, wrote to
Admiral Robinson that although Ericsson and the monitor
party controlled the Northern press, the ships themselves
were intensely unpopular with those officers who had to
serve in them. McKay assured the controller: "One thing,
Admiral, you can tell your friends in Parliament who exalted the 'monitor' so highly last year, that they need have
no fear of 'Ericsson' visiting the Thames or Downing Street
as stated in the press so politely, after the victory over the
Merrimac, a vessel covered with cross-strapped iron and
railroad bars." [25]

A month later Rear Admiral Milne, Commander in
Chief of the North American and West Indies Squadron,
reported that the monitors' turrets were liable to jam in
action, that concussion inside the turrets could be severe
while firing the guns, and that flying nuts and bolts constituted a great danger even if no shot penetrated.[26] The next
year Admiral Milne concluded "that the monitors as a class
are failures." He added slowness of fire, lock of stowage,

and unhealthy living conditions to his previous criticisms of the monitors.[27] Even the ability of monitors to attack forts in protected waters came to be questioned when a Foreign Office memorandum listed all such actions involving monitors to date, and decided that in all the monitors had failed.[28] And from at least one official federal source came confirmation. After the repulse of a monitor fleet by Confederate batteries at Charleston (when one semi-monitor was riddled and sunk by fire from Fort Sumter), the captains of the turret ships and their Commanding Officer, Admiral Du Pont, agreed that their ships would be useless for such actions.[29]

The Admiralty was still interested in Coles's work, even though it could see no way of retaining masts and yards while still enjoying the benefits of all-around fire in a cruising turret ship.[30] But the controller was willing to consider suggestions on some way to skirt this difficulty. And in its communications to Captain Coles, the Admiralty expressed its willingness to consider any "mature" plan Coles might have.[31] To facilitate his work, Admiral Robinson generously lent Captain Coles a draughtsman, Nathanial Barnaby, from his hard-pressed department, "to carry out his views with reference to a design for a sea-going turret ship, which he is to prepare for the consideration of Their Lordships." [32] Here was the second attempt of the controller's department to work with Coles on a seagoing turret ship design.

It should be noted that part of Coles's persistence stemmed from another invention of his—the tripod mast. In this device, shrouds supporting the masts would be eliminated, enabling the turrets to swing in a wider arc of command for the guns. But again Coles had underestimated the technical difficulties involved. And again the controller's department advised caution. While conceding that Coles's designs for tripod masts reflected "great credit" on the inventor, Admiral Robinson was dubious about the great spread of canvas that would be hung upon a heavy iron tripod arrangement, perhaps endangering stability, and he concluded that its installation in any of the proposed turret ships would constitute a "very hazardous and expensive experiment to make." [33] The system was never adopted in the Royal Navy on any scale, having been fitted, on an experimental basis only, in H.M.S. *Wyvern*, one of the famous "Birkenhead rams", purchased by the Admiralty in 1863, and finally, in H.M.S. *Captain*.

The *Wyvern* and her sister ship, the *Scorpion*, were masted turret ships of low freeboard that were secretly contracted for and built for Confederate agents at Messrs. Laird's Birkenhead yards. For the purpose that the Confederate States government had in mind, the breaking of the federal blockade and of other coastal operations, turret ships were admirable. Just what part Captain Coles played in the design of these two small turret ships is uncertain, but the chief Confederate agent wrote on 10 September 1862 that he had secured working drawings of Coles's turrets for the ships, presumably something he would not have come by without the permission of the inventor. [34] Work progressed but slowly, and by the fall of 1862, Lord Russell, Foreign Secretary, wrote to Lord Palmerston that the suspicious conduct of those who had contracted for the Birkenhead ironclads (supposedly for Egypt) had led him to feel that it would be necessary to detain them in order to avoid a repetition of the *Alabama*'s escape from a British yard to a career of privateering against the North. [35]

Russell's suspicions were undoubtedly reinforced by Charles Francis Adams, United States Minister to Great Britain, who excitedly wrote to Secretary of State Seward: "The new vessels which the Lairds are preparing must, therefore, be expected to enter Portland, Boston, New York, or if they prefer, must attempt to break the blockade at Charleston, or to ascend the Mississippi." On the same day Adams's justifiable fears were translated into resolute action. If the rams were allowed to sail, he wrote in his famous note to Russell, "it would be superfluous in me to point out to your Lordship that this is war." Fortunately,

Russell had capitulated two days previously, detaining the turret rams.[36]

The question remained as to what to do with them. Palmerston strongly urged that they be purchased for the navy, for "if the Federals get them they will strengthen the Yankees against us if they should be disposed and able next year to execute their threatened vengeance for all the forbearance we have shown them." [37] Turning southward, the bellicose prime minister thought that the ironclads could "run down and sink the Russian ships in the Black Sea if

H.M.S. *Scorpion* or *Wyvern*. The Birkenhead rams, turret ironclad rams designed by Captain Coles for the Confederate Navy, but taken into Royal Navy service. NATIONAL MARITIME MUSEUM, LONDON.

need were." [38] But the First Lord of the Admiralty, the Duke of Somerset, had far less sanguinary hopes. He doubted that the Laird rams would be of much use at sea, and disapproved of their "inferior" construction.[39] They might, however, "furnish the means of testing the qualities of a masted turret ship at sea." [40] But Somerset agreed that the purchase of the rams would serve to keep the peace with America, and he was further determined that "such a trick as the *Alabama* must not be successful a second time." [41]

Thus the first masted turret ships entered the Royal Navy. They could not be considered a success, despite some contrary opinions of The *Times*.[42] Six years later the captain of the *Scorpion* had to report to their lordships that his ship's company "have declined respectfully but firmly to put to sea in the ship" for a projected voyage to Bermuda.[43] Meanwhile the Admiralty controller and the constructor continued to receive disparaging reports on the American turret monitors. Admirals Du Pont and Farragut were reported as definitely antimonitor. Farragut called for "a ship with broadside guns, *high speed*, and all good fighting men." [44] Donald McKay also had not changed his opinion, contending that even the federal naval constructors basically disapproved of the monitor. As for the supposed seagoing monitors, *Dictator* and *Puritan*—those "you may set down as perfect failures." [45] Whether the monitors were a failure is not so important here as the fact that the reports from America, by both British and American authorities, almost uniformly wrote off the Ericsson monitor as practically useless, particularly for sea service. Such reports could only strengthen the resolve of the controller and the chief constructor and most of the board against any precipitate oceanic turret-ship program. Coles himself termed the federal monitors *wretched vessels*.[46]

In correspondence with Captain Coles, the Admiralty continued to make it clear that they were not prepared to build a seagoing turret ship until the *Royal Sovereign*, the *Prince Albert*, and now the *Wyvern* and the *Scorpion* were tested at sea. This seemed unfair to Captain Coles since neither of his turret ships had been built for high-seas cruising, since the Birkenhead rams were little better than masted coastal-defense ironclads,[47] and since apparently the Coles-Barnaby high-seas turret ship design was completely ignored and forgotten. Well could Coles grumble that "at this moment Her Majesty's Navy does not possess a single cupola ship adapted for the navigation and police of the high seas." [48]

Much of 1864 was taken up by trials of the *Royal Sovereign*. In these, some of the more fatuous objections to turret ships were dispelled. Concussion in the turrets was negligible, decks were relatively unscoured by firing across them, and the ship generally suffered remarkably little, considering that it was designed as a 130-gun wooden ship-of-the-line rather than as a five-gun turret ironclad. The only major defect lay in the fact that the gun carriages were of wood rather than of iron. After describing her as more than a match for any ironclad on the broadside system, her captain, Sherard Osborne, concluded a report by asserting that "her handiness, speed, weight of broadside [the *Royal Sovereign* carried the heaviest guns to date of any British warship], and the small target she offers, increase tenfold her powers of assault and retreat." [49] Captain Osborne was an old friend of Captain Coles and, according to the Duke of Somerset, "had an especial predilection for turret ships." [50] Nonetheless, Osborne's reports served finally to clear away prejudices against the working of heavy guns and turrets themselves, and to show the superiority of the Coles's turret over Ericsson's. The Admiralty was now ready to try Captain Coles's invention where it belonged—on the high seas.

On 8 October 1864 a conference was summoned at the Admiralty to consider the building of a seagoing turret ship. Most of the Admiralty Board was present, as were Reed, Coles, Robinson, and Osborne. Following agreement on the necessity for a seagoing turret ship of the type urged by Captain Coles, the inventor was given the floor for his suggestions and requests. He asked that he be given the plans of the *Pallas*, a small, wooden, box-battery ironclad, on which he would design his seagoing turret ship. But Reed objected that the lines of the *Pallas* were unsuitable for an iron-built warship. Instead he urged upon Coles his plans for the *Bellerophon*, an iron box-battery vessel.[51] But Coles remained obdurate, insisting that the *Bellerophon* was unnecessarily large for his purpose. It will be remembered that in favor of the turret ship, according to its supporters, were the supposed lower-manning requirement and the contention that a greater offensive power could be packed into a smaller tonnage than in the broadside system. On this inconclusive note the conference ended, but Coles had been given to understand that now the Admiralty was seriously interested in his designs.

Two days after the conference Coles wrote to the Admiralty, blandly requesting plans and specifications of the *Pallas* "in accordance with their [lordships'] promise." [52] Apparently the chief constructor's objections to this procedure, based on his unrivaled technical knowledge, was to be ignored, for the Admiralty replied by return post that Captain Coles would indeed be supplied with the particulars of the said *Pallas*. Realizing his penchant for publicity, however, their lordships emphasized that the information was "not to be made public." [53]

At the conference in the Admiralty and on public occasions Coles had disclaimed any ability as a naval designer. Although he could draw up excellent general sketches of his ships, the technical details he left to others, often omitting the bottom of his vessels, for example. Therefore he now requested the aid of an Admiralty draughtsman in his new project. At the same time he declared that he was "perfectly ready to design a vessel representing [his] views." [54] Reed, deeply suspicious of Coles's ability as a naval architect, wondered just what part Coles would have in the design. For it was on the understanding that Coles would not design the turret ship as a whole, but probably just the turrets and their fittings, that the begrudged *Pallas* plans and the new draughtsman were to be made available to him.[55] Coles reassured the Admiralty that he meant that he would design his ship in conjunction with a competent draughtsman, and was duly given the services of a Mr. Scullard of the Portsmouth yards.[56] At the same time he suggested that his ship be constructed as a competitor to the Reed box-battery ships now being built, and that a committee, half of whom Coles should nominate, would judge the merits of his design. This proposal, according to Coles, would eliminate the unfair influence in favor of the broadside in the constructor's department. "The only great difficulty I see at present is that the Constructor of the Navy is opposed to the turret system, which he has publicly denounced, and is a strong advocate of his own rival scheme," [57] he charged. But their lordships quickly scouted the idea that Coles's ship should in any way be considered to compete with Reed's ship designs and refused to consider the committee urged by Coles to judge his plans.[58]

Throughout the first quarter of 1865 a voluminous correspondence passed between the Admiralty and Captain Coles, mostly concerning weights and other details of the *Pallas*, on which the lines of the new turret ship would be based. Robinson hesitated in giving such information to "irresponsible persons" who had "a total want of candour and fairness and who thereby injured the reputation of Admiralty designers." [59]

The reputation of Admiralty designers was mauled also in Parliament as the Opposition gleefully used Captain Coles's supposed martyrdom at the hands of an unimaginative and obstructive officialdom as a club to beat the government. Coles was lauded for his courage, and Reed condemned for his sinister opposition. In place of the recognized talent of the Constructors' Corps of the past, now the naval designs were supposedly the responsibility of a "single and undisciplined mind," that is, Reed.[60] Sir John Pakington, First Lord of the Admiralty under the Conservative Derby administration, and under whose regime H.M.S. *Warrior* was laid down, espied a "secret influence at the

Admiralty, which is opposed to the turret principle." [61] The Admiralty spokesman, Lord Henry Lennox, Parliamentary Secretary, could only reply that the problems of a seagoing turret ship had not yet been solved by any means, although the principle was fully accepted for coastal defense. "Captain Coles himself will tell you that I am one of the most devoted adherents of turret ships for coast defence." [62] Coles replied sardonically, and not completely accurately, that he was "excessively glad to hear that His Lordship is one of *my* devoted adherents." [63]

On 3 April 1865, Coles submitted to the Admiralty his and Scullard's designs for a seagoing turret ship. But for once he had lost his cocksureness, for he wrote that "it is for Their Lordships to decide whether this vessel meets their needs." His projected ship mounted one turret only, displaced 2,409 tons, mounted two six-hundred-pound (twenty-tons) muzzle-loading rifles, and carried a full spread of canvas on three tripod masts.[64] According to E. J. Reed's preliminary report on the design, all of Captain Coles's calculations were in error. Reed further maintained that Coles had used the machinery and the dimensions of the *Pallas* and the method of construction of the *Bellerophon*, thus helping "to remove out of Captain Coles's way some of the greatest difficulties which opposed the construction of a fast sea-going turret ship of moderate dimensions." [65] Whether Reed meant that Coles had removed these difficulties by a clever piece of manipulation, or that he had indeed discovered real answers to the problem, is unclear, although in the context Reed was certainly not impressed by the design. In a later report he complained that Coles had utilized many of Reed's own inventions and developments from the *Pallas* and *Bellerophon*, although the distinct understanding was that Coles should alter only the above-water plans of the hulls in order to enable them to receive turrets. Reed was obviously annoyed by such cavalier treatment of his discoveries and developments, worked out over a period of years. Yet he was willing to waive all objections "in order that no obstacle might be placed in the way of Captain Coles." [66] So much for the "secret influence" against turret ships.

Admiral Robinson, with his broader knowledge of naval warfare, was more critical of the general design. His main objection was to the single turret, the concentrating of all armament in one confined area, slowing the rate of fire and leaving the vessel defenseless in her hind quarters.[67] Guns of the size planned, twenty tons, were "unknown and untried." And Robinson, despite the *Royal Sovereign*'s successful tests in coastal waters, was still not convinced that turret guns would be worked efficiently in a seaway, and he wondered whether more numerous and lighter guns would not be an improvement.[68]

Reversing its previous opposition to a committee to judge Coles's turret ship, the Admiralty informed Coles that a board of naval officers had been appointed, entirely by the Admiralty, to do this. Coles, ungenerously in view of the fact that the Admiralty had originally refused to appoint such a committee at all, protested against the decision not to allow him to nominate any committee officers. But their lordships felt that they had made enough concessions to the half-pay captain. In the end, Coles was not able to attend any of the committee's sittings because of illness, and he refused even to appoint a representative.[69]

The committee sat from May to June 1865, taking evidence and opinion on turret ships from naval constructors, gunners, and officers, as well as from Reed and Robinson. It is unnecessary to follow all of the technical discussions over a warship that was never built, and this study will be confined to the evidence that bore upon the problems of turret ships in general. The testimony of John Scott Russell carried great weight when he recommended the two-turret principle, rather than the one-turret vessel proposed by Coles and Scullard.[70] On the other hand, Captain Cooper Key of H.M.S. *Excellent*, ever the conservative, testified that the broadside system would remain superior, as mechanical means for working heavy guns were perfected.[71] Admiral Robinson revealed much of departmental thinking about the best method of mounting heavy guns in an iron-clad. Unreservedly condemning the turret principle for any cruising (fully-masted) warship, the controller stated that the box-battery system was still the best method of combining armament and seaworthiness. He insisted that the turret ship would need more armor to protect similar tonnage than would a box-battery warship. Furthermore, the turret ship would be liable to destruction, he reasoned, if a shot were to penetrate below the armored turret base and strike the turning gear. Finally, there was the irresistible argument that neither the French nor the Americans had any seagoing turret ships, and the French Chief Constructor, M. Depuy de Lôme, "who is without doubt the greatest naval constructor in the world," [72] disapproved of a sea-going ship with movable turrets. The British chief constructor, in spite of his apparently taking second place now to M. de Lôme, reinforced Robinson's opinion, stating flatly that "no sea-going turret ship of moderate dimensions and of high speed could be satisfactorily built, if an attempt was made to preserve even a near approach to that all-round fire" that was one of the major advantages of the turret warship.[73] Robinson then produced the design of a full-rigged box-battery ironclad, drawn up, like Captain Coles's turret ship, on the plans of the *Pallas* and, according to the controller, "presenting fewer points of weakness and fewer imperfections." [74]

In its report the committee opened with an expression of regret that Captain Coles had fallen ill and thus could not personally defend his designs, and then passed on to a summation of the advantages and disadvantages of the turret system. To the members of the committee the advantages, briefly, were that the turret was the "most efficient mode of carrying and working heavy guns in a sea-way," and that in the training, loading, protection, aiming, elevating, and steadiness of guns it was superior to the broadside system.

Its disadvantages lay in the supposed vulnerability of the turret to shots directed at its base, in boarders jamming the turret with wedges (!), the length of deck to be fired across, the difficulty of working the guns on a low freeboard in a heavy sea, and the general unseaworthiness of a low freeboard. The committee recognized the turret ship's unrivaled advantages in coastal defense, but insisted that these merits were curtailed in a seagoing cruiser because of the need for high freeboard to keep the ship dry and seaworthy, and because of the necessity (so the committee reasoned) for masts and rigging for economy and safety.

The Coles-Scullard design was rejected primarily because of its single turret, "although great pains have evidently been bestowed upon the preparation of that design." But the most important part of the report lay in the recommendation that "we consider it most desirable that a conclusive trial should be given to the system in a sea-going ship to be armed with *two* turrets, capable of carrying two 12-ton guns in each turret." In this recommendation, as apparently in others, the committee followed closely the opinions of Reed who stated in his evidence that "my own feeling has always been that it is very desirable that the best sea-going turret ship that can be produced should be produced and sent to sea for some months, and reported upon for the guidance of Their Lordships and others." [75]

A truncated form of the committee's report was sent off to Coles on 5 June 1865, listing in thirty-one terse paragraphs the Turret Ship Committee's objections to the Coles-Scullard plans. This action was taken on the grounds that the complete evidence was confidential and must first be passed on to the lords of the Admiralty. [76] But Captain Coles insisted that he would be quite unable to answer these thirty-one objections if he were not permitted to see the minutes of evidence upon which they were based. Coles subtly threatened to arouse unfavorable publicity if he did not receive the complete minutes by informing the Admiralty that he did not consider the question of turret ships as "one between Their Lordships and me, but a public and a national one." A little over a week later Coles received the minutes of evidence.[77] Acknowledging receipt, he enthusiastically agreed to collaborate fully on the committee's recommendation to build a seagoing turret ship.[78]

On the same day that Coles was sent the minutes of evidence, the Admiralty instructed the controller to submit his recommendation on some of the points to be considered in the designing of a seagoing turret ship. On 13 July Admiral Robinson replied, and in his recommendation laid down the general lines on which was to be built the first seagoing turret ship, H.M.S. *Monarch*. The important question of the turrets on this projected ironclad was one their lordships would have to decide for themselves, noted Robinson. If they were to be placed near the extremities, an uninterrupted range of fire could be secured, for then masts and rigging could be fitted between the turrets. But serious difficulties would arise if this course were followed. The bow in particular would tend to plunge deeply into oncoming waves if subjected to so great a weight as an armored turret carrying two twenty-five-ton rifled guns. A far greater expanse and weight of armor-plating would be necessary to cover the distance between the two turrets. Placing the turrets amidships would obviously reverse these conditions. Greater seaworthiness and less armor-plating would then be obtained, but at the cost of all-around fire. Freeboard was also an important problem. Admiral Robinson held out for a high freeboard, noting that "sixteen feet is not too much." By comparison, the Coles-Scullard design called for a mere eight feet of freeboard. Yet this high freeboard presented new problems of armoring. Since high sides could not be completely covered, a belt at the waterline had to be substituted. This arrangement, however, left large areas vulnerable to shot above the waterline.

In consequence, Robinson was unenthusiastic about the projected Admiralty turret ship, merely allowing that if the board should resolve the problems of turret placement,

H.M.S. *Monarch*. Reed seagoing, masted turret ship. OFFICIAL U.S. NAVY PHOTOGRAPH.

armoring, and masting, "the Constructors could enter upon a design that might possibly prove a powerful sea-going turret ship." [79] To reinforce his doubts, Robinson referred with approval to a report by Captain Key on the *Royal Sovereign* gunnery trials: "I am of opinion that for harbour defense and short voyages for the purpose of attacking a fortified position, the turret would be of great value." But he believed that the turret system would be inferior to the box battery or even the broadside if applied to all the ships of the fleet, particularly to those intended for long distance cruising. [80]

Two months later, in reply to a letter from Coles complaining that no answer had been given to his offer to aid in the design of a double-turreted, seagoing warship, the Admiralty informed him that the controller had been working on just such a vessel. Coles was to receive the plans when completed, and would be permitted to assist "in the arrangement of the details." [81] Querulously, Coles reminded their lordships that a similar plan had been agreed to two years previously, but that it had come to nothing. As for the "serious problems" in designing a seagoing turret ship to which the Admiralty had referred, Coles protested: "I am kept in ignorance of what they are." He noted that the *Royal Sovereign* tests had verified his claims for the turret ship—a totally irrelevant observation since the Admiralty were now concerned with seagoing, masted turret ships, something the *Royal Sovereign* obviously was not.[82]

At the end of the month, Coles submitted his reply to the objections of the Turret Ship Committee to his design— but in the form of a pamphlet. The substance of Coles's reply was predictable, answering the committee's objections with a mixture of technical knowledge and his own opinions. Generally, he was writing as an expert on all matters dealing with his turrets, and as a raw amateur when discussing naval architecture.[83] The Admiralty was outraged that Coles had released his pamphlet to the press (although it was labeled "for private circulation"). Admiral Grey, First Sea Lord, recommended that Coles be dropped from his consultative post for his impudence, denouncing this "most unusual proceeding" in issuing a pamphlet "containing erroneous, and I must say disingenuous statements." Particularly galling to the Admiral was Coles's reiteration that "my designs were for a sea-going turret ship to compete with the *Pallas*." Now the Admiralty had distinctly repudiated this interpretation by Captain Coles in their letter of 24 November 1864. Yet Coles had omitted to publish that letter, or to refer to it in any way.[84]

Admiral Robinson also commented on Coles's reply to the Turret Ship Committee. He claimed that the inventor had not really answered basic objections raised by the committee to lack of protection; to the problems of boarders, fighting, and training the big guns; to the possibilities of jamming; and to the dangers of low freeboard. Coles had considerably weakened his case by continually comparing the powers of his theoretical warship with those of the

Pallas, an ironclad that was, in the words of Robinson, "a ship of a special type, designed seventeen months before, to be built of timber . . . and not intended to be repeated."[85] Coles's design was discredited from the start by his stubborn insistence on utilizing the plans of the unsuitable *Pallas*, against the advice of Reed. His motives for so doing probably stemmed from the desire to keep dimensions as small as possible, and to compete directly with a Reed-designed warship.

Meanwhile plans had progressed on the new Admiralty turret ship, after the board had settled the various questions Admiral Robinson had posed. Instructions were issued to the controller on 13 October 1865 "that to obtain a good sea-going vessel the fore and aft fire of the turrets should be given up," that the turrets should be located close together amidships, and that a forecastle and possibly a poop were to be fitted. Following the controller's advice, the board ordered a freeboard of not less than fourteen feet, and a waterline armor belt of five-and-one-half inches, extending up to the bases of the turrets. The question of the guns was still left open, but they were to be of at least fifteen-tons weight. Finally, sail power was to be considered "as only auxiliary," and Coles's tripod masts could be fitted to give the guns a clearer field of fire.[86] Robinson accepted these conditions for the building of the ironclad, although the rapidly changing technology of the day necessitated increases in gun size and armor-plate thickness. The decision to utilize sail as auxiliary to steam was almost completely reversed later, and the sail plan was to be full-scale. On Robinson's advice, a courteous letter was sent to Coles informing him that plans of the ship were nearly complete and would be referred to him.[87]

True to their undertaking, the Admiralty requested Coles to submit plans for the turrets of the ship. On 20 November 1865 Coles sent in his plans, and thereafter he and Admiral Robinson cooperated amiably enough in settling by post details of the turrets and their fittings.[88]

On 10 January 1866 the completed plans and specifications were submitted for the board's approval. Robinson pointed out that here was a ship of compromises as far as armor and distribution of armament were concerned, and he was anything but optimistic about her powers. Unwilling to sacrifice high freeboard, Robinson admitted that the iron-clad stood out as a fine target since it was armored merely with a waterline belt that extended up to the gunwales only beneath the turrets.[89] Of course, the design was actually the work of the chief constructor, who himself was never enthusiastic about the *Monarch*.

Yet the *Monarch* remained in service for thirty-seven years and was considered one of Reed's most successful ventures. Her only combat experience was in the bombardment of the Alexandria Forts in 1882. Since the Egyptian forts were in poor condition, the *Monarch*'s supposed shortcomings and compromises were hardly put to the supreme test.

Admiral Robinson concluded his comments by recommending that tracings of the entire plan be sent to Captain Coles.[90] Yet on the very day that Robinson had recommended that Coles be given plans of the *Monarch*, the controller, the Admiralty, and the chief constructor were the objects of a vicious attack by Captain Coles in the *Standard*. Coles renewed his familiar charges of deliberate obstruction and incompetence in the controller's department, and demanded provocatively: "Give me a hundredth part of the encouragement and assistance Mr. Reed is given." [91] Admiralty reaction was swift, for the memory of Coles's other publicizing ventures was still fresh. Robinson pointed out the "grossest inaccuracies" of the article, particularly those concerned with facts of speed, time of construction, and seaworthiness of Admiralty-designed warships. On 19 January 1866, having received no satisfactory explanation, the Admiralty in a stinging letter dismissed Coles from his post.[92] As with so many policy decisions affecting Coles, this action was taken on the recommendation of the controller.[93]

Coles's first reply to the Admiralty insisted that the agreement with the board dating from 1862 gave him liberty to expound his invention by means of lectures, models, and publications. This provision, he added solicitously, "has probably escaped Their Lordships' attention."[94] But the Admiralty's main objection was to Coles's attacks on fellow officers of the same Service, particularly Admiral Robinson. Coles later truculently asserted that as a half-pay officer and an Englishman he was entitled to free speech, but that if he had seemed to attack the controller, he must have been "misunderstood."[95] In cutting off Coles from his consultative position, the pay of three guineas per diem due to him was also stopped. On this point Coles took legal advice and informed the Admiralty that this payment was for the relinquishing of his patent rights on turrets, and that therefore he could not legally be deprived of this money. The board refused to agree to this interpretation, but since Captain Coles had reluctantly apologized for his personal attacks, he was reinstated upon his undertaking "to conduct the advocacy of (his) inventions . . . without attacking the officers of this department."[96] and to "carry on [his] duties in an officer-like manner, and in a spirit of cordial co-operation."[97] Perhaps the threatened loss of his remuneration forced Coles into a more conciliatory attitude, for he had a wife and ten children to support on a half-pay captain's salary.

The Coles partisans renewed their agitation with increased zeal after the inventor's supposed arbitrary treatment. Sir John Pakington, in his capacity as president of the Institution of Naval Architects, had already demanded fair treatment for Coles,[98] while a motion was carried in the Commons to place the report of the Turret Ship Committee before the House of Lords.[99]

Still the turret ship controversy continued to rage, in and out of the Admiralty. Admiral Robinson wrote disparagingly of the small Peruvian turret ironclad *Huascar*, built by Laird's according to Captain Coles's designs, comparing it unfavorably with the *Scorpion* and the *Wyvern*.[100] These turret rams were, in turn, described in Parliament by the Parliamentary Secretary of the Navy, Lord Lennox, as "two of the greatest failures ever known."[101] But it is worth noting that all of these warships enjoyed a long career. The chief constructor also remained dubious about the prospects for seagoing turret ships. For various technical reasons, he had rejected out of hand a plan by Samuda's yard for such a vessel.[102]

II

Parallel with Coles's proposals, the campaign waged by Charles Henwood to convert old wooden line-of-battleships into fully-masted, seagoing monitors further taxed the patience of Reed and Admiral Robinson. Henwood, like Coles, enjoyed widespread public support; no less than seven popular and three Service periodicals, and also The *Times*, carried on his agitation.[103] Here was seen an economical method of using up useless steam-powered wooden warships. The timber-hulled broadside ironclads had proved efficient; why could not timber-hulled monitors also? As was also the case with Coles's proposals, Admiral Robinson posed no objection to converted coastal timber monitors.[104] But both Robinson and Reed could see no value but much danger in such cobbled-up vessels fitted for ocean cruising. Henwood's proposals were unsound, for the wooden hulls were decayed and weak, their engines of low power and high coal consumption. Any such ironclad would be of deep draught and dangerously low freeboard. Their construction would prove a false economy, for they would be almost as expensive to convert as iron coastal warships built as such from the keel up. Particularly irritating to the meticulous Reed and to Robinson were Henwood's faulty calculations, although he was accounted a reputable naval designer.[105] Furthermore, Reed took pains to prove mathematically that the combination of low freeboard and full sailing rig would lead to instability.[106] The *Army and Navy Gazette* (a pro-Reed journal) succinctly predicted the fate that in fact befell the low-freeboard, heavily masted *Captain* three years later: "Mr. Henwood's converted vessels would capsize in the first strong breeze they met and go to the bottom." [107] Despite some powerful newspaper and periodical backing, the Henwood plans never materialized.

A similar fate befell the ideas of Admiral E. Pellew Halsted, who publicized his plans for a fantastic, low-freeboard, fully-masted, iron ship of no less than seven turrets.[108] The only lasting effect of the agitation for the Henwood and Halsted turret ships was that they may well have impelled Reed to draw up plans of his own for a breastwork, converted, mastless monitor. The "breastwork," an armored shelf that raised turrets and uptakes above the low-lying upper deck, will be described below. For in this tentative design can be found one of the main threads that was to lead to the *Devastation*.[109]

III

Coles still had his allies in Parliament Opposition Members, who continued to find the turret issue useful for political purposes. Sir John Pakington insisted that "while Captain Coles' proposal for a sea-going turret ship has never up to this hour been fairly tried," the Reed broadside system had been given the cloak of official approval and encouragement.[110] Mr. Ferrand thundered that "the country would not be satisfied unless Captain Coles had every power given to him for the building of a turret ship," [111] while the First Lord of the Admiralty, the Duke of Somerset, could not defend his department in the Commons, and had to be content to reply in the far more genteel debate of the Lords.[112]

The *Times* had continued its qualified support of Coles

and, in a thoughtful leading article for the new year, 1866, expounded: "But here are the hard facts before us—that whereas guns are getting heavier and heavier, turrets can carry any weight, and that though the Americans have not built a good turret ship, we have an architect who declares that he can." [113] More avowed partisans of Coles, of course, were less restrained. The *United Service Gazette* declared that "the country is being deliberately and openly robbed, and nothing short of impeachment is due to a minister or a Board which dares to deal with public matters as His Grace the Duke of Somerset, or the Admiralty, or both, have dealt with the construction of ships for the Royal Navy." [114]

On March 8 1866 the plans and specifications of the *Monarch* were sent to Coles, now reinstated in his consultative position. Undoubtedly bearing in mind Coles's recent activities, Robinson took pains to emphasize that "there exists in this department the most anxious desire to meet your wishes whenever it will be possible to do so." [115]

After examining the plans, Coles was keenly disappointed. Primarily, he found the *Monarch* too large and too high out of the water, thus negating some of the basic arguments in favor of turret ships. Also, the *Monarch*'s all-around fire from her turret guns would be seriously compromised by the planned forecastle. In all, Coles seems to have found the Admiralty effort little more than another of Reed's box-battery ironclads, with turrets. He continued to complain of unfair treatment by the Admiralty and concluded petulantly that "from the incomplete drawings and information hitherto received, I consider she will not fairly represent my views of a sea-going turret ship." However, not wishing to cut himself off completely from Admiralty patronage, and the three-guinea per diem payments, he agreed to continue to work with the controller on the turrets and fittings of the *Monarch*.[116] Any change in the design of the *Monarch* was out of the question now, their lordships informed Coles. "I trust she will prove as great a success as Their Lordships may desire,"[117] Coles politely conceded.

In the same letter, however, in which the board had refused to consider any changes in the Monarch's design, Coles was informed in an almost offhand manner that he would be given "the opportunity of reducing to practice [his] own version of what a sea-going turret ship should be," and he was authorized to "put [himself] in communication with any of the firms named in the accompanying list for a sea-going ship to carry not less than two turrets," making adequate provision for protection, health, and comfort of the crew.[118] This offer, seen against the background of what had happened previously in Admiralty relations with Captain Coles, and subsequent testimony indicated a desire on the part of the Admiralty to put an end to the continuous barrage of public criticism from Coles and his supporters, and to settle finally the question of the practicability of seagoing turret ships. Neither Reed nor Robinson had ever said that such a ship was impossible to build; they had said only that Captain Coles seemed to display a cavalier disregard of some very real impediments in the working of plans into reality. After almost a century of success with turret ships, the difficulties foreseen by Reed and Robinson appear exaggerated. But the technical obstructions were real enough in the 1860s, and not until the perfecting of the marine engine and the abolition of sail would turret ships be fit for the high seas.

Coles gladly accepted the Admiralty offer, choosing Messrs. Laird as his builder, since they had constructed the greatest number of turret ships.[119] By 14 July 1866 he was able to forward a design for a two-turret ironclad worked out by himself and Messrs. Laird. On the 20th, E. J. Reed made a preliminary report on the design. He considered the ship "well designed and proportioned" and, surprisingly enough, that it "conforms exactly to the views which have been entertained for years past in this department," and that had been utilized in the Monarch. But in view of the low freeboard proposed and the notorious inability of shipbuilders to construct hulls to carry the necessary weights, it would be well that a sharp account be kept of all weight worked into the proposed ironclad.[120] Admiral Robinson agreed with Reed's evaluation of the ship, and, like Reed, noted with surprise Coles's acceptance of features that he had denounced in other designs. He called for close scrutiny of any contract drawn up.[121] On the strength of these obvervations, the Admiralty submitted the estimates for the vessel to Parliament, and devised the formula by which the responsibilities of those concerned with its design and construction were apportioned: "My Lords approve of this ship being built as proposed, on the entire responsibility of Captain Coles and Messrs. Laird, under the usual Admiralty inspections as to workmanship and material." [122] Coles, in a carefully worded reply, accepted "any joint responsibility which may fairly belong to me," and took the "sole responsibility of strongly recommending Their Lordships to build this ship as designed." [123]

In the meantime the Admiralty had conducted a somewhat anachronistic experiment to determine the ability of turrets to withstand fire from modern rifled artillery. For a target the board selected the *Royal Sovereign*, completed in 1864. Reed's newest box-battery ironclad, H.M.S. *Bellerophon*, was drawn up at a distance of two hundred yards to fire three shots from her twelve-and-one-half-ton rifles at the ten-inch protection of the *Royal Sovereign*'s turrets. All three shots hit the target ship, one near the turret gun port, another at a junction of the armor plates on the turret, while the third scoured the deck and flew overboard. Like most such experiments, the results could be interpreted in more than one way. Coles and his supporters were gratified that the turrets revolved freely after the bombardment, thus apparently vindicating their contention that Coles's turrets would not jam under fire as did Ericsson's.[124] Reed, however, remained unconvinced, pointing out later that the *Bellerophon*'s twelve-inch gun had indeed roughly handled the turrets, even if it had not prevented their rotation.[125] Robinson claimed that the *Royal Sovereign*'s turrets would have been penetrated by a few more shots, while the nine-inch armor of a target representing Reed's newest box-battery warship, the *Hercules*, had completely withstood the same gun at the same distance in trials at Shoeburyness. Even the rotation of the turrets could have been arrested, Robinson insisted, if one of the shots had hit the *Royal Sovereign* at the juncture of turret and deck.[126] But, in fairness to Captain Coles, it must be remembered that the turret ship's armor had been forged two years previously, and in the rapidly changing technology of the 1860s this could have made it obsolescent.

Later in the summer of 1866 the chief constructor had become somewhat uneasy about the arrangements for building the *Captain*—as the Coles-Laird ship was to be named—and about the distribution of responsibility for it. His next report is worth attention in some detail because the question of responsibility for the *Captain* was to assume tragic significance within a few years. Reed specifically absolved his department from responsibility for details of construction, since Admiralty accountability was to be confined to materials and workmanship. He questioned how Captain Coles, admittedly no shipbuilder, could supervise all the unspecified details of building a warship, particularly in the face of Admiralty experience, which showed that contractors would often prefer the cheapest method of construction to the best or the strongest. Reed continued to worry about the weight of the hull and suggested that a full list of weights be included in the contract. Although in his first report he had no fears for the stability of the ship, he now found "that the centre of gravity of ships armed and plated in the proposed manner, is situated higher than would appear probable at first sight," and urged that since a large spread of canvas was proposed, Laird's should thoroughly satisfy themselves on this point.[127]

On 10 August the Admiralty formally communicated to

Laird's its requirements, based on Reed's reports of 20
July and 2 August, for the construction of the *Captain*.
Their lordships informed the Birkenhead firm: "It is in
contemplation to place on you and Captain Coles the entire
responsibility of the design." An Admiralty inspector would
be assigned to reject imperfect workmanship or inferior
materials only, and Laird's were to "thoroughly satisfy
[themselves] in regard to the weights and the position of
the centre of gravity." [128]

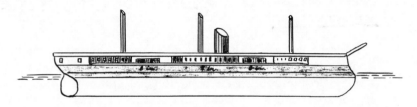

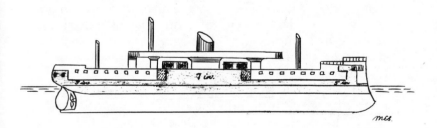

H.M.S. *Captain* and *Monarch* compared.

Messrs. Laird quickly replied that they would accept
joint responsibility with Coles for "having recommended
Their Lordships to build a warship on the plans submitted."
This was not the same as accepting responsibility for the
details of construction not found in the plans. Laird's also

brushed aside suggestions of any lack of stability.[129] Since the firm failed to take responsibility for details of construction, Coles was informed that the Admiralty wished to place him in supervision of the *Captain*'s construction, generally fulfilling the duties of the controller's department in interpreting the contract and specifications and details of construction, and in certifying the ship ready for sea.[130] Coles naturally balked at such responsibility, but in his haste to see his ship completed, he agreed to assume the position, with the provision that the ship be stored and equipped in a government yard. To this the Admiralty agreed, for they were determined that the *Captain* should be built exactly to Coles's plans so that he could no longer complain in public about Admiralty indifference and hostility.[131] The general tenor of correspondence among Reed, Robinson, Coles, and the board seems to indicate that the Admiralty was more concerned about avoiding the extra payments and litigation arising from differences of opinion over who was responsible for what work, than for any fears for the ironclad's safety. Robinson, in particular, had pointed out the difficulties of constructing so novel a ship in a private yard. Even in the case of more conventional ironclads, endless difficulties over the meanings of contracts and responsibility for work had developed.[132] This was only to be expected, because the building of ironclads was unknown a decade previous.

On the day the Admiralty gave its approval to Coles's proviso, he wrote to inform the board that further discussions of his supervision at the Birkenhead yard would be useless because: "I am obliged, under medical advice, to decline any responsibility or engagement which would involve my residence or attendance at Birkenhead in the winter or spring."[133] For Robinson, any further delay seemed "almost a calamity." Magnanimously, in view of his objections to many features of the Coles-Laird design, Robinson offered to take Coles's place and to be responsible for the supervision of details of construction. He hoped that it would be possible to follow Captain Coles's wishes in the design, but, he admitted, "the experience of five years has taught me how small a chance I have of succeeding or of avoiding most unpleasant communications." Rather pathetically he asked for their lordships' support, "and for, I may say, their protection." [134] The Admiralty agreed to this modification of their original outline of responsibility and again wrote to Coles: "The responsibility of the design and specifications, must, therefore, [since neither met with the full approval of the Controller] rest with you and Messrs. Laird, and nothing but the duty of seeing the design rigidly adhered to, and worked out faithfully, both as regards materials and labour, will be entrusted to the Controller of the Navy's Department." [135]

Far from attempting to hinder the *Captain*'s design and construction, Robinson was now in a positive haste to begin, worrying about Coles's balking at the question of responsibility, and insisting that "energetic means should be at once taken to get on with the construction of that design." [136] Such anxiety must not be interpreted as a conversion to Coles's ideas. On the contrary, in the spring of 1867, Admiral Robinson declared in a discussion after a lecture by Coles at the Royal United Service Institution that it was only "possible to have a sea-going turret ship if you give up the low freeboard." [137] Rather, it would seem that Robinson and Reed were confident that the *Captain* would prove to be a failure and be relegated to a backwater, along with Coles.[138] But, for his part, Coles was more concerned about pecuniary responsibility that might attach itself to him, than about any premonition of failure. On this point, Robinson advised the board to reassure Coles.[139]

As a further complication, Coles suddenly demanded that he be consulted on all those details not in the plans and specifications, a duty that was now in Robinson's hands.[140] Robinson pointed out this anomaly to the board, and the impracticability of Laird's referring details to the controller's department, their sending it to the bedridden Coles, and his returning it to the controller and on to Laird's again. Robinson suggested, instead, that these details be settled between Laird's and Coles.[141] This arrangement shifted some of the responsibility from the controller back to Coles. Such fragmentation of responsibility, in its tortuous complexity, is unique in the history of the Royal Navy, and seemed destined from the start to foster misunderstanding, expense, and delay.[142] Here was an arrangement to construct something as complex and novel as a seagoing turret ship on the responsibility of no less than three authorities, separated by scores of miles from each other, and between at least two of whom positive distrust festered.

Laird's were informed accordingly that all details that came under the heading in the contract of "to be done as directed" were to be referred to Captain Coles, rather than to the controller. Their lordships were careful to state that no payment would be allowed for expense above the contract price for any work performed without Admiralty permission.[143]

Robinson had advocated rendering all possible assistance to Coles in order to test the validity of his claims, but he could still gain no respite from the dynamic inventor. Two months after the *Captain*'s contract was sent to Laird's, Coles sent the Admiralty plans for a fleet of turret ships, a rather ominous change from the single ironclads he had advocated previously. Would he now publicly demand that a whole squadron of turret ships be built? Once again he explained in detail the advantages of the turret system over the broadside, in case the controller of the board had not yet been made aware of them. Wearily, their lordships replied that Coles's latest proposal had "received their serious consideration," but that it could not as yet be put into practice.[144]

In a lengthy lecture at the Royal United Service Institution, under the belligerent title "The Turret *vs.* the Broadside System," Coles interpreted the findings of the Turret Ship Committee of 1865 as originating with the "anti-turret party," which had prevented a fair trial for the Coles-Scullard design. Both Reed and Robinson were present and took part in the debate following the lecture. Reed pointed out that, far from being the head of the "anti-turret" forces, he had encouraged Coles to build his turret ship on the dimensions of the *Bellerophon*, and Coles had only himself to blame if he had chosen to copy so unsuitable an ironclad as the *Pallas*.

Coles's lecture itself was unexceptional, primarily a re-iteration of the advantages of the turret over the broadside (illuminated by his excellent drawings), but he did apply to turret ships the distinction between the cruiser that possessed good steam for war but trusted much to her sails, and the warship designed for European waters but capable of long voyages and lightly masted.[145]

The *Captain* and *Monarch* projects were not enough to satisfy many of Coles's supporters. Captain Sherard Os-borne, late captain of the *Royal Sovereign*, denounced the *Monarch*'s high freeboard, and rudely wrote in the *Times* that "her turrets might as well be mounted on the top of the First Lord's old hat as fifteen feet high" and suggested that such an excuse for a turret ship was "fresh proof of the rottenness of the present Board of Admiralty system of governing the Navy."[146] It might be noted that Osborne was a full-pay officer supposedly under Admiralty discipline.

Yet, a year earlier, the Admiralty had called for tenders from prominent shipbuilders for either a turret or broad-side ship, laying down fifteen conditions to be fulfilled if a turret ship were to be designed. The height of freeboard was not specified. The designers were only to see that it was "carefully considered." Sail power was essential, speed not to be less than thirteen-and-one-half knots, and the ironclad must carry two turrets. Twelve conditions were laid down for any proposed broadside warship. The armament was to consist of not less than ten muzzle-loading rifles, with one or more guns able to command every point of the horizon. Armor-plating, tonnage, speed, sail power, and iron construction were to be similar to those requirements for turret ships.[147]

By 10 September 1867 all builders competing had submitted designs, and the controller, on the technical advice of the chief constructor, was to recommend one plan to the board. Robinson, painfully aware that the Coles controversy had by no means abated, longed to submit the designs to "some unofficial tribunal which should have been beyond even the suspicion of partiality." If a turret design were not chosen over a broadside, the Coles partisans would denounce, with even greater vigor, the imagined bias of the "anti-turret party"—Reed and himself. Nonetheless, he had to defer to their lordships' directions, and in so doing eliminated three designs: one broadside, one compound of two systems, and a broadside and movable-battery plan. Three plans, two for turrets and one broadside design, were considered in detail. In summarizing their strong and weak points, Robinson was gratified to note that none of the private designs was able to improve on Admiralty plans. None could carry the required amount of armament, power, and armor on a smaller warship, something Coles and his supporters always claimed that his designs were able to do.

Most of the designs were subjected to severe criticism. Millwall's, for example, was "as unsightly as it [was] faulty." The shortcomings lay mainly in stability, weights, constructional details, and freeboard. Reed considered Messrs. Laird's design to be the best, and he recommended that both as a seagoing ship and as a fighting ship it deserved careful consideration.[148] He still had serious doubts about the low freeboard of the design, but at least did not reject it out of hand.

Actually, Reed's praise of the Laird entry was the more disinterested considering that he had previously designed a masted turret ship that he belived would have been superior to both the *Monarch* and the *Captain*. In his planned vessel, Reed concentrated his weights amidship to give his turrets free range of fire. The turrets themselves were raised on a

breastwork to bring them twelve feet above the waterline.
The ironclad was to carry a full sailing rig and four hundred
fifty tons of coal. As seemed to have been the case with so
many designs of this era, Reed did not enjoy a free hand.
Therefore he was compelled to design his turret ship within
a limit of 3,774 tons. He maintained that "with larger
dimensions it would be easy, of course, to produce a better
ship." [149] Admiral Robinson agreed that "if they chose to
have a turret ship of 3,774 tons, the design produced is
probably as good as can be made." [150] Unfortunately, no
plans of this ironclad have been found.

Rejecting both Reed's and the competition ships, the
board, acting on the recommendation of the controller,
decided to build the *Invincible* class of box-battery ironclads
instead. According to Robinson, none of the competition
turret ships enjoyed any great advantage over the broadside system.[151]

In order to forestall the expected repercussions to their
decision in Parliament, the Admiralty requested eleven
high-ranking officers to submit their opinions of turret ships.
Their replies generally were cautiously optimistic toward the
turret principle, but the majority thought that the best
course would be to wait until the tests of the *Monarch* and
Capain had been evaluated. Only two officers came out unreservedly for the turret.[152] Thus armed, the Parliamentary
secretary was able to argue effectively against an Opposition resolution calling for a scientific committee to review
the Admiralty's entire shipbuilding and design policy. Lord
Lennox rightly argued that such a resolution, if passed,
would weaken the Admiralty's responsibility to Parliament.
The government's policy of waiting for the performance of
the *Monarch* and *Captain* before further committing itself
to turret ships was sustained by a majority of ten.[153]

Construction on the two seagoing turret ships continued,
although relations remained strained between the Admiralty
and Coles, who was still attempting to change the design of
the *Monarch*. Robinson, suspicious of Coles, refused to give

him information on any particulars except those of the turrets.[154] But work on the *Captain* proceeded satisfactorily and rapidly, for it was in the hands of enthusiastic master builders. Nathaniel Barnaby, a future Chief Constructor, found Laird's work "well and truly done" but noted the extravagant use of material.[155] Here was the first indication of the tragedy that was literally being built into the turret ship. Laird's and Coles, anxious to make the ship structurally sound and to prevent any possibility of failure, utilized extra-heavy materials on a lavish scale for her construction. As mentioned earlier, the Admiralty inspectors at Laird's were to check only on workmanship and materials, not on weights.

Even with the *Captain* well in hand Coles was not satisfied. In September 1868 he called upon the Admiralty to redeem its "pledge" to give a full and fair trial to the turret system. It seemed rank ingratitude to the Admiralty that Captain Coles had not even mentioned the *Captain* in his letter, and their lordships felt that they had been more than generous to a half-pay captain. They had authorized him, they responded, "to construct a turret ship in accordance with your own plans and views, free from all interference, allowing you to select your own builders." [156]

On 27 March 1869 the *Captain* was floated out of dock. There were even cheers for Coles, Laird's, and the ladies, too, at the ceremony over which Childers presided.[157] Frederick Barnes of the Admiralty construction department quickly calculated that the *Captain* with all her weights on board would float thirteen inches below her intended waterline, reducing her freeboard to six feet, eleven inches, from the planned eight feet.[158] This reduction of freeboard should not have come as a surprise to the Admiralty. In September 1867 Robinson had noted that "in building ships in private yards a less vigilant supervision or less minute direction and inspection necessarily takes place, the calculated displacement constantly proves insufficient" to carry intended weights.[159] With the Barnes report before him, Reed did not hesitate to pronounce the *Captain* "utterly unsafe." [160] An unhappy Admiralty was now faced with the prospect of an unsatisfactory and perhaps unsafe warship if it accepted the *Captain*, and lengthy litigation (particularly in view of the complicated allocation of responsibility) and a storm of unfavorable publicity if it did not. In this dilemma, the board even considered commissioning the *Captain* without her guns, although for what purpose is not clear.[161]

The *Captain*, in the meanwhile, was fitted for sea during the remainder of 1869, and in so doing her freeboard continued to decrease. Even the *Times* noted that much of the work on the ship "appears far too massive" but concluded optimistically that this "may be of little consequence." [162]

In February 1870 the *Captain* proceeded to Portsmouth for steam trials, her freeboard now down to six feet, seven inches. In consequence, Reed recommended that final payment for the turret ship be withheld from Laird's.[163] The controller disagreed with his chief constructor and felt that the Admiralty was bound by the terms of the contract to make full payment in the light of the *Captain*'s successful trials and excellent workmanship. Coles, in accordance with the contract, certified that the *Captain* had been built to his entire satisfaction—except for the increased draught.[164] Since the primary aim of the entire *Captain* project was to build a warship exactly to Captain Coles's satisfaction, it seems strange that the Admiralty or Coles would have accepted a ship that fell so far short of this aim in so important a detail. Thus the original intentions of the Admiralty had been modified several times: when the controller had agreed to supervise details of construction beyond those merely of workmanship and materials, when Coles was allowed a partial share in this arrangement with Laird's, and when Captain Coles only partially approved of the *Captain*. Any of these concessions could conceivably allow Coles to be exculpated were the *Captain* to prove a failure.

The ready acceptance of this arrangement may be explained in large part by the fact that the First Lord of the

Admiralty in the new Gladstone administration, Hugh C. B. Childers, was a strong believer in turret ships. Childers had imbibed the extreme principles of economy associated with the Manchester School and apparently came to his belief in turret ships primarily as an economy measure. From his first days in office he had hoped to keep down the estimates for seamen by building the type of ship that Coles and his supporters claimed would need fewer sailors.[165] Naturally he could be expected to come into conflict with the constructor and the Controller. An autocratic bearing and marked ineptitude in his dealings with subordinates exacerbated a tense situation. To the stupefaction of the naval officers involved, Childers actually took personal command of the Reserve Squadron's maneuvers in 1869, an unprecedented and possibly illegal usurpation of authority. By the end of 1870 the chief constructor and the civil lord had resigned, and the controller and the third sea lord had threatened to follow.[166] One authority termed Childers "a legislator of the type that regards disagreement with professional colleagues as a true indication of statesmanship."[167]

Perhaps uneasy about the diminished freeboard of the *Captain*, Messrs. Laird had suggested in February 1870 that the warship be inclined with weights to locate her center of gravity more accurately than would be possible by calculation. However, Reed minuted this suggestion by submitting that these tests be postponed until the weather improved and steam trials were completed.[168] Messrs. Laird never repeated the suggestion, which was most sensible in the light of the *Captain*'s novelty.

Yet Reed continued to have misgivings about the *Captain*, and in March wrote: "I am unable any longer to anticipate a satisfactory result to the trials of this ship in such seas as the *Monarch* has had to encounter."[169] A year later Admiral Robinson was to explain that neither he nor Reed foresaw "any unavoidable peril." It is likely that Reed and Robinson felt that the deck and turrets would be swamped in heavy seas, rendering the *Captain* uninhabitable and her

guns useless. That nothing worse than failure was anticipated is shown by Robinson's request, refused by Childers,
to go to sea with the *Captain* for a two-month cruise.[170]
   To settle the differences of opinion about the sea-keeping
abilities of turret ships, the *Monarch* and *Captain* were
sent on a cruise with the broadside and box-battery ships
of the Channel Squadron. The comparison was not exactly
fair between the two turret ships since the *Monarch* had
already made a transatlantic voyage (bearing the body of
Samuel Peabody to New York), and her crew was therefore better coordinated and more experienced, whereas the
Captain was a new ship with a new crew. But Coles had
subjected the *Monarch* to virulent abuse and had always
insisted that his ships were built to compete with those of
Reed. It was only natural that all observers would look
upon the cruise as a trial between the two seagoing turret
ships. On this cruise the *Captain* certainly did not triumphantly vindicate her designer, and signally failed to impress
Admiral Robinson with her merits. Great masses of green
water rushed across the upper deck, in any sea, crashing
against the turrets. The *Monarch* remained bone-dry, Robinson noted. The *Captain* was able to open her gun ports
and fire blank charges, however, even when seemingly
swamped. Under steam the *Monarch* was the more economical and the faster, as she was under sail, and sail and
steam combined. But it should be noted that the *Captain*
was equipped with twin screws, an immeasurable advantage
in combat over the *Monarch*'s single screw, enabling the
former to turn almost upon her axis, and giving her a
reserve engine in case one were disabled. But these twin
screws retarded the *Captain*'s speed under sail and rendered
her slightly inferior in steaming-speed and economy. Finally,
for some reason, the *Captain*'s screws could not be disconnected, thus preventing them from revolving freely under
sail and increasing hull resistance. Since sailing qualities
meant so much in the 1860s and early 1870s, the *Captain*
was thus condemned by many.
   Far more significant were the observations of a Lieu-

tenant Rice, who accompanied Admiral Robinson in the *Monarch*. Noting the *Captain*'s sluggish behavior, Lieutenant Rice concluded: "The *Captain* is not a ship which should be much pressed under sail. A heel of 14 degrees will bring her gunwale to the water, and from that point, of course, her stability would very rapidly decrease." Robinson carefully included Lieutenant Rice's remarks in his relatively unfavorable report on the *Captain*. Praising Captain Coles's "highly practical inventive, and ingenious" mind, and expressing unjustified confidence that the argument of the turret versus the broadside system was now "a long extinguished controversy," Admiral Robinson proceeded to demonstrate the shortcomings of the *Captain* as opposed to the *Monarch*. In summary, he noted: "The *Monarch* has fulfilled in every respect the intention of her designers, the *Captain* has not." The latter turret ship was superior only in smooth water, and this superiority was obtained at the cost of her qualities as a high-seas vessel. Robinson, in fact, rejected the *Captain* completely, contending that the low-freeboard turret ship of the future would be of the mastless *Devastation* type, not that of the *Captain*. For ocean cruising, the high-freeboard *Monarch* should be the model. Robinson believed that he had at last found the answer to the vexing problem of how to utilize Coles's invention.[171]

But a far more favorable report on the *Captain* was submitted by Vice Adm. Sir Thomas Symonds, Commander of the Channel Squadron. Admiral Symonds emphasized the ability of the *Captain* to fire her guns in heavy seas, and noted that some of the broadside ships were nearly as wet in rough weather. He concluded that the *Captain* could destroy all of them "in detail."[172]

Reed, of course, took strong exception to these opinions, particularly the last, which seemed to reflect on his and Robinson's designs. He considered that Admiral Symonds was misled by the fact that, on this cruise, the *Captain* was lighter, thus bringing her guns farther out of the water, and that the Admiral entertained "widely different views from those expressed by captains and commanders" with whom Reed had discussed the cruise upon its completion. The constructor hinted that Admiral Symonds's impending retirement had induced him to make somewhat irresponsible statements. Admiral Robinson replied in similar vein, and the Admiralty laid Admiral Symonds and Robinson's reports on the table of the House of Commons.[173]

The *Times* at first seemed to think the *Monarch* a slightly superior vessel on the strength of the Channel Squadron cruise, and went so far as to call the *Captain* an "unsuccessfully built" warship. Nine days later the "Thunderer" clarified its turret-ship policy by affirming that the *Captain* was just as good, if not a better ship, than the *Monarch*, and provocatively asserted that until the turret-ship question was resolved, "we shall refuse to admit that the Board of Admiralty are sincere and straightforward in their policy of naval construction."[174]

After the *Captain*'s third cruise in July 1870, Captain Coles and the ironclad's commander, Capt. Hugh Burgoyne, V.C., submitted reports that found little or no fault with their turret ship.[175]

But Admiral Robinson's doubts as to the *Captain*'s efficiency found more definite expression when he stated that since the ship's immersion had been so miscalculated, any mathematical determination of her center of gravity would be suspect. On 23 July, acting on Admiral Robinson's orders, Admiralty officers finally carried out inclining experiments on the *Captain* at Portsmouth dockyard. These experiments showed that the Laird's calculations as to the metacenter and the center of gravity were indeed correct.[176] The preliminary report on these experiments was submitted to the board on 23 August. It noted that the *Captain*'s stability would be jeopardized when light, due to her topweights and low freeboard, but that this condition could easily be corrected by the taking of water into the boilers or the double bottom.[177]

Previous to these experiments, Reed had resigned his

post in disgust at "the very low estimate which all governments put upon mechanical and scientific skill." While his
resistance to the *Captain* was not the cause of Reed's actual
resignation, "this cause had its weight," he remarked
later.[178]

Still later, Reed elaborated that "with the advent of this
[Gladstone] government to power there commenced a system of pressure upon the Chief Constructor which was
utterly unknown before, which greatly influenced my work,
and which at last forced me to resign in order to retain my
dignity as a scientific man."[179] The pro-Coles press adopted
a surprisingly moderate tone in reporting the fall of the
archenemy of progress. All offered wildly conflicting reasons
for his resignation.[180]

Free from the restraints of office, Reed harshly attacked
the *Captain* and the blunders of her builders, in space
obligingly given by the *Times*. His experienced designer's
eye revolted against the ungainly ship's "mere mass of unarmoured houses, casing, decks, and hammock boxes piled
up before, between, abaft, and over the turrets."[181] The
controversy had become exceedingly bitter by now. Captain
Osborne raved of the "almost criminal opposition" to the
turret principle, and denounced the *Monarch* as "a mere
dodge to stay progress."[182]

Assistant Constructor Frederick K. Barnes had meanwhile continued his calculations on the curves of stability of
the *Captain*. His preliminary report, based on the inclining
tests, were determined on the assumption that the poop and
forecastle had been destroyed in combat. Now he worked
from the more likely assumption that they were intact.
Barnes found that these structures added only one degree
to the range of stability of the *Captain*, and that this
stability was less than that of any other Royal Navy warship. The maximum righting force was reached at fourteen
degrees, at which angle the upper deck was immersed; it
increased at a slower rate until twenty-one degrees was
reached. Beyond that angle stability decreased at an accel-

erating rate until fifty-four-and-a-half degrees was attained,
at which point stability vanished. Barnes reported that the
Captain would be "quite safe," however, to the angle of
thirty-four degrees, a fair margin of safety. But he noted
at the end of his report "that a force which if applied
steadily will hold a ship inclined at a definite angle, would
if applied to the ship suddenly, incline her to double that
angle." [183] So, if the *Captain* were not carefully managed,
she could be capsized by a sudden gust of wind. If the
Captain were sailed at an angle of fifteen degrees, for
example, a gust of wind could put her over to thirty
degrees, perilously close to her limits of safety. On the
other hand, one of Coles's reasons for preferring low-
freeboard turret ships was that they would roll far less
than ships of high freeboard.

Admiral Robinson reported these conclusions to the
board, and suggested that in consequence Messrs. Laird
should be made aware of their lordships' displeasure at the
"serious and unexampled error" in the miscalculation of
weights that had so undermined the turret ship's stability.
Yet, Robinson recommended that the Admiralty should
accept the ship, since it had passed its acceptance trials.[184]

Robinson felt that Barnes's still-incomplete report on the
stability of the *Captain* proved that the ship was safe
enough up to the point at which her gunwale was immersed
—fourteen degrees. "I had no doubt that with common
prudence such an approach to danger need never have
occurred," he wrote afterwards.[185] The controller possessed
neither the plans of the *Captain* (they were the property of
Laird's) nor the time and personnel required to work out
for himself more detailed calculations on the ironclad's
stability. Reed was unofficially shown Barnes's preliminary
report and he found it satisfactory. But he did not see the
calculations on which it was based.[186] Admiral Robinson
later insisted, as did Reed, that Captains Coles and John
Burgoyne, V.C., knew the limits of stability of their own
ship, and that the turret ship having been to sea on two

cruises had stood up to rough weather. In the tortuous prose of the controller: "There was therefore no reason connected with the apprehension of immediate danger, which made it specially urgent that those problems of her construction over which doubt had been thrown by the miscalculations of Messrs. Laird," should prevent the winding-up of the *Captain*'s contract.[187] On 2 September 1870 the order was given for the payment of the final installment of the *Captain*'s cost to Messrs. Laird.

H.M.S. *Captain*. Fitting-out. OFFICIAL U.S. NAVY PHOTOGRAPH.

Meanwhile, the *Captain* had put to sea on 4 August for a cruise with the Mediterranean Fleet under Admiral Alexander Milne.[188] She behaved strangely on the outward leg of the voyage to Gibraltar. Always a crank ship (likely to heel under sail), her lee gunwale now was *immersed* in the sea, as the ship heeled at a more or less permanent angle of from twelve to fourteen degrees. As he came aboard for a tour of the new ironclad, Admiral Milne, on the morning of 6 September, experienced the rather startling sensation of stepping out of his cutter directly onto a warship's upper deck. "I cannot reconcile myself to this state of things so very unusual in all my experience," the Admiral remarked to Coles. Rather tactlessly, Captain Coles answered that there was not the slightest danger, that the water could safely go over to the ladder at the base of the bridge, eight or ten feet from the gunwale. Milne retorted that he was worried about the ship's inclination and her full spread of sail, and not about any danger to himself. Coles did admit that he was "certain the guns ought to be from two feet to two feet six inches higher," perhaps a tacit admission of chagrin at the warship's low freeboard.[189]

Admiral Milne carefully observed the sailing qualities of the ironclad, and was as startled by these as by her low freeboard. The yards were braced up at a very sharp angle in order to catch as much wind as possible, the probable cause of the *Captain*'s startling list. Coles, however, was oblivious to any imagined faults of his project.[190] In what is probably the last surviving scrap of his voluminous correspondence, he had poetically exulted: "She walks the waters like a thing of life."[191]

Admiral Milne's flag lieutenant, Robert Hastings Harris, has recorded how the ship's behavior "seemed to us very uneasy and startling," and noticed her "very slow recovery from every lurch she gave."[192] But Milne did not press unduly his misgivings upon Coles, and left the ship after a tour of inspection.

The next morning the *Captain* had vanished. An account later was pieced together from the one gunner and seventeen seamen who survived; the *Captain*, along with the rest of the fleet, had been in a moderate gale. A heavy gust of wind seems to have heeled over the turret ship, and before sail could be taken in to relieve the pressure of the wind, she had capsized, about twenty miles to the westward of Cape Finisterre. Those below decks were lost to a man,

H.M.S. *Captain*. On board the doomed ironclad. The presence of debris suggests that the photographs were taken while the ironclad was still in the builders' hands. Note old boot atop turret. NATIONAL MARITIME MUSEUM, LONDON.

and the survivors, thrown clear from the upper and hurricane decks, could hear their hideous shrieks as they were scalded and crushed as the ship's machinery broke loose. Captain Burgoyne managed to stay afloat for a brief time, then drifted away to his death. Captain Coles, seen by no one, probably perished in his cabin. He had lived just long enough to experience the total destruction of all his dreams and plans. With Coles also perished the eldest son of Childers, a son of Lord Northbrook, a nephew of Sir John Pakington, a son of Lord Herbert of Lea, and the only son of Field Marshal Sir John F. Burgoyne.

The first reaction to this disaster, the worst in peacetime British naval history, was one of stunned apprehension. Were other ironclads also doomed?

A court martial was quickly assembled, ostensibly to try the survivors. This was a pure formality, the main purpose of the court being to discover the cause of the disaster. The survivors gave their account of what had happened on that night of 6/7 September 1870. The gunner seemed to corroborate the Barnes report of 23 August, in which it was stated that the ship would be in some danger if a strong gust of wind acted in conjunction with wave action. Gunner May recollected that he had felt "a heavy sea strike her on the weather side." [193] Some survivors remembered seeing Captain Burgoyne, in a state of semi-undress that suggested that he had come on deck quickly, call out to the seaman who was watching the inclinometer: "How many degrees is she heeling?" The seaman's reply was "18 degrees." This exchange indicates that some of Captain Burgoyne's confidence had evaporated, for that angle of heel would not have given the captain of any other ship a moment's pause. He may well have remembered Captain Osborne's warning "at all costs not to hesitate if caught in bad weather to furl all sail, and bring the ship under steam, with her bow to the sea." [194] With the *Captain* heeled over to eighteen degrees by the wind, a sudden gust could have doubled that heel and brought the ironclad perilously close to the end of her stability; the heave of the sea could well have completed the process.   .

All those connected with the design and building of the turret ship were called to testify, with the strange exceptions of Admiral Robinson and Childers. Henry Laird could give no satisfactory explanation for the *Captain*'s increased draught, and attributed the loss to some unknown cause, as did his brother, William Laird.

E. J. Reed explained why he had not given to Captain Burgoyne official information reflecting upon the stability of the *Captain*. He, along with Robinson, assumed that the ship would have enjoyed the highest praises to begin with, that she would be carefully nursed through her early career, to be quietly condemned when her deficiencies became obvious. Reed might have also pointed out that he was no longer employed in the Admiralty when the exact calculations of the *Captain*'s stability, with all her weights, were made.[195]

But it was established that the *Captain*'s increased immersion was not enough in itself to capsize her. From the testimony of her supervisors, the *Captain* seemed to have been literally blown over, assisted by the choppy sea. Yet it was also testified that the sails would have been blown out of an ordinary ironclad before it could be brought to so great a heel as to capsize it; every ship in the squadron lost canvas and spars on that night, except the *Captain*. Perhaps here, as in the hull, weights were the cause. The Laird brothers testified that Captain Coles was responsible for the design of the spars, and the surviving crewmen agreed with Admiral Milne that the ship seemed too heavily built in her masts and spars.[196] Instead of blowing away, as they did on the other ships in the squadron, the sails acted as a fatal wind trap. Coles, like Laird's, must have wished to insure against any possibility of failure, and so had not spared material to make his work as strong as possible. Laird's and Coles, free from any Admiralty inspection other than for workmanship, quality of materials, and details of construction, and anxious to prove the turret ship, had determined to build her of the highest quality. In those early days of iron shipbuilding, quality meant weight, but weight meant increased immersion and spars that would not give way when necessary. Finally, Coles's patented iron tripod masts added topside weight, particularly because the mizzen and fore tripod extended only to the hurricane deck.

A strong suspicion was entertained that the *Captain* was not only overbuilt, but also over-sailed. Pointed questions were asked about the sail carried by ships of the squadron. The *Captain* carried double-reefed topsails and fore-top-mast staysail, no more than any other ship in the squadron. But since the *Captain* was an experimental and crank type, with fears expressed for her stability, would it not have been prudent for Captain Burgoyne to have shortened sail in the face of the gale? No definite conclusion was reached on this speculative question. But there was no doubt that the ironclad had not been able to furl her sail so rapidly as the other warships. When Captain Burgoyne hurriedly attempted to lower sail, the heel of the deck made it impossible.

The storm on the night of 6/7 September was considered by almost all witnesses to have been less severe than one that the *Captain* had weathered in May. But in the September storm a confused sea was running that built up into pyramids on occasion, and it may have been such a wave that destroyed the last vestige of stability of a warship already undermined by low freeboard, heavy rig, and close sailing.

After eleven days of testimony the court returned its verdict in which it concluded that "her Majesty's ship *Captain* was capsized on the morning of the 7th September, 1870, by pressure of sail, assisted by the heave of the sea; and that the sail carried at the time of her loss . . . was insufficient to have endangered a ship endowed with a proper amount of stability." Furthermore, "the *Captain* was built in deference to public opinion expressed in Parliament, and through other channels, and in opposition to the views and opinions of the Controller and his Department, and that the evidence all tends to show that they generally disapproved of her construction." After rebuking Messrs. Laird for their "grave error" in miscalculating the ship's freeboard and thereby imperiling its stability, the court concluded by expressing its regret that the facts about the *Captain*'s reduced stability "were not communicated to the officer in command of the ship," and that further experiments were not carried out on her. The survivors were praised for their conduct, and discharged.[197]

The *Times*, which had called for another *Captain* when first reporting the news of the turret ship's loss, now commented: "The case against the *Captain* as an experiment in naval architecture comes out worse than was ever anticipated."[198]

The strange history of the *Captain* was about to take an even stranger course. That the court martial would vaguely censure unnamed persons for dereliction of duty was unusual. But the Admiralty then replied in a public minute, rebuking the court for its "conditional and not altogether clear, opinion." Their lordships pointed out that the often-quoted statement that the *Captain* was "built in deference to public opinion" rested on the opinion of three men—Reed and two subordinates of Admiral Robinson. No member of either of the boards concerned with the *Captain* was ever called upon to testify. The minute concluded by insisting that Captains Coles and Burgoyne were aware of the limits of safety of their ship. This was only the opening phase of a bitter dispute.[199]

In retrospect, the court's findings seem only partially valid. Increased immersion did reduce the *Captain*'s stability, but not fatally so; at any rate the blunder was as much the fault of the Admiralty for drawing up so complicated a division of responsibility, as of Laird's. Messrs. Laird were responsible for the over-masting, even if it was based on the plans of Captain Coles. The sail plan was also faulty in that it was not carried down to the upper deck but to the hurricane deck. This raised the center of wind pressure by ten feet, while the tripod masts added further weight aloft.[200] The *Captain*'s extraordinary ratio of length to beam, the greatest until the *Dreadnought* of 1906, may also have been a contributory factor.[201] That the *Captain* was over-sailed on her last voyage is more than just conjecture. She had made a mediocre showing in her trials with the *Monarch*, and on this last cruise, according to Admiral Robert Hastings Harris, Coles had told him as they stood on Southsea pier before embarking: "We will make her sail like a witch this time." [202] Admiral Milne had testified that Burgoyne had told him that it was Coles's idea to sail as close to the wind as possible; this would account for the permanent heel of the *Captain*, which brought her lee gunwale underwater and reduced her stability.[203] None of these points was decided upon by the court martial. Furthermore, it was later established that the *Captain*'s reduced freeboard, for which Laird's were responsible, had undermined her entire range of stability.[204]

The controller was quick to reply to the court martial's intimation of dereliction of duty, which he believed was directed at himself. In a memorandum that apparently was never published, he attributed the disaster to a combination of factors, most of them reflecting adversely on Captain Burgoyne. After describing the crankiness of the ship on her last voyage and the immersion of her gunwale, Robinson concluded: "No ship could have been less cautiously handled than the unfortunate *Captain* on the night of her loss." [205] Robinson's opinions were special pleading. But disinterested evidence has already been given of the *Captain*'s unusual sailing on her final cruise. Robinson's conclusions were based on the private findings, none of which were made public, of Adm. Sir James Hope, president of the court martial.

Childers was certainly not the sort of public servant to accept criticism, however ambiguous, without demur. In a detailed minute summarizing the decisions that led to the sending of the *Captain* to sea, Childers blamed Reed for failing to inform the controller and himself of his apprehensions about stability. Admiral Robinson also came under censure for not calling the attention of Childers and the first sea lord to the Barnes preliminary report. Childers' action was unprecedented, for the minute was issued in his name alone, yet was under the Admiralty imprimatur. Hence great confusion existed as to whether the minute represented the private views of an interested party or those of the Admiralty itself.[206]

Robinson was quick to reply, this time in a public minute of his own. He denied that he had failed to call the attention of Childers and the first sea lord to the dangers inherent in the *Captain*. Childers, in his minute, had quoted a proposal submitted by Robinson in such a way as to emphasize Robinson's responsibility. After the Barnes report was received, Robinson, according to Childers, had written: "I propose that Messrs. Laird should be written to as follows. . . . " Robinson had actually written: "The Barnes report referred to has now been enclosed. I propose, in consequence, that Messrs. Laird should be written to as follows. . . . " The second version, of course, draws their lordships' attention to the report enclosed. It was then their duty to determine what action to take. Considering that neither Robinson nor Reed had predicted disaster for the *Captain*, this course seems defensible.[207] Robinson's responsibility—and Childers's integrity—were seen in a different light. At any rate, the science of stability, despite some brilliant work by Reed and Nathaniel Barnaby, was in its infancy. The constructor's department admitted that they were working in an unknown field.[208] Yet Childers blamed Reed and Robinson for failing to give him precise information that the *Captain* would capsize.

Reed also defended himself. After glumly conceding that "we should have given definite shape to our vague apprehensions," he pointed out that most of his communication

with Childers was oral. The first lord's reorganization of
the Admiralty had broken down lines of communication and
liaison. Even if Reed and Robinson had sensed imminent
disaster and had given Childers warning, it is entirely possible that it would have been lost in the administrative
chaos.[209]

All this airing of Admiralty antagonisms must have
seemed confusing to the public, particularly since the navy
appeared to speak with about five official voices, all on
Admiralty letterhead. Certainly this confusion was mirrored
in Parliament, where the public was treated to the spectacle
of a recent first lord of the Admiralty's apparently en-
couraging seamen not to serve in ships of which he dis·
approved.[210] Foreseeing this public dissection of the navy's
ships, Childers had set up a Committee on Designs to evaluate ships being built or planned. This committee will be
described below, but it again reveals the autocratic and
strangely irresponsible character of the first lord. The more
acceptable course could have been for Childers to defend
himself, and the ships designed or constructed under his
authority, before the House. The action he took seemed to
cast doubt on previous naval designs and on departments
that could not defend themselves in public or in Parliament.[211]

As a final act before resigning office, broken in mind and
body by the *Captain* controversy and the loss of his son,
Childers dismissed Admiral Robinson.[212]

But the *Captain* episode is not the mere account of a
naval tragedy. Captain Coles's turret would dominate the
designs of warships for almost a century to come.

H. M. S. *Devastation*

I

By 1868, despite the dead end of H.M.S. *Captain*, naval architecture and technical progress had reached the stage where the outlines of the modern capital ship could be discerned. Previous developments in design, weapons, deployment, propulsion, and the turret, would combine to produce Reed's masterpiece, H.M.S. *Devastation*, the first seagoing, mastless, capital ship. The size of the gun had grown to the point that only turrets would be able to handle them efficiently; a few very heavy rifles could be far more efficient when mounted in a turret than a score of smaller pieces arranged in a box-battery. The emphasis upon the defense of the waters surrounding the British Isles, and the recognition that the major naval threat must come from Europe, rendered the sacrifice of masts and sails and of some habitability of little consequence. The recognized need for twin screws, both for maneuverability and as a measure of safety, and the steady improvement of engines strengthened Reed's and Robinson's—and to a lesser extent the Board of Admiralty's—resolve to abolish sails in the *Devastation* class. Finally, the experiences of the *Scorpion*, *Wyvern*, *Monarch*, and *Captain* had shown just how unsatisfactory a compromise a masted turret ship would be. A high-freeboard turret ship was an anachronism, but a low-freeboard one could not be combined with sails without gravely endangering stability and efficiency. When sail was done away with, a host of problems evaporated, as would, in fact, the box-battery ironclad, whose main raison d'être was its ability to carry sails without interfering with its guns.

The *Devastation* was the germ of all future battleships; the credit for its design must go to Reed, for all of the factors described above were still not fully accepted by the board, who, indeed, returned to a more conservative and unsatisfactory policy soon after Reed's resignation. Relying upon its twin screws rather than upon sails, carrying a few heavy rifled guns in revolving turrets on a low-lying hull, this basic ironclad type would remain the dominant naval weapons system, with drastic improvements and increases in tonnage, until it was superseded by the aircraft carrier.

But the genius of Reed's bold departure is far more readily seen when it is compared with the *Devastation*'s predecessors. The *Warrior* was an elongated iron frigate with a section of armor amidships. The *Bellerophon* was a greatly improved *Warrior* with provision for axial fire, and a hull design better adapted for carrying armor-plating and a fewer number of heavier guns. Both carried single screws and relied as much upon sail as upon steam for movement. But the *Devastation* abolished the entire paraphernalia of masts, yards, and rigging, was propelled by twin screws, and carried her guns in two turrets, one at either extremity. Although this ironclad was not the first to carry any one of these innovations, it did pioneer their combination.

It is well known that Drake's seamen would have felt more or less at home aboard H.M.S. *Victory*. It is less obvious that, with instruction in the new gunnery, they could have discharged their duties aboard H.M.S. *Warrior*, or perhaps even H.M.S. *Bellerophon*. The *Devastation*, however, (like the *Monitor*), would have represented nothing to them but a hopelessly confusing mass of machinery. Yet this basic transformation had been effected within the span of a decade, from the laying down of the *Warrior* on 25 May 1859, to the clinching of the first rivet in the keel of the *Devastation*, 12 November 1869. The magnitude of Reed's departure may be seen in the fact that another decade was to elapse before the Admiralty totally accepted the new concept, still preferring in the meantime to tinker with box-battery and sailing rigs. Only with the commencement of the "Admiral" class of the early 1880s was the thread of progressive development seized once again, this time permanently. At the height of the *Dreadnought* controversy, when Admiral Fisher's creation was the cynosure of international naval interest, Fred T. Jane could assert: "The *Dreadnought* of more or less these times was nothing in the way of novelty compared to the *Devastation* of the later '60s."[1] Reed designed numerous ships for foreign governments after his resignation as chief constructor, but he maintained that his last Admiralty design was the precursor of all subsequent ironclad designs.[2]

Neither the *Monarch*, nor certainly the *Captain*, had fulfilled Reed's concept of the ideal turret ship. Both he and Admiral Dacres, First Sea Lord, agreed that sail power vitiated any advantages offered by the turret.[3] According to Admiral Robinson, he and Reed had urged the new Conservative government (1866) to lay down mastless turret ships fit for oceanic cruising.[4] In that year Reed drew up sketches for a monster turret ship of no less than twenty-two thousand tons and a coal capacity of ten thousand tons, well over twice the displacement of any previous ironclad. The coal capacity was over five times that even of the *Devastation*. Even Robinson was taken aback by Reed's startling proposal: "I think everybody would admit that that was going rather far and fast."[5]

Some evidence exists that Reed cooperated in that year with John Ericsson, whose biographer related that John Bourne, Ericsson's publicist in Britain, suggested that Reed forward hs turret-ship plans to Ericsson for revision. According to this account: "Mr. Reed jumped at" this suggestion.[6] But considering the basic differences between Coles's turrets and Ericsson's designs, the account must be accepted with reserve. Whether Reed's ideas were vetted by Ericsson

or not, by November 1866 Reed had completed designs for
"a first-class monitor turret ship," a mere five months following the laying down of the *Monarch*'s keel. Abolishing
sail power, Reed relied upon twin screws and large coal
capacity "to enable her to make long voyages across the
sea." On the advice of Admiral Robinson, who preferred
a broadside ironclad on the same displacement, this turret
ironclad was not built.[7] But Reed, still calling for less reliance upon sail, advocated the laying down of a class of
turret ships combining the best features of both the Coles
and Ericsson designs.[8] There is certainly paradox here, with
Reed, denounced as a conservative reactionary, calling for
the abolition of traditional sail power, while Coles the "progressive" was designing the towering wind trap for H.M.S.
Captain. In July 1867 Reed submitted plans for a seagoing
turret ship with moderate masting, perhaps feeling that it
would be possible to remove the rig later when the Board
of Admiralty grew less conservative.[9] But the plans for
this small turret ship were filed away and never acted upon.

Undeterred by these repeated rebuffs, Reed continued
to study the problem of the seagoing turret ship. He
soon realized that if Captain Coles's turrets, rather than
Ericsson's, were to be used (and reports on the American
monitors made this choice definite), then a fundamental
departure must be made from the monitor pattern. Ericsson's turret rested upon the upper deck and was connected
to its machinery by a single iron spindle. The Coles turret
rested upon the lower deck and was carried up through a
large opening in the upper deck. If Coles's turrets were
mounted on the extremely low freeboard of the Ericsson
monitor, a serious danger of swamping would exist. The
turret must be carried higher out of the water, but how
could this be accomplished while maintaining the low freeboard that permitted complete thick-armor protection and
steadiness? Both Reed and Coles proposed solutions to this
problem in the same year, 1867. As Coles explained his
concept, "You can have a low freeboard and a gun a great

height out of the water . . . you have only . . . to slope the deck considerably."[10] Reed, on the other hand, proposed a "breastwork" or step-up rising from the middle of the upper deck, carrying the turrets, and encasing ventilators, uptakes, and hatches.[11] Reed's was obviously the more practical solution, and later Coles was to claim the credit for its suggestion.[12]

Late in 1868 Coles submitted plans for a mastless, seagoing turret ironclad, carrying its guns on a sloping deck twelve feet above the waterline, displacing 4,272 tons and bunkering one thousand tons of coal.[13] Robinson, reporting on the design, summarized Coles's design principles behind this ironclad: "The gallant Captain maintains that we can afford at once to sweep away the masts, gear, and rigging as antagonistic to the steaming and fighting powers of warships."[14] This opinion may appear to be in conflict with Coles's insistence upon full-sail power for the *Captain*, then under construction. But Coles maintained that from 1860 he had appreciated "that we must have two distinct classes of ironclads, the seagoing turret cruiser with full sail power and full steam, and the turret ship with full steam and auxiliary sail power."[15] There is nothing in Coles's writings to suggest that he had ever produced any matured plans for a first-class, mastless turret ship before 1868. Nonetheless, he must be given credit for being among the first to advocate the abolition of masts in capital ships, and his mastless turret ships bore a rather close resemblance to the *Devastation*, which was almost a year in the future. As proof that his was not merely another coastal mastless ironclad, Coles planned a coal capacity of one thousand tons, four hundred more than that of the *Captain*, but little more than half that of the *Devastation*.

Reed's breastwork principle was first incorporated in the diminutive colonial-defense harbor ironclad H.M.S. *Cerberus*. Other than receiving his royalty on the turrets, Coles had nothing to do with this warship, a matter of some annoyance and apprehension to the inventor, who deeply

H.M.S. *Cerberus*. Reed-designed dwarf coastal-defense ironclad. Precursor of H.M.S. *Devastation*. NATIONAL MARITIME MUSEUM, LONDON.

distrusted the ability of the chief constructor to design even a harbor turret ship.[16]

The *Cerberus* type of breastwork turret ship proved an efficient means of overcoming serious objections to the low-freeboard monitor. No difficulties now stood in the way of applying the principle to a seagoing mastless turret ship. According to Admiral Robinson, the decision to build such an ironclad was taken in early 1869, when he was informed by the First Lord (Childers) that pressure from the House of Commons had dictated that any new ironclads must be fitted with turrets. With considerations of economy ever paramount, Childers limited weight to a mere three thousand tons. Yet upon this ludicrous tonnage he called for forty- to forty-five-ton guns (almost twice the size of any existing heavy ordnance), coal for an ocean voyage at full speed, limited sail power, extensive watertight integrity, and a speed of fourteen knots. Only the armor was permitted to be below first-class standard. This ironclad was to be only one hundred tons heavier than the *Cerberus*, a ship that carried only four eighteen-ton guns, a maximum of two hundred ten tons of coal, and a speed of 9.75 knots. Admiral Robinson immediately objected to Childers' fantasy, but a few days later the first lord presented his particulars to the chief constructor.[17] Reed also dismissed this attempt to pour a quart into a pint pot for the sake of economy: "It will be obvious, on a moment's reflection that this outline comprises conditions which have never yet been fulfilled in any actual ship." Reed concluded his critique by predicting that "exact calculations would probably force me to say the certainty of the ship's capsizing in a breeze or a gust." He then submitted his own proposal that outlined the subsequent design of the *Devastation*. Calling for an end to masts and sails, the substitution of twin screws for Childers's single propeller, and a coal capacity for a four-thousand-mile radius, Reed asserted that tonnage could not be less than four thousand tons. On this design Reed could guarantee moderate costs, a comparatively small complement, steadiness at sea, and ramming and counter-ramming powers. The planned monitor would be utilized primarily in European waters, but with transatlantic range "considered" in the design by the inclusion of great coal capacity.[18] Even so, Reed and Robinson considered that they were still seriously hampered by tonnage restrictions. Reed later stated that the earlier drawings for the *Devastation* were "for a much larger ship, intended to be much faster."[19] Robinson bitterly charged that he and Reed "had to mould an impractical design, insisted on with much pertinacity, into as good a one as could be got from the limited tonnage."[20]

Childers next took the unusual step of presenting Reed's designs before a committee composed of the constructor's great rival, Captain Coles; the first sea lord; Admiral Dacres (a Coles supporter); the earl of Lauderdale; Adm. Cooper Key; Sir Joseph Whitworth; Dr. Wooley the mathematician; William Fairbairn; and Admiral Yelverton. The committee members' individual opinions were not recorded, but it is obvious that withal a majority supported Reed's design and encouraged the board to accept it.[21]

Admiral Robinson strongly urged Reed's design upon the first lord and the board in a memorandum of convincing lucidity. Robinson's and Reed's motives for building the warship were those which should always have been followed by any great naval power: "to produce an armour-plated ship combining powers of offence and defence greater than those possessed by other ships she is likely to meet." Following this, the controller wrote that at least ten inches of armor would be needed to resist the latest French ordnance, and twelve inches would be more desirable. Only the monitor form could carry such a weight of protection. To carry the heaviest means of offense, the turret system "followed as a matter of course." But the monitor was neither efficient nor safe under sail, so the projected ironclad must be without masts and depend entirely upon her engines, twin screws, and a supply of coal that would give a radius of action (at ten knots) quadruple that of any previous capital ship design. Robinson's summary of the *Devastation*'s qualities provided a succinct description of all subsequent British capital ships (with some unfortunate exceptions in the decade immediately following): "We have come, therefore, of necessity, to ships of low freeboard, thick shot-resisting armour, guns few in number, but of the heaviest known power, revolving in turrets, with an uncompromised all-around fire, twin-screws, double engines, and vast stores of coal." [22]

Eventually Childers acquiesced to Reed's proposals, and the *Devastation* was laid down in November 1869 and launched in July 1871. The *Devastation* and her sister ship, the *Thunderer*, endured the usual barrage of criticism so common in those days to all new ironclads. Since the design was such a break with traditional practice, the criticism was the more savage. While the *Times* rejoiced that "the old combination of irreconcilable qualities which spoilt our former turret ships has been at last rejected,"[23] the *United Service Gazette* denounced the ironclad for her lack of sailing rig, and considered that native dash and élan would be far more valuable in a naval battle than heavy armor.[24] In the Commons, Admiral Erskine raised the argument that was to be used against Fisher's *Dreadnought* forty years later, namely, that all naval powers were now reduced to a position of relative equality by such radical innovation.[25] A former first lord suggested that "the Royal Humane Society should be called in to stop the building of vessels to be sent to sea without masts and sails."[26] Childers, in order to forestall further criticism, insisted that the *Devastation* class was simply an improved *Glatton,* surely an egregious example of either a politician's craftiness or of his complete ignorance of naval matters, for in no possible sense could the *Devastation* be compared with that small coastal monitor of limited range and usefulness to which Childers referred.[27] Just prior to the *Devastation's* launching, Sir Thomas Brassey had called for postponement of work upon her and the substitution of a program of thirty-six coastal-defense ironclads.[28] The *Annual* of the Royal School of Naval Architecture warned that "there exists great difference of opinion respecting the propriety of sending to sea vessels having steam power only, even when the coal supply is so exceptionally large."[29] George Goschen, Childers' successor as First Lord, was compelled one year after the *Captain* disaster to refer to the class as Channel or Baltic ironclads.[30] By 1873 he was willing to speak of them as seagoing fighting ships, but still considered the class "experimental" and concluded that "we should not be safe if we possessed unmasted turret ships alone."[31] Suspicion of the mastless turret ship was not confined to the press and Parliament. A possibly apocryphal story affixed to the gangway of the *Devastation* the notice "Letters for the *Captain* may be posted aboard."[32]

Even the designers of the *Devastation* proved hesitant as to her true power. Reed confined the ironclad to "carrying war to any European port, or in an emergency, across the Atlantic, in addition to defending our own shores when threatened."[33] Despite these omnibus duties envisaged for the *Devastation*, Reed still wished to retain the old distinction between the ironclad designed primarily for European waters, and the cruising, fully-rigged warship, represented by H.M.S. *Monarch*.[34]

Both Reed and Robinson limited the *Devastation* to an action radius of several thousand miles from the British Isles,[35] although the class was bunkered for forty-seven hundred miles, steaming at ten knots. If the speed were cut to five-and-one-half knots, the ironclads possessed the phenomenal radius of ninty-two hundred miles, as compared with the *Monarch*'s fifty-four hundred under similar circumstances.[36] Yet Reed's successor also confined the *Devastation* to European waters,[37] and not for another decade and a half, when all masts and sailing impediment had been swept away for capital ships, did an ironclad enjoy a greater steam-operating radius.

John Ericsson in America labored under no illusions as to the oceanic possibilities of the *Devastation*. The naval inventor sounded a note curiously similar to those imaginative British coastal merchants who feared for the safety of their commercial enterprises at the advent of the federal monitor. "The *Devastation* and *Thunderer* may steam up the Hudson in spite of our batteries and our monitors, and dictate terms off Castle Garden," he warned.[38]

A major part of the hesitation felt by the Admiralty toward the *Devastation* as an oceanic cruiser may be attributed to her low freeboard, which could cause flooding and a generally poor sea-keeping capability. But even before the first two ships of the class had been completed, their sides had been raised by the addition of light iron structures, which added to the ironclads' dryness and living quarters. Reed would have preferred simply to have extended the breastwork out to the sides, but had been prevented by the ubiquitous tonnage restrictions.[39]

The year following the acceptance of the *Devastation*

H.M.S. *Devastation*. World's first seagoing, mastless, turret warship.
OFFICIAL U.S. NAVY PHOTOGRAPH.

design, Childers, who by now must have acceded to Reed's
pleas for a freer hand in design and tonnage, waived such
restrictions and allowed the chief constructor to draw up
plans for a larger and faster *Devastation*.[40] But work was
suspended during the sittings of the Committee on Designs.
In order to carry out the recommendations of the committee
in regard to armor, armament, and stability, the board
canceled all of Reed's plans and called upon William White,
the future Director of Naval Construction, to redesign the
ironclad along the lines recommended by the committee.
As a result, the breastwork was carried out to the sides
(Reed's idea from the beginning), and light iron filled in
the space fore and aft the armored citadel, thus raising the
freeboard and eliminating the *Devastation*'s and the *Thunderer*'s "step" appearance. Compound engines, thicker
armor, and heavier ordnance comprised the other major
improvements upon the *Devastation*. But the basic design

was still Reed's, and the *Devastation* the prototype. Certainly all the improvements in the *Dreadnought*, as the third, and final, ship of the class was named, were those long urged by Reed.

The *Devastation* class was the last official design by Reed to be accepted by the Board of Admiralty. Reed resigned in July 1870, and Robinson was forced out of office the following year. Thus passed the two men who had guided the Royal Navy through the brief period of its most profound materiel transformation.

II

The entire design policy of the Reed and Robinson era, 1863–71, fell under close scrutiny following the *Captain* disaster, with a subsequent public distrust of all recent Admiralty ironclads, particularly those of the *Devastation* class.[41]

In 1871 Hugh Childers instituted an enquiry by Royal Commission into Admiralty ironclad designs, the well-known Committee on Designs, which consisted of prominent naval officers, designers, and mathematicians. Such a course is now common enough, but at the time, coming on the heels of the first lord's notorious minute, which appeared to shift all blame for the *Captain* from himself to Admiral Robinson and E. J. Reed, the action seemed further proof of Childers's irresponsibility, and appeared likely to do the Service enormous harm. Robinson, stunned by this second blow from his superior (the third would be his dismissal from office), termed the appointment of the committee "an expression of doubt on the part of the Admiralty of the day, whether they, their predecessors, or their servants were competent to fill the posts entrusted to them."[42] Reed denounced the summoning of the committee, which "had its origins in the mean and contemptible necessities of party politicians," but only mildly criticized its findings and composition. He asserted that this would be a "committee of

strangers," for no one could unravel the skein of confer-
ences, discussions, and board meetings that had ultimately
resulted in the building of the ironclads.[43] Robinson, Reed,
Barnaby, and most of the prominent naval and civilian
authorities responsible in any way for the design of warships were summoned to testify.

Perhaps the most far-reaching of the committee's recommendations was that calling for the abolition of sails in all
future men-of-war. A majority of the committee recognized
that it was almost impossible "to unite in one ship a very
high degree of offensive and defensive power with real
efficiency under sail."[44]

In its appreciation of the *Devastation*, the committee performed another lasting service. It recognized that "the
Devastation class represents in its broad features the first-
class fighting ship of the immediate future," and realized
that the sailing box-battery and broadside ironclads now
represented a dead end in naval architecture, serving their
purpose only as long as sail was necessary. Even the later
sailing ironclads, *Hercules*, *Sultan*, and *Monarch* (the last
design of which the committee accurately considered a box-
battery with turrets mounted), had been rendered obsolete
by the mastless *Devastation*.

A majority of the committee foresaw that "we appear
to be closely approaching a period when the gun will assert
a final and definitive superiority." Refusing, however, to
assent to Sir William Armstrong's suggestion that future
warships be stripped of practically all armor, the committee
wisely realized that an armored ship would always be able
to choose its range and penetrate an unarmored adversary,
while impervious itself to shot. But the progress of artillery
had reached a point where twenty-four-inch plates were
required to keep out projectiles. It was therefore proposed
that this heavy armor be concentrated amidships in a
"central citadel" buoyed up by minutely subdivided and cork-
filled ends, ensuring watertight integrity and stability.

Since compound engines were quite common in the merchant fleet and had been installed in a few navy ships, the committee urged their adoption for all ironclads. Greater coal capacity, with a subsequent reduced need for sail power, thicker armor, greater speed, and a smaller, cheaper warship were thus promised.

With the fiery fate of the *Palestro* at Lissa in mind, the committee recommended that all fittings in warships be rendered incombustible. The confusion attending "Builders Old Measurement" and "nominal horsepower" were to be done away with by the substitution of the simple "displacement" and the more accurate "indicated horsepower." Flying in the face of the "single-blow" school of naval artillery that called for ever-larger (and ever more slowly working) ordnance, the committee recommended secondary batteries of light, quick-firing guns, undoubtedly to meet the new menace from torpedo boats.

Almost without exception these major recommendations of the Committee on Designs were sound and requisite. If the Admiralty did not choose to implement immediately its recommendations for the abolition of sail power and the adoption of the *Devastation* type as the future standard for first-class ironclads, the fault lay not with the committee, but with conservative influence in the Admiralty and economy-mided political leaders in Westminster.

In much of the committee's work can be seen a complete vindication of Reed's work as chief constructor. Not only in the recognition of the *Devastation* class, but in its opinions on the need for as complete armor protection as possible, the committee followed Reed's basic principles of steady improvements that culminated in the *Devastation*. At the same time, the committee recorded no serious criticism of Reed's previous box-battery types. Certainly no thought was expressed, either in the testimony taken or in the report, that called for any return to the long ironclads of Reed's predecessors.

The reports of the Committee on Designs composed farseeing documents that William White, looking back on thirty years of naval development of which he was the chief innovator, termed "classics." He further agreed that they were generally "most reassuring" that the progress in design of the early ironclad era had been sound and worth continuing.[45] The committee had been criticized for neglecting the gun and for relying upon heavy armor plate alone to meet any increase in ordnance. But the gun was not included within the committee's terms of reference and, by its endorsement of the *Devastation* type, it recognized that this design, improved over the years, would prove the most efficient means for utilizing the heaviest ordnance, and for defense against it.

III

Long before the Committee on Designs had presented its findings, of course, Reed had resigned from his post as chief constructor. It would be a simplification to assert that the subsequent stagnation in British warship design, lasting until, approximately, the appointment of Sir William White as Director of Naval Construction (1886), was due to the removal of Reed and Robinson from office. The "Dark Ages of the Victorian Navy," as one authority calls the period between Reed and White,[46] was as much the result of excessive cheese-paring in Westminster, as of a continued lack of any strategic or tactical doctrine worthy of the name in the Royal Navy. The comment by N. A. M. Rodger on this period is worth quoting: "Political and even naval lords were apt to regard planning for war with the jaundiced eye of a Victorian bishop viewing a popular Millenarian movement."[47]

Reed and Robinson had been able to ensure that ironclads of Britain would be the most powerful in the world. Reed's successor, Nathaniel Barnaby, exerted far less influence upon the board and the controller, and he must be held responsible for a personal conservatism that could write favorably of wood as a warship builder's material in the twentieth century.[48] Part of the reason for the stagnation of the 1870s may have been a general ennui with naval subjects; after the exciting days of the introduction of the ironclad and the monitor, and the turret ship controversy, the years following must have seemed dull indeed. Only the quickening pulse of empire in the later 1880s brought about a renewed interest in the Royal Navy and its ships.

Public opinion, inflamed by such skillful propagandists as W. T. Stead and Lord Charles Beresford, and informed by the writings of Mahan and Lord Brassey, was then willing to make the sacrifices necessary for a two-power standard of global sea power. The Naval Defense Act of 1889, with its systematic program of building toward this end was the first material expression of a reawakened interest in the Royal Navy that would serve Britain well in the years to come. But without the work of Edward Reed and Adm. Sir Robert Spencer Robinson, naval powers might well have faced almost insoluble problems in the design of ironclads. As it was, they had simply to improve now upon the *Devastation*, the prototype of the modern battleship.

Appendixes

Appendix A: The Board of Admiralty, 1863–70

The First Lord of the Admiralty
    A political appointee, usually a civilian. Ultimately responsible for the entire policy of the Board of Admiralty.

First Sea Lord
    The highest naval position, whose incumbent acted as professional adviser to the First Lord. Responsible for the movement, personnel, and conditions of the Fleet.

Junior Sea Lord
    Responsible for transports, medical services, stores, victualling, chaplaincy, accountancy.

Third Lord, and the Controller
    Responsible for the materiél of the fleet, engines, ordnance, design, dockyards. The controller was made a member of the board under the Childers reorganization period, but throughout the 1860s retained the right to attend board meetings when designs or any of his business was under discussion. Under his authority was the vital chief constructor.

Civil Lord
    Responsible for works and civil personnel.

First or Parliamentary Secretary
    Attended board meeting, and noted on papers that were read the decisions arrived at.

Second or Permanent Secretary

Called by Admiral Hamilton "the nerve centre" of the board, he coordinated Admiralty departments and was responsible for the efficient working of the entire Admiralty apparatus. Throughout the 1860s the position was held by one official, W. G. Romaine.

The Board of Admiralty followed the British Cabinet tradition of public unanimity of decision, secrecy, and undivided responsibility and, like the Cabinet, was changed, except for its permanent officers, with each government.

The best sources for Admiralty administration in the ironclad era are Sir John Briggs, *Naval Administration* (London, 1897); Adm. Sir R. Vesey Hamilton, *Naval Administration* (London, 1896), Leslie Gardiner, *The British Admiralty* (Edinburgh, 1968). Adm. Sir Robert S. Robinson, *Results of Admiralty Organization as Established by Sir James Graham and Mr. Childers, with suggestions for Improvement* (London, 1871); Thomas Brassey, *Naval Administration* (London, 1872). A large number of pamphlets and articles of the time severely criticize the Admiralty for inefficiency and ultraconservative sterility, but there is little evidence to prove these contentions, and much to show the opposite.

Lords Commissioners of the Board of Admiralty, 1863–70

27 March 1863

First Lord of the Admiralty—The Duke of Somerset
First Sea Lord— Vice Adm. Sir F. W. Grey
Second Sea Lord— Rear Adm. Charles Eden
Junior Sea Lord— Rear Adm. Charles Frederick
Third Lord— Capt. J. R. Drummond
Civil Lord— The Marquis of Hartington
1st Secretary— Rear Adm. Lord Clarence Paget
2nd Secretary— W. G. Romaine, M.P.

5 May 1863

Civil Lord— James Stansfeld (for Marquis of
Hartington)

22 April 1864

Civil Lord—   Hugh C. E. Childers (for Stansfeld)

25 March 1865

Junior Sea Lord—   Rear Adm. E. G. Fanshawe
       (for Frederick)

23 January 1866

Civil Lord—   H. Fenwick (for Childers)

10 April 1866

1st Secretary—   T. G. Baring, M.P. (for Paget)
Civil Lord—   Capt. Lord John May, M.P.
       (for Fenwick)

9 May 1866

Third Lord—   Lord John Hay (for Drummond)
Civil Lord—   G. J. Shaw Lefevre, M.P. (for Hay)

13 July 1866

First Lord of the Admiralty—Sir John Pakington
First Sea Lord—   Vice Adm. Sir Alexander Milne
Second Sea Lord—   Vice Adm. Sir Sidney Dacres
Third Lord—   Rear Adm. G. H. Seymour
Junior Sea Lord—   Rear Adm. Sir J. C. D. Hay, M.P.
Civil Lord—   Charles Du Cane, M.P.
1st Secretary—   Lord H. G. Lennox, M.P.
2nd Secretary—   W. G. Romaine

8 March 1867

First Lord of the Admiralty—H. T. L. Corry (for Sir John
       Pakington)

3 September 1868

Civil Lord—   Hon F. A. Stanley, M.P. (for
       Du Cane)

18 December 1868*

First Lord of the Admiralty—Rt. Hon. Hugh C. E. Childers
First Naval Lord— Vice Adm. Sir Sidney Dacres
Third Lord and Controller— Vice Adm. Sir Robert S. Robinson
Junior Naval Lord— Capt. Lord John Hay, M.P.
Civil Lord— G. O. Trevelyan, M.P.
1st Secretary— W. E. Baxter, M.P.
2nd Secretary— W. G Romaine

29 July 1869

Permanent Secretary   Vernon Lushington (for Romaine)
(2nd Secretary)—

12 July 1870

Civil Lord—   The Earl of Camperdown
                            (for Trevelyan)

From: *List of the Lord High Admiral and Commissioners for Executing That Office, Which Have Been from Time to Time Appointed, Since the Year 1660.* Admiralty Library.

*During the Childers Administration the following changes were made:
First Sea Lord became First Naval Lord.
Second Sea Lord was replaced by the Third Lord and Controller.
1st Secretary became Parliamentary Secretary (1870).
2nd Secretary became Permanent Secretary (1870).

Appendix B: Finance

The charge of "bloated armaments" could hardly in fairness be leveled at the ironclad program of the Royal Navy in the 1860s. While total navy estimates were to remain lower than those for the army until the great Anglo-German naval race, the cost of ironclads was a mere fraction of navy estimates. The ironclad expenditure for the term of office of E. J. Reed as chief constructor follows.*

1863–64 Appropriations for: *Royal Oak Prince Consort, Hector, Caledonia, Enterprise, Research,*

> *Favorite, Ocean, Valiant, Prince Albert, Achilles, Royal Alfred, Zealous, Agincourt, Minotaur, Northumberland.*

For ironclad construction: £630,203
Total naval estimates: £10,736,036

1864–65 Appropriations for: *Bellerophon, Lord Clyde, Lord Warden, Pallas.*

For ironclad construction: £384,412
For purchase of Laird rams: £220,000
Total ironclad expenditure:` £604,412
Total naval estimates: £10,708,651

1865–66 Appropriations for: *Royal Sovereign, Scorpion, Wyvern.*

For ironclad construction: £130,000
Total naval estimates: £10,392,225

1866–67 Appropriations for: *Monarch, Hercules.*

For ironclad construction: £60,000
Total naval estimates: £10,434,000

1867–68 Appropriations for: *Monarch, Hercules, Repulse, Penelope, Inconstant.*

For ironclad construction: £344,000
Total naval estimates: £10,976,253

1868–69 Appropriations for: *Captain, Audacious, Invincible, Vanguard.*

For ironclad construction: £680,000
Total naval estimates: £10,973,998

1869–70 Appropriations for: *Devastation, Thunderer.*

For ironclad construction: £420,000
For naval estimates: £9,996,641

From: Estimates, Navy, *Parliamentary Papers* 35 (1863): 1; 37 (1864): 1; 35 (1865), pt. 1, p. 1; 45 (1866): 1; 44 (1867): 1; 45 (1867–68): 1; 37 (1868–69): 1. This information is collected in *Navy Estimates*, Admiralty Library, for each year. Cf. also C. J. Bartlett, "The Mid-Victorian Reappraisal of Naval Policy," in

Studies in International History, ed. K. Bourne and D. C. Watt (London, 1967), for political and strategic background of naval estimates. Bartlett, noting the 25 percent decline in expenditures, 1863–85, rightly comments: "It is doubtful whether Britain was able at any other time to purchase security at so cheap a price." Ibid., p. 189.

Appendix C: Relative Ironclad Strength of Britain and France; Ships Completed by End of Year

	Britain	Ratio	France
1863	*Warrior, Black Prince, Defence, Resistance, Royal Oak**	5:6	*Gloire, Couronne, Magenta, Invincible, Normandie, Solferino*
1864	*Achilles, Hector, Research, Prince Consort*, Enterprize,* Royal Sovereign**	11:7	*Savoie*
1865	*Caledonia,* Scorpion, Wyvern*	14:11	*Flandre, Heroïne, Magnamie, Provence*
1866	*Bellerophon, Lord Clyde,* Ocean,* Zealous,* Favorite,* Pallas,* Prince Albert*	21:14	*Guyenne, Belliqueuse, Taureau*
1867	*Minotaur, Lord Warden,* Royal Alfred**	24:21	*Surveillante, Valeureuse, Rochambeau, Galoise, Revanche, Onondaga, Armide*
1868	*Agincourt, Northumberland, Valiant,* Hercules, Penelope*	29:24	*Thetis, Cerbère, Jeanne d'Arc*
1869	*Monarch*	30:27	*Montcalm, Alma, Reine Blanche*

| 1870 | *Invincible, Vanguard, Audacious, Repulse,** *Captain* | 35:28 | *Ocean* |

From: *Complete List of the Steamships, Steam Launches, and Sailing Ships on the List of the Navy* (1863–70).

Admiralty Library: *Nominal Lists of all Ironclads and Date of Their First Completion for Sea, Parl. Papers* 38 (1874); *List of the Navy,* Admiralty Library; Marine et Colonies *Liste de la Flotte*; Admiralty, *Iron-Cased Ships of France* (1867); De Balincourt and Vincent-Brechignac, "La Marine Française d'Hier," *Revue Maritime* (May 1930), pp. 577–95; (March 1931), pp. 289–317.

* Timber construction.

Notes

Chapter 1 : The Shape of Ships

1. Outside of Europe one armored warship of the ironclad era survives. She is the *Huascar*, a Coles type of turret coastal ironclad, built in the United Kingdom in 1866 and sold to Peru. A veteran of an indecisive clash with a Royal Navy cruiser and of a ferocious battle with two Chilean ironclads, the *Huascar* is now preserved as a memorial, although still technically in commission with the Chilean Navy. Monitor *Tecumseh*, apparently well preserved, lies in relatively shallow water beneath Mobile Bay, a potential treasure trove for marine archaeologists and historians.

2. James P. Baxter III, *The Introduction of the Ironclad Warship* (Cambridge, Mass., 1933; 1968), p. 3.

3. For descriptions and details of these vessels and all other Royal Navy warships mentioned here, see *Ships' Covers*, National Maritime Museum; *Steamships of the Navy, 1868–1884*, Admiralty Library, Ministry of Defence; Oscar Parkes, *British Battleships, 1860–1950* (London, 1957; 1966), Adm. G. A. Ballard, irregular series on the ironclads of the 1860s, *Mariner's Mirror* 15–21 (1929–35). (Publication of these articles in book form is anticipated soon.)

4. Baxter, *Introduction of the Ironclad Warship*, p. 176.; Parkes, *British Battleships*, pp. 49–58; Ballard, *Mariner's Mirror* 17 (1932): 5–31.

5. In the Duke of Somerset's words: "I was convinced that there must be means of obtaining shorter vessels with the necessary flotation, and I therefore resolved to bring in a new person, and charge him with this construction." Hansard, *Parliamentary Debates* 175 (1867): 130. Adm. Sir Robert Spencer Robinson agreed with this interpretation of Reed's appointment. See his testimony before the Select Committee of the House of Lords on the Board of Admiralty, *Parliamentary Papers* (1871): 43; and his submission to the Board, Admiralty I, 6061 (1 Jan-

uary 1867), supporting Reed's claims for increased emoluments. One of the first calls for moderate dimensions for ironclads came from the *Cornhill Magazine*, which presaged much of Reed's work. "On a Further Reconstruction of the Navy," *Cornhill Magazine* (December 1861), pp. 715–24.

6. Thomas Brassey, *The British Navy* (London, 1882), 1: 82.

7. Fred T. Jane, *The British Battlefleet* (London, 1912), p. 1814.

8. E. J. Reed, "On Long and Short Ironclads"; *Transactions of the Institution of Naval Architects* 10 (1869) : 39–91. For Reed design concepts, see also idem, *Our Iron-Clad Ships* (London, 1869) ; idem *Theory and Practice of Hydro-Mechanics* (London, 1885), pp. 183–204; idem, "On Iron-Clad Ships," *Proceedings of the Royal Institution of Great Britain* 6 (1870–72): 95–99; idem, "Armour-Plated Ships," *Nautical Magazine* 36 (1867): 19–26. Reed succinctly summarized his opinions to the then First Lord, H. L. Corry, one day after the latter took office: "The importance of the new method consists in making the ship short, cheap, and handy, and giving her a small increase of steam power as a compensation." Confidentially printed Board Minute, 9 March 1868, Milne MSS, National Maritime Museum, Greenwich. Reed's genius extended to flying machines, which most later nineteenth-century inventors studied, but he must have been among the first to realize that flight was more a question of a powerful, lightweight engine than of an imitation of the birds. "On the Value of Science to Ship-Builders," *Annual of the Royal School of Naval Architecture* 2 (1872): 12.

9. At the end of his own career, Robinson was to complain: "I think it is a very great mistake that the Board of Admiralty has always made in limiting the naval architect in tonnage and dimension. . . . I hardly know of a case in which we have built a ship in the manner we would have liked to build it." Testimony before Committee on Designs, *Parl. Papers* 14 (1872): 7. E. J. Reed agreed, noting that the *Bellerophon* was the only ship he had designed that was unrestricted in its tonnage. Ibid., p. 133.

10. E. J. Reed, "On Iron-Cased Ships of War," *Transactions of I.N.A.*, 4 (1863): 31–38.

11. *Kentish Mercury*, 5 December 1863. Reed's conversion to moderate tonnage was reenforced later by the famous American clipper ship designer and builder Donald McKay, who wrote to Reed agreeing that "the shortest ship in an engagement will always have the advantages, providing she has the same speed." McKay to Reed, 18 April 1865, Duke of Somerset MSS, Buckinghamshire Record Office, Aylesbury.

12. Reed, *Our Iron-Clad Ships*, p. 20. Reed's successor, Nathaniel Barnaby, agreed on this point. See Barnaby, *Naval Development of the Century* (London, 1904), p. 68.

13. *Transactions of I.N.A.* 10 (1869) : 78–80.

14. These ironclads were apparently to be of iron when originally submitted by Reed, but budgetary restrictions limited them to wooden construction. Draft letter from Admiralty to Treasury, Adm. I, 6061 [1867?]; Ballard, "The Three British Armoured Cruisers," *Mariner's Mirror* 30 (1935) : 15–19; *Transactions of I.N.A.* 4 (1863) : 39, and 9 (1868) : 195, 31; Reed to Admiralty, Adm. I, 6061 (20 April 1868). These small warships may be said to have secured for Reed the post of chief constructor, for according to Admiral Robinson the Admiralty had tried time and again to obtain from its previous constructors designs for wooden ironclads that would not exceed the dimensions of the older *Caledonia* class of converted wooden ironclads. Soon afterward, Reed submitted his designs for the *Favorite*, while supervising the cutting down and conversion of the *Research* and *Enterprise*, also to his designs. The board, already favorably impressed with Reed's work, pensioned off the incumbent constructors, Isaac Watts and Mr. Abthell, who were over seventy years old anyway. Robinson to Board, Adm. I, 6061 (5 May 1867). Such proceedings led some of Reed's enemies to hint darkly that research and enterprise had less to do with Reed's accession than did favoritism.

15. According to Adm. Phipps Hornby, the *Enterprise* had large "blind" areas where her guns could not bear even in calm waters. Report of the Admiralty Committee on Turret Ships *Parl. Papers* 47 (1866) : p. 52.

16. The Duke of Somerset, on the other hand, saw the *Pallas* as designed for protection of commerce from raiders. Somerset to Palmerston, June 1863, Palmerston MSS., National Registry of Archives. Cf. also Report of the Admiralty Committee on Turret Ships, *Parl. Papers* 47 (1866) : p. 69; Reed, *Our Iron-Clad Ships*, p. 71. Referring to the *Lord Warden* class, the Admiralty praised its "several highly important advantages which could not otherwise be secured, among which were increased thickness of armor plating, increased height of port, and the most formidable bow-fire yet possessed by any class of ship," Admiralty to Treasury, Adm. I, 6061 [1867].

17. For Reed's opinion of the *Bellerophon*, see his *Our Iron-Clad Ships*, pp. 167–71.

18. William Fairbairn, *Treatise on Iron Shipbuilding* (London, 1865), pp. 213–14; cf. also *Colburn's United Service Magazine* (1865), pt. 2, pp. 213–14.

19. Reed's description of the bracket-frame principle is found in his *Shipbuilding in Iron and Steel* (London, 1869), pp. 110–34; and idem, *Our Iron-Clad Ships*, pp. 80–86. Cf. also "The Structure of Iron Ships," *Naval Science* 1 (1872) : 81–82. *Naval Science* was a Reed venture, expiring in 1875.

20. W. John, "On the Cellular Construction of Merchant Ships," *Trans-*

actions of I.N.A. 21 (1880) : 165. This opinion still held as late as 1906, when a speaker before the Institution of Civil Engineers said of the *Bellerophon* that the design "was novel and ingenius, and it has been followed in principle, in the later battleships and cruisers of the British Navy, and adopted all over the world." *Proceedings of the I.C.E.* 168 (1906–7), pt. 2, p. 350.

21. Somerset to Palmerston, 14 December 1865, Palmerston MSS. But Henry Laird, of Messrs. Laird, Birkenhead, was not so impressed by the *Bellerophon*, probably because of his strong partisanship of the Coles turret principle. Reed, by way of rebuttal, pointed out that the new turret ship, H.M.S. *Captain*, was to be built in Laird's yard according to the bracket-frame method. Laird to Admiralty, Adm. I, 5997 (18 July 1866) ; Reed to Board, ibid. (26 July 1866). Admiral Farragut, whose opposition to monitors was notorious, called for a "quick-working" warship, carrying a few heavy broadside guns. Reed was quick to point out that such was the principle upon which the *Pallas* and the *Bellerophon* had been designed. McKay to Reed, 18 April 1865, Somerset MSS.

22. Fairbairn, *Treatise*, pp. 112–14; Navy (Channel Fleet), *Parl. Papers* 45 (1868). *Times* (London), 29 May 1865, p. 12.

23. Reports, etc. Relative to Trials of the Channel Fleet in 1867, *Parl. Papers* 45 (1867–68) : 321–22.

24. Ibid., p. 13 ; Reed to Controller, Adm. I, 6018 (2 August 1867).

25. This pressure for economy is emphasized in the correspondence between Gladstone, Chancellor of the Exchequer, and Lord Paget, Parliamentary Secretary for the Admiralty, and the Duke of Somerset. Gladstone MSS, Reference Division, British Library.

26. "Modern Ships of War," *Journal of the Royal United Service Institution* 16 (1872) : 60.

27. Quoted in Frederick Manning, *Life of Sir William White* (London, 1923), p. 40 ; cf. also White's Presidential Address before the Institution of Civil Engineers, *Proceedings of I.C.E.* 155 (1903) : 30 ; Thomas Brassey paid high tribute to the successive controllers of the navy, pp. xii–xiii. Adm. Sir Frederick W. Grey, First Sea Lord, 1863–66, wrote that the ironclad progress of that period was due in large measure to the controller and his department. Grey, *Admiralty Administration, 1861–1866* (London, 1866), p. 13.

28. Testimony before Committee on Designs, *Parl. Papers* 14 (1872) : 167–68.

29. Ibid., p. 571.

30. Ibid., pp. 52, 55. Robinson fully supported Reed when the latter applied to the Admiralty for compensation for the designs that were submitted by him to the board before his appointment; although paid for the work he performed, he had received nothing for the many new

inventions and methods it embodied. In the end, Reed was given a cash gratuity of five hundred pounds and an increase in salary. Robinson to Board, Adm. I, 5840 (4 March 1863) ; Robinson to Reed, Adm. I, 5840 (3 March 1863). The final disposition of Reed's case is contained in Adm. I, 6061. Reed was particularly galled by the generous financial settlement made with Captain Coles for his turret patents.

31. The term *frigate* was rather loosely used to describe any seagoing ironclad, since none of them then boasted more than one gun deck.
32. Admiralty to Treasury, Adm. I, 6081 (4 January 1867).
33. Hansard, *Parl. Debates* 169 (1863): pp. 198, 705, 801, 802, 878.
34. *United Service Gazette*, 31 January 1863, p. 4; cf. also ibid., 14 and 28 February and 2 May 1863.
35. *Times* (London), 29 July 1864, p. 5.
36. Hansard, *Parl. Debates* 177 (1865): 1185–86.
37. John Scott Russell, *The Modern System of Naval Architecture*, (London, 1865), p. 566.
38. *Naval and Military Gazette*, 27 August 1864, p. 553.
39. *Times* (London), 27 June 1870; *Globe*, 12 August 1869; *London Review*, 11 March 1865, p. 267.
40. John Scott Russell, "The Fleet of the Future, For Commerce—For War," *Transactions of I.N.A.* 11 (1870): 74–75. The lateness of Russell's proposal, ten years after the launching of the *Warrior*, is instructive. Reed confided that he was often tempted to resign in the face of such "an amount of misrepresentation which but few professional persons are called upon to bear." Reed to Board, Adm. I, 6061 (31 June 1867).
41. Reed, "On Iron-Cased Ships of War," p. 39.
42. *Transactions of I.N.A.* 6 (1865): 91; *Standard*, 16 April 1868; *Punch*, 27 June 1868.
43. *United Service Gazette*, 16 April 1870, p. 4. *Nautical Magazine* worried about the effect on the navy of such disparagement of its new warships and hoped that no naval war would arise before confidence would be restored. "Armour-Plated Ships," *Nautical Magazine* 36 (1867): 21.
44. Quoted by (then) Lord Hailsham, *Transactions of I.N.A.* 102 (1960): xlvii.
45. Practical training was available in the royal dockyards and private shipbuilding yards, but such training made little concession to any theoretical or mathematical education. The standard of instruction also varied widely.
46. For the early history of the institution see Kenneth C. Barnaby, *The Institution of Naval Architects, 1860–1960* (London, 1960), pp. 1–29; *Transactions of I.N.A.* 1 (1860), 52 (1911), 102 (1960); William H.

White, "The History of the Institution of Naval Architects and of Scientific Education in Naval Architecture," *Transactions of I.N.A.* 52 (1911).

47. John Scott Russell, "On the Education of Naval Architects in England and France," *Transactions of I.N.A.* 4 (1863): 162.

48. Evidence of Sir John Pakington's pressure upon the Board of Admiralty can be found in Somerset MSS, 12 June 1863, and Letter Book, passim.

49. Board Memorandum, Adm. I, 5890 (17 June 1864).

50. Hansard, *Parl. Debates* 173 (1864): 1308–11; ibid. 176 (1864): 498–505; for Paget's replies, see ibid. 176 (1864): 501–5.

51. *Naval and Military Gazette*, 9 July 1864, p. 441.

52. Patrick Barry, *Dockyard Economy and Naval Power* (London, 1863), p. 121.

53. White, "History of Institution of Naval Architects," p. 20. See also [William H. White], "Three English Schools of Naval Architecture," *Annual of Royal School of Naval Architecture* 4 (1874): 7–26; Manning, *Life of White*, pp. 8–24.

54. John Scott Russell, "On the Technical Education of Naval Architects in England," *Transactions of I.N.A.* 8 (1867): 223–43. See also White, "Three Schools," p. 18; White, "On the Course of Study in the Royal Naval College, Greenwich," *Transactions of I.N.A.* 18 (1877): 360–78; W. John, "On the Royal Naval College and the Mercantile Marine," *Transactions of I.N.A.* 19 (1878): 120–36.

55. W. Gowings, "Technical Education of Naval Architects," *Annual of Royal School of Naval Architecture* 2 (1872): 24–25.

56. "In the race of competition among shipbuilders it is probable that inferior materials and bad workmanship are admitted into ships." Reed before *Royal Commission on Unseaworthy Ships, Parl. Papers* 36 (1873): xiv; *Final Report, Parl. Papers* 34 (1874); Copy of Report From Institution of Naval Architects to the Board of Trade in April, 1867, Respecting the Construction, Equipment, and Freeboard of Ships, *Parl. Papers* 60 (1870): 479; "Royal Commission on Unsound Ships," *Naval Science* 3 (1874): 387–400; E. J. Reed, "On the Value of Science to Shipbuilders," *Annual of Royal School of Naval Architecture* 2 (1872): 7; Robert Murray, *Shipbuilding in Iron and Wood* (Edinburgh, 1863), p. 30; "On the Building of Iron Merchant Vessels," *Naval Science* 3 (1874): 145–57; Samuel Plimsoll, *Our Seamen, An Appeal* (London, 1873), pp. 36–39.

57. White, Presidential Address, *Proceedings of I.C.E.* 155 (1903): 69.

58. Ibid.

59. Corry to Disraeli 11 January 1867, Disraeli MSS, Hughenden, B/XXII/C/442; a few months previous Disraeli had written to the fourteenth earl of Derby, then Prime Minister, in regard to the Ad-

miralty: "It is useless to reason with them; you must command. The whole system of Administration is palsied by their mutinous spirit." George E. Buckle and William F. Monypenny, *The Life of Benjamin Disraeli, Earl of Beaconsfield,* 6 vols. (London, 1916), 4: 478. A perusal of the Gladstone MSS in the British Museum indicates that that statesman was almost exclusively concerned with economy in his dealings with the navy. The Palmerston MSS, National Registry of Archives, shows that Palmerston's policy was one of fits and starts to meet the foreign threat.

60. N. A. M. Rodger, "The Dark Ages of the Admiralty, 1869–1885," pt. 2, *Mariner's Mirror* (February 1976), p. 37.

61. Sir John Briggs, *Naval Administration* (London, 1897), p. xxi. According to Briggs, the Derby regime was as economy-minded in naval matters as were the Liberals, p. 154.

62. Adm. Lord Clarence Paget, *Autobiography,* ed. Sir Arthur Otway (London, 1896), pp. 361–62. Adm. Sir R. Vesey Hamilton, *Naval Administration* (London, 1896), pp. 72–74; Robinson, testimony before Committee on Designs, p. 315; Sir Frederick Grey, testimony before Select Committee of the House of Lords on the Board of Admiralty, *Parl. Papers* 7 (1871): vii; letter by Admiral Robinson in *Pall Mall Gazette,* 7 June 1864.

63. Hansard, *Parl. Debates* 174 (1864): 434. Lord Clarence Paget claimed that dockyard-built ships were superior in quality to those from the private yards, although somewhat more expensive, and that changes could be made in the dockyard ships without financial penalties. Ibid., 176 (1864): 1762 and 181 (1866): 1149.

64. Robinson to Board, Adm. I, 6081 (5 August 1868).

65. [Duke of Somerset], *The Naval Expenditure From 1860 to 1866* (London, 1867), p. 3. In the same vein, the admiralty controller of victualling wrote: "It is hard to say which has received the greater condemnation, the Admiralty as it is—or the Admiralty as it *was.*" Memorandum, [February 1872], Admiralty Library, p. 480.

66. Leslie Gardiner, *The British Admiralty* (Edinburgh and London, 1968), p. 275. Anthony Trollope amiably recorded that it was a good idea "to rub up the officials of the Admiralty by a little wholesome abuse. Trollope, *The Prime Minister,* 2 vols. (London: Oxford University Press, 1938), 2: 179.

67. *Naval and Military Gazette,* 2 May 1868, p. 281.

68. *United Service Gazette,* 22 August 1863, p. 4; also ibid., 29 August 1863, p. 4. Five years later this relatively moderate journal called the Admiralty "without exception, the most incapable and mischievous department existing in any government of the world" (8 August 1868, p. 4). Perhaps the most telling criticism came from the commission charged with the investigation of royal dockyards. The commission

found serious inefficiency and blamed the Admiralty organization. Cf. Gardiner, *British Admiralty*, p. 276.

69. [William Willis], *Remarks on Naval Administration* (London, 1871). Captain Sherard Osborne, Coles's closest friend, waxed lyrical on the "car of Juggernaut," as he termed the Admiralty, crushing new inventions and inventors, "upheld and dragged along by the high priesthood of ancient custom and vested interest." Osborne, "Our Admiralty," *Fortnightly Review* (February 1867), p. 146.

70. Hansard, *Parl. Debates* 185 (1867): 604. Could Pakington (who was the most favorable to Coles of all the first lords in this period) have had in mind Osborne's "Juggernaut"?

71. Ibid. 242 (1874): 1429.

72. One month before the *Captain* disaster the respected journal *Engineer* termed the higher Admiralty officials, including the board members, the controller, and the chief constructor, "practically irresponsible," due to self-interest, prejudice, and jealousies. "The Captain and the Monarch," *Engineer* 20 (5 August 1870): 103. For Gladstone's unfavorable opinion of the Admiralty, see Gladstone to Lord Goschen, 23 September 1871, in Arthur O. Elliott, *Life of Lord Goschen* (London, 1911), pp. 118–19; also Disraeli to Lord Derby, 28 January 1868, in Buckle and Monypenny, *Life of Disraeli*, 4: 579; Thomas Brassey, *Recent Naval Administration* (London, 1872), p. 6; "Admiralty Reform," *Macmillan's Magazine* (January 1870), p. 193; Admiral Robinson wrote that since 1832 there had been only five years of efficient and progressive Admiralty administration, 1860–66. Robinson to Adm. Sir F. W. Grey, 26 June 1871, Admiralty Library, p. 48. In reply to such a barrage of criticism, Admiral Grey, First Sea Lord, 1863–66, was apparently commissioned to write a rebuttal. He asserted that an expenditure of less than three million pounds per annum had sufficed to "create an ironclad fleet . . . equal to any possessed by any other power and some of them superior to any yet built elsewhere." Grey, *Admiralty Administration*, p. 15.

73. Hansard, *Parl. Debates* 169 (1863): 1351.

74. Somerset to Palmerston, 4 March 1863, Palmerston MSS.

75. Parkes, *British Battleships*, p. 160; Reed, *Our Iron-Clad Ships*, pp. 78, 100; Comdr. W. B. Rowbatham, "The Loss of H.M.S. *Magaera*," *Journal of R.U.S.I.* 100 (1955): 58–68; Robert Mallet, "On the Corrosion and Fouling of Iron Ships," *Transactions of I.N.A.* 13 (1872): 90–162.

76. Controller to Board, Adm. I, 5980 (September 1864).

77. Hansard, *Parl. Debates* 169 (1863): 676.

78. Ibid., p. 846. The Board of Admiralty, in turn, insisted that the constructor's department "adapt some at least of the wooden ships either built or partly built" to ironclads. Robinson to Board, Adm. I, 6061 (5 January 1867). Such pressure is understandable, for the wooden

ships consumed large sums in maintenance and skeleton crews. Even breaking them up was not the final solution, for the Duke of Somerset pointed out that this would take twelve years to complete. Somerset to Russell, 7 December 1863, Russell MSS, P.R.O. 30/22 (26).

79. Hansard, *Parl. Debates* 177 (1865) : 1411.

80. It should be noted that all of the French timber ironclads were designed as such from the keel up.

81. Statement Relating to the Advantages of Iron and Wood in Construction of Ships (Navy), *Parl. Papers* 36 (1863). See also Robinson to Board, Adm. I, 5849 (11 February 1863).

82. *Transactions of I.N.A.* 9 (1868) : 244; Reed, *Our Iron-Clad Ships*, pp. 70–79.

83. See Navy (Channel Fleet), *Parl. Papers* 45 (1867–68) : 303; *Mariner's Mirror* 17 (1932) : 5–31.

84. Hansard, *Parl. Debates* 177 (1865) : 1,182, and 169 (1863) : p. 844.

85. Disraeli to Lord Derby, 20 August 1866, in Buckle and Monypenny, *Life of Disraeli*, 4: 474–75.

86. Somerset to Pakington, 1 June 1862, Palmerston MSS.

87. Robinson complained that "the controller's correspondence with the Board is frightful to contemplate." Lords' Committee on Board of Admiralty, *Parl. Papers* 7 (1871) : 48. The Duke of Somerset noted that as early as 1860 the correspondence passing through the controller's department had grown from 6,885 pieces in 1848 to 36,296 in 1860. Somerset MSS, n.d. Robinson generously proposed that three assistants be given to Reed to ease his burdens. Robinson to Board, Adm. I, 5889 (23 March 1864). Their lordships were not inclined to undue sympathy, although they acknowledged that "the duties of the Chief Constructor are extremely arduous". Draft letter to Treasury requesting grant to Reed, and raise of salary Adm. I, 6061 [1867?]. The Lords Committee on Admiralty Administration established that almost all of the higher Admiralty members were grossly overworked, *Parl. Papers* 7 (1871) : 74. Lord Clarence Paget stated that during his term of office, 1859–66, two lords of the Admiralty died from overwork, and two were forced to resign for the same reason. Sir Arthur Otway, *Autobiography and Journals of Admiral of Lord Clarence E. Paget* (London, 1896), p. 364. It is small wonder that important questions raised about H.M.S. *Captain* and *Magaera* were not fully resolved until after tragedy struck.

88. Robinson to Board, Adm. I, 5980 (5 September 1866). Reed, *Our Iron-Clad Ships*, p. 5, expresses similar views.

89. *Transactions of I.N.A.* 9 (1868) : 148.

90. *Standard*, 17 July 1868.

91. *Kentish Mercury*, 5 December 1863; also Reed, *Our Iron-Clad Ships*, pp. 1–2, 22.

92. Memorandum by Controller, 13 December 1863, Palmerston MSS. See

also Adm. Sir Robert Spencer Robinson, "General Remarks on the Classification, Distribution, and Construction of Armour-Plated Ships," [1866?], Milne MSS, MLN p/b/3. John Scott Russell produced a similar classification, calling for three fleets: 1) turret ships for coast defense-offense; 2) ocean cruisers (ironclad) with broadside guns; 3) cruisers, carrying the minimum of armor. *Transactions of I.N.A.* 12 (1872): 35.

93. Capt. T. E. Symonds, "The Combined 'End-On' and Broadside Principle," *Journal of R.U.S.I.* 11 (1867): 485.

94. Comdr. Philip H. Colomb, *Memoirs of Admiral Sir Astley Cooper Key* London, 1898), pp. 370-76.

95. Reed, *Our Iron-Clad Ships*, pp. 231-36. See also remarks of Captain Symonds in *Proceedings of I.C.E.* 26 (1866-67): 222.

Chapter 2: Foreign Competition

1. Oddly, evidence of an awareness of Great Britain's industrial lead as a vital naval asset is singularly lacking.

2. Confidential paper, December 1867; Milne MSS, MLN/P/B lcc. John C. Paget reminisced that the idea was prevalent at the time that steam and iron had been "levelling up the naval powers," and that England could have lost her power through one great naval disaster, a not uncommon sentiment in later years. Paget, *Naval Powers and Their Policies* (London, 1876), p. vii.

3. Robinson to Board, Admiralty I, 5840 (11 February 1862).

4. Memorandum [1863], Somerset MSS.

5. Hansard, *Parliamentary Debates* 169 (1863): 669. Estimates, Navy, *Parliamentary Papers* 35 (1863-64): 1.

6. Hansard, *Parl. Debates*, 3d ser., 173 (1864): 1289-90. Baxter was rewarded by Gladstone for his keen knowledge of naval affairs by being appointed secretary to the Admiralty, where he distinguished himself by his zeal for economy and retrenchment. Cf. also Palmerston to Somerset, 2 October 1863, Somerset MSS.

7. Sir Robert Spencer Robinson, *On the State of the British Navy*, (London, 1874), p. 5.

8. Controller's Office, "A Return of the Armoured Ships and Batteries Built and Building," Adm. I, 5840 (27 April 1863).

9. See, for example, Iron-Plated Ships and Batteries, *Parl. Papers*, 35 (1865): 2, which gives the ironclad strength of the fleet as seventeen, whereas it was actually fourteen. Nominal Lists of All Ironclads and Date of their First Completion For Sea, *Parl. Papers* 37 (1874): 525. Unless otherwise indicated, figures of British ironclad strength and dates of commission are taken from *Nominal Lists*.

10. "Ships and Guns," *Colburn's United Service Magazine* (1866), pt. 3, p. 505.

11. *Times* (London), 1 January 1863, p. 11.

12. Sir Arthur Otway, *Autobiography and Journals of Admiral Lord Clarence E. Paget* (London, 1896), pp. 195–96. Even then Lord Clarence managed to bring back false information, for he wrote that he took "careful note of the turret which stared me in the face." He obviously had confounded the armored conning tower with a turret. On the other hand, the minister of marine gave one Patrick Barry carte blanche to inspect public and private dockyards and shipbuilding facilities. Barry returned with hugely exaggerated accounts of the naval might of the third empire and of corresponding British peril. Patrick Barry, *The Dockyards, Shipyards, and Marine of France* (London, 1864).

13. Admiralty memorandum, Adm. I, 5977 (19 September 1866).

14. Adm. Sir Frederick W. Grey, *Admiralty Administration, 1861–1866.* (London, 1866), p. 8.

15. Hansard, *Parl. Debates* 174 (1864) : 1301. Two years later the shipbuilder J. D. Samuda called for a fleet "at least equal to that of all the fleets of Europe put together." The idea was criticized as one no administration had ever even attempted to follow. Hansard, *Parl. Debates*, 3d ser. 184: 1190. The same year Lord John Hay called for precisely the same goal, but neither proposition seems to have influenced Admiralty policy. Milne MSS, National Maritime Museum, NLN/p/b/1 December 1866. Cf. also Capt. J. C. R. Colomb, *On The Distribution of Our War Forces* (London, 1869), p. 28.

16. Lord Halifax to Gladstone, 16 December 1870, Gladstone MSS, British Museum, Add. MSS 44185, f. 111.

17. "Our Armoured Fleet," *Annual of Royal School of Naval Architecture* 1 (1871) : 24.

18. Committee on Designs, *Parl. Papers* 14 (1872) : ix.

19. Confidential printed Cabinet memorandum, 16 June 1862, Palmerston MSS, National Registry of Archives; Somerset to Palmerston, 23 May 1862, Palmerston MSS.

20. Quoted by Lord Clarence Paget, Hansard, *Parl. Debates* 169 (1863) : 1346.

21. The French were supposed by some to have built in wood as a defense against ramming. Capt. C. B. Brackenbury, *European Armaments in 1867* (London, 1867), p. 108 ; Robinson to Board, 13 December 1864, Palmerston MSS ; French ironclad particulars and numbers based on : Commandants de Balincourt and Vincent de Brechignac, "La Marine Française d'Hier," *La Revue Maritime* (January 1931), pp. 289–317 ; Marine et Colonies, *Liste de La Flotte* (Paris, 1868) ; Admiralty, *Iron-Cased Ships of France*, 4 December 1867.

22. See Admiralty memorandum, 20 January 1865, Palmerston MSS.

23. *Times* (London), 19 August 1865, p. 10.

24. "A General Outline of the Wants of the Navy at the Present Moment with Reference to Ships," confidential memorandum, August 1865, Adm. I, 5981; Robinson to Board, Adm. I, 5982 (20 November 1866).

25. Admiralty Second Secretary to Sir John Pakington, Adm. I, 5977 (19 September 1866).

26. Robinson to Board, Adm. I, 5982 (20 November 1866).

27. *Journal of the Royal United Service Institution* 10 (1866): 32. Reed's successor expressed identical sentiments in 1873. Nathaniel Barnaby, "Our UnArmoured Ships," *Colburn's United Service Magazine* (1873), pt. 3, p. 1.

28. Lennox to Disraeli, 12 December 1867, Disraeli MSS, B/XX/LX/256.

29. Milne memorandum, March 1867, Milne MSS, MLN/P/B/1. Yet almost simultaneously, the Admiralty's *Iron-Cased Ships of France* (1867) dismissed the first six ships in the French ironclad program as "obsolete as sea-going ships" (p. 2).

30. de Balincourt and de Brechignac, "La Marine Française d'Hier," pp. 439–42.

31. Confidential printed memorandum, December 1867, Milne MSS, MLN/P/B/1 (c). Corry feared that France would widen the gap in coastal ironclads.

32. George E. Buckle and William F. Monypenny, *The Life of Benjamin Disraeli, Earl of Beaconsfield*, 6 vols. (London, 1916), 4: 579.

33. Lord Lennox, for example, warned the Commons that the French fleet was on an equality with the Royal Navy. Hansard, *Parl. Debates* 193 (1868): 1,134. The actual figure was twenty-four completed French ironclads to twenty-nine British. By the year 1870 the margin would widen to twenty-eight French ironclads to thirty-five British.

34. In the late 1870s and early 1880s the French again approached equality, but the French fleet was permanently eclipsed by the British Naval Defense Act of 1889.

35. James P. Baxter III, *The Introduction of the Ironclad Warship* (Cambridge, Mass., 1933; 1968), pp. 311–13.

36. *New York Herald*, 24 November 1862. Cf. also C. B. Boynton, *The Navies of England, America, France, and Russia* (New York, 1865), a panegyric to the American monitor.

37. Ephraim D. Adams, *Great Britain and the American Civil War* (New York, 1925) 1: 176. This period in Britain is described with corrosive bitterness by Brooks Adams, son of Charles Francis, in his "The Seizure of the Laird Rams," *Proceedings of the Massachusetts Historical Society* 45 (1911–12): 247, and Sarah A. Wallace and Frances E. Gillespie, eds., *The Journal of Benjamin Moran* (Chicago, 1949).

38. Robinson to Board, Adm. I, 5840 (3 January 1863). For U.S. monitors the authoritative source is *Dictionary of American Naval Fighting*

Ships, vol. 3 (Department of the Navy, Washington, D. C., 1968), app. 2, abstracted in R. H. Webber, *Monitors of the U.S. Navy* (Department of the Navy, Washington, D.C., 1969). Cf. also typescript "Our Navy's Ships and Their Builders, 1775–1885" ("With the Approval and Cooperation of the Bureau of Ships, U.S. Navy, Washington, D.C., 1962"). Arnold R. Shapack, "Oak to Iron-Monitors in United States Navy History" (Master's thesis, University of Maryland, 1973).

39. Adm. Sir James Hope to Duke of Somerset, 12 January 1864, Somerset MSS. Admiral Hope accurately foresaw that the United States would demand indemnification for the *Alabama*'s and *Florida*'s depredations, and feared that refusal of this demand would be considered a *casus belli* by America. The Duke of Somerset, however, had been attempting to smooth over Anglo-American tensions. He had been a willing ally in the Admiral Commanding, North American Station, Sir Alexander Milne, who had just been received with marked civility by Lincoln and Seward. Somerset assured Milne: "We have as yet, however, no ground for believing that the Government of North America wishes for a quarrel with this country." Somerset to Milne, 25 April 1863, Milne MSS, MLN 107.

40. Palmerston to Somerset, 6 September 1864, Palmerston MSS.

41. Admiral Hope to Somerset, 26 March 1866, Somerset MSS.

42. Lennox to Disraeli, 27 October 1866, Disraeli MSS, B/XX/LX/245.

43. *Report of the Secretary of the Navy, 1866* (Washington, D.C., 1866), p. 23.

44. *Times* (London), 19 June 1866, p. 13; 28 June 1866, p. 12.

45. Captain Bythsea report, Adm. I, 5992 (20 June 1866). On the basis of this report, Lord Derby wrote Disraeli that Britain was "far superior" to the United States in its ironclad strength, and added the curious postscript that it would be best not to tell Lord Salisbury "or he will want to go to war." Lord Derby to Disraeli, 12 December 1866, Disraeli MSS, B/XX/S/758.

46. Foreign Office to Admiralty, Adm. I, 5992 (6 December 1866).

47. Robinson to Board, Adm. I, 6018 (6 March 1867).

48. Disraeli to Lord Derby, 28 January 1868, in Buckle and Monypenny, *Life of Disraeli*, 4: 578.

49. Russell to Childers, 12 February 1869. Spencer Childers, *Life and Correspondence of the Rt. Honourable Hugh C. E. Childers* (London, 1921) 2: 171–72. Childers to Russell, ibid., p. 172.

50. Admiralty, "Report of the Condition of the United States Navy in 1869." MSS report in Admiralty Library, p. 552. Captain Goodenough in 1872 reported that basic faults in design and construction had led the Americans themselves to neglect the monitor. Captain Goodenough to Admiral Robinson, Adm. I, 6198 (19 July 1872).

51. Stanley Sandler, "A Navy in Decay," *Military Affairs* 25, no. 4 (December 1971).

52. During the renaissance of the United States Navy, plans were bought from Britain, particularly in the case of the U.S.S. *Texas*, constructed under the Act of 1886.

53. For early Russian ironclad policy, see p. 78. "The Russian Ironclad Fleet," *Proceedings of the Royal Artillery Institution*, (1864), translation from the Russian *Military Magazine*; Fred T. Jane, *The Imperial Russian Navy* (London, 1899), pp. 154–71; Thomas Brassey, *The British Navy* (London, 1882), 1: 157–61; Admiralty, "Report of Shipbuilding Department of Russian Admiralty for 1862" (London, 1862); Reports of Captain Goodenough on Foreign Navies, 1871–72, Adm. I, 6171; J. F. Von Kronenfels, *Das Schwimmende Flotten-Material* (Vienna: 1881), pp. 483–528; C. B. Boynton, *Navies*, pp. 6–7; J .W. Kipp, "Consequences of Defeat: Modernizing the Russian Navy, 1856–1863," *Jahrbucher fur Geschichte Osteuropas* (June 1971), pp. 210–25.

54. This policy may have been the result of more than mere admiration from afar, for the British Consul at Odessa reported that he had seen plans of H.M.S. *Magdala* (a forerunner of the *Devastation*) in the Nicolaieff Admiralty office and believed that the Russians possessed others as well. Reports of Captain Ward, Adm. I, 6171 (17 November 1870).

55. See "Our Naval Defences, Where Are We," *Blackwood's* 101 (January 1867): 10, for an account of the financial consequences of a highly imagined Russo-American monitor demonstration in the North Sea.

56. Captain Thompson to Admiralty, 15 March 1868, Milne MSS, MLN P/A/1. Cf. also Capt. J. C. R. Colomb, *The Protection of Our Commerce and Distribution of Our Naval Forces Considered* (London, 1867).

57. Captain Goodenough to British Ambassador at St. Petersburg, Adm. I, 6198 (October 1871).

58. Letter from E. J. Reed in the *Times* (London), 17 November 1872, p. 12, in reply to anonymous letter of 9 November 1872. The ship's workmanship, and that of Russian yards in general, are described in Brassey, *The British Navy*, pp. 361–62; Chief Engineer King, U.S.N., *The WarShips and Navies of the World* (London, 1878), p. 323; Jane, *Imperial Russian Navy*, who held a high opinion of the Russian Navy, nevertheless writes of the battleship *Gangoot*, which foundered after target practice. Although some held that an anarchist bomb was to blame, Jane admits that the ship was badly built, p. 240. The best English description of the *Peter the Great* comes from the Admiralty Intelligence Department, "Russia, War Vessels, 1906," a Russian compilation captured by the Japanese at Tsushima and passed on to their ally. As late as 1912, the American military attaché witnessed Russian

workmen pounding rivets with hand sledges! U. S. National Archives, R.G. 165. 6566-20.

59. "Circular Ironclads," *Colburn's United Service Magazine* (1875) pt. 3, pp. 427-72.

60. Jane, *Imperial Russian Navy*, p. 175. Reed's adventures are contained in his "On Circular Ironclads," *Journal of R.U.S.I.* 20 (1876) : 85-109. Cf. also discussion following E. E. Goulaeff, "On Circular Ironclads," *Transactions of the Institution of Naval Architects* 17 (1876) : 29-61. Cf. also A. A. Kraeuskii, ed., *Sbor'nik statei o krugykh sudakh* (St. Petersburg, 1875), for *Popoffkas*. The Russians were peculiarly receptive to advanced prototypes of dubious practicality such as the Winans's "cigar boat" of 1862, tested in the Finnish Gulf in 1862. The Russian naval authority J. W. Kipp notes that the *Popoffkas* were plagued with weak engines and by the treacherous currents of the Bug River at the new naval base at Nikolaev. Letter to author, 25 January 1973. For further sources of nineteenth-century Russian naval development cf. also: Iv. Shokol'skii, "Sistematicheskii katalog Biblioteki morskogo ministerstua: otdely moenno morskoi i voennyi" ("The Systematic Catalogue of the Library of the Naval and Military Sections" (Petrogradi Tipografiia Morskogo Ministerstua, 1916)). K. A. Mann, ed., "Obzor delatel'nosti morskogo upravleniia n. Rossii n. pervoe dvadtsatiletie B. Imp. Alexsandra Nikolaevicha, 1855-1880 gg." (St. Petersburg: tipografiia morskogo ministerstua, 1880) 2 vols. (good on technology). E. Arem, "Rol'flota n.voein 1877-1878 gg." ("The Role of the Fleet in the War of 1877-1878") (St. Petersburg: Tipografiia Morskogo Ministerstua, 1903).

61. Captain James Graham Goodenough, "Report on Foreign Navies," Admiralty Library MSS, 1871-72, p. 43. Kipp maintains that the Russian Navy, after a century of consistent naval triumphs over the Turks, were not impressed by their enemy's naval might, and at the same time feared that a vigorous naval offensive in the Black Sea might once again draw in France and Great Britain. It is not in dispute that the Czarist Black Sea Fleet neutralized a technologically superior Turkish armada. Ibid.

62. "M.H.W." to Controller, Adm. I, 6198 (19 July 1872).

63. Hansard, *Parl. Debates* 178 (1865) : 1400.

64. Somerset memorandum (n.d.) [1865], Somerset MSS.

65. *The Armed Strength of Italy* (trans. from the German by Lt. W. A. Hare, R.E. for the Intelligence Branch of the Quartermaster-General's Department, 1875), p. 140.

66. Goodenough, "Report on Foreign Navies," p. 245.

67. Italy, Marina, *Ufficio Storico Le Navi Di Linea Italiane, 1861-1961* (Rome, 1969), pp. 1-116.

68. Cf. an article attributed to the Emperor Maximillian of Mexico calling

for a great Austrian naval expansion and an alliance with Britain. "The Austrian Navy," *Colburn's United Service Magazine* (1868), pt. 2, pp. 534–48.

69. *Naval and Military Gazette*, 22 April 1865, p. 253. Cf. p. 85.

70. Goodenough, "Foreign Navies," pp. 147, 54, 97, 157; Lt. Thomas Very, *Navies of the World* (New York, 1880), pp. 73–81; King, *Warships and Navies of the World*, pp. 301–19.

Chapter 3: Propulsion

1. E. C. Smith, *A Short History of Marine Engineering* (London, 1938), p. 162; Admiralty, *Quarterly List of the Navy* (1877). Even mass production was not unknown. One hundred fifty sets of engines were assembled for the Crimean gunboat program. G. A. Osbon, "The Crimean Gunboats," *Mariner's Mirror* 50 (1965): 106–8.

2. Detached Squadron (*Cruise Round the World*), *Parliamentary Papers*, 40 (1871): 621–39; Adm. G. T. Phipps Hornby, *The Cruise Round the World of the Flying Squadron* (London, 1871).

3. Mrs. Fred Egerton, *Admiral of the Fleet Sir Geoffrey Phipps Hornby* (London, 1896), p. 120.

4. *Times* (London), 29 December 1869, p. 9.

5. C. F. Henwood, *Textbook to the Turret and Tripod Systems of Captain Cowper P. Coles* (Paris, 1867), p. 25. See also *Transactions of the Institution of Naval Architects* 9 (1868): 115–43; Memorandum by Captain Key and Lord John Hay, Admiralty I, 5981 (11 August 1866).

6. Adm. Percy Scott recalled that the pressure for coal economy, even for distillation, was so great that one captain was driven to the revolting expedient of a "suck tap" for his crew's water supply. G. Penn, *Fifty Years in the Royal Navy* (London, 1919), p. 6.

7. E. J. Reed, *Our Iron-Clad Ships* (London, 1869), p. 108. Reed maintained before the Committee on Designs that the *Hercules* expended a mere one-and-three-quarters pound of coal per indicated horsepower per hour. *Parl. Papers* 14 (1872): 140.

8. Capt. J. C. R. Colomb, *The Protection of our Commerce and Distribution of our Naval Forces Considered* (London, 1867), p. 39.

9. Comdr. Philip H. Colomb, "Steam-Power *vs.* Sail Power for Men of War," *Journal of the Royal United Service Institution* 22 (1878): 530–55.

10. Navy (Channel Fleet), *Parl. Papers*, 45 (1867–68): 5.

11. The most accurate source for the performance of ironclads under steam can be found in Admiralty publication *Results of Trials Made in Her Majesty's Screw Ships and Vessels* (1867, 1868, 1870). Cf. also Channel Fleet *Parl. Papers*, 44 (1867): 19.

12. Vice Adm. Sir Henry J. Oram, "Fifty Years' Changes in British Warship Machinery," *Transactions of I.N.A.* 52 (1911) : 98–101; Oram and Richard Sennet, *The Marine Steam Engine* (London, 1900). pp. 10–13; Adm. G. A. Ballard, "The Black Battlefleet," *Mariner's Mirror* 15 (1929) : 111–15.

13. *Proceedings of the Institution of Civil Engineers* 26 (1866–67) : 206. Until the coming of the turbine engine with Fisher's *Dreadnought*, every day's steaming at high speed with the old reciprocating engine compelled several days' harbor overhaul of machinery. Arthur J. Marder, *From the Dreadnought to Scapa Flow* (London, 1961) 1:43–44.

14. Cf. Board Minute, Channel and Mediterranean Squadron, *Parl. Papers* 44 (1870) : 15. Even John Ericsson, designer of the mastless *Monitor*, denounced the "absurd idea of employing vessels without sails" for long-distance cruising. Letter to Engineering, 18 February 1870, p. 103. U.S. naval strategic concepts of the time are discussed in Stanley Sandler, "A Navy in Decay," *Military Affairs* 35, no. 4 (1971). The fate of H.M.S. *Captain* seemed vivid proof of the folly of masting low-freeboard, turret warships.

15. Committee on Designs. *Parl. Papers* 14 (1872) : 66, 68, 71, 131; Reed, "Armour-Plated Ships," *Nautical Magazine* 70 (1867) : 25–26, a call for less reliance on sail power.

16. E. J. Reed, "An Amateur Naval Designer," *Naval Science* 2 (1873) : 361–62.

17. Reed, *Our Iron-Clad Ships*, p. 132.

18. Committee on Designs, App. E, *Parl. Papers* 14 (1872) : 342.

19. See Channel Fleet, *Parl. Papers* 44 (1867) : 15. In the words of a Board Minute: "As perfect efficiency as a steam-ship is found incompatible with perfect efficiency as a sailing ship, in ironclad vessels of war, the practical result to arrive at is the best and most useful compromise between these antagonistic qualities." Channel and Mediterranean Squadrons, 1869, *Parl. Papers* 44 (1870) : 15.

20. Ballard, "British Battleships of 1870," *Mariner's Mirror* 19 (1913) : 265.

21. Admiralty, "Correspondence Respecting New Designs for Armoured Ships" (2 March 1869) p. 6. One year after Admiral Dacres's observations on the disadvantages of masts and rigging in battle, the Prussian *Meteor* was unable to pursue the stricken French *Bouvet* because her screw had been fouled by her rigging after a successful ramming had brought down top hamper. H. W. Wilson, *Ironclads in Action* (London, 1896), p. 1:279.

22. Robinson to Board, Adm. I, 5941 (26 April 1865). Cf. also his submission of September 5 1866, Adm. I, 5981, in which the controller contended that well-trained officers and men "would not need the stimulus of a full rig outfit to shew the ancient valour of their race."

23. Committee on Designs, *Parl. Papers* 14 (1872) : 168.

24. Ibid., p. xiv.

25. "X," "Our Armoured Fleet," *Annual of the Royal School of Naval Architecture* (1871): 18.
26. Channel Fleet, *Parl. Papers* 44 (1867).
27. Oscar Parkes, *British Battleships, 1860–1950* (London, 1957; 1966), p. 139
28. Ibid., pp. 276–80.
29. Channel and Mediterranean Squadrons, 1869, *Parl. Papers* 44 (1870): 15. As early as October 1865, in laying down design principles of the *Monarch*, the board wrote that "the masts should be considered as wholly auxiliary." But the *Monarch's* sail plan was increased substantially when her great rival, H.M.S. *Captain*, was given the fullest sail rig ever mounted on a British ironclad. Minute of the First Lord on the Loss of H.M.S. Captain *Parl. Papers* 40 (1871): 52.
30. Committee on Designs, *Parl. Papers* 14 (1872): 77. Reed's and Robinson's similar opinions are found on pp. 129 and 74, respectively.
31. Memorandum by Robinson, Committee on Designs, *Parl. Papers* p. 317. Frederick L. Robertson, *The Evolution of Naval Armament* (London, 1921), p. 281.
32. Admiralty, "Correspondence Respecting New Designs," p. 2.
33. Committee on Designs, *Parl. Papers* 14 (1872): 797–804. Smith, *Short History of Marine Engineering*, p. 174. K. T. Rowland, *Steam at Sea* (New York, 1970), pp. 119–22.
34. Committee on Designs, *Parl. Papers* 14 (1872): xi.
35. Capt. C. Penrose Fitzgerald, "Mastless Ships of War," *Journal of R.U.S.I.* 31 (1887): 115–33.

Chapter 4: Weapons

1. The unsatisfactory situation in the field of naval armament was a reflection of the backward and conservative state of British arms manufacturing generally. Authorities agree that the major cause of such backwardness was the stranglehold of the master general of the ordnance and the authorities at the Woolwich Arsenal upon production and procurement of heavy armaments. Confirmation of this thesis can be found in the fact that after 1880 British ordnance developed rapidly to a position of world leadership, precisely at a time when the state monopoly was being progressively dismantled. Cf. Clive Trebilcock, "Armaments and Industry," *Economic History Review*, 2d ser. 22, no. 3 (December 1969): 12–69. S. B. Saul, "The Market and the Development of the Mechanical Engineering Industries in Britain, 1860–1914," ibid. 2d ser. 20 (April 1967), asserts the superiority of the British small arms industry, but concedes the backwardness of heavy armament. Further evidence cited below in this chapter.

2. Commdr. Philip H. Colomb, *Memoirs of Admiral Sir Astley Cooper Key* (London, 1898), pp. 326-28.

3. Report from the Select Committee on Ordnance, *Parliamentary Papers* 11 (1864) : 249.

4. Arthur J. Marder, *Fear God and Dreadnought* (London, 1952), 1:73.

5. Rear Adm. Sir R. Vesey Hamilton, *Naval Administration* (London, 1896), pp. 79-85. Admiral Robinson testified that the War Department differed with the Admiralty over gun carriages and refused to supply the carriages and slides needed. Lord's Committee on Admiralty Administration, *Parl. Papers* 7 (1871) : 58.

6. *Times* (London), 28 July 1866, p. 5; *Naval and Military Gazette*, 13 October 1866, p. 51.

7. "Correspondence Respecting New Designs for Armour-Clad Ships," Admiralty memorandum, 2 March 1869, Admiralty Library, p. 1. The Duke of Somerset publicly defended the system before the Ordnance Select Committee, *Parl. Papers* 11 (1863) : 254.

8. See Controller's submission, Admiralty I, 6082 (24 November 1868). The possible effects of gun salvos were described by Capt. J. H. Selwyn, but his work went unheeded. "On the Future of Naval Attack and Defence," *Journal of the Royal United Service Institution* 7 (1863): 17-18. Electrical firing was included in *A Manual of Gunnery for Her Majesty's Fleet* (1873) for the first time, as was prize firing (pp. 30, 61, 134-38).

9. [M. H. Jansen], *The Revolution in Naval Warfare* (London, 1867) ; p. 144.

10. Comdr. Philip H. Colomb, "The Attack and Defense of Fleets," *Journal of R.U.S.I.* 15 (1871) : 412-14. Capt. W. H. Hood, Key's successor in H.M.S. *Excellent,* asserted that H.M.S. *Hercules* would be fortunate if her gunnery could hit a target eight feet by twelve at a range of two hundred yards. Committee on 'Gibraltar' Shields, *Parl. Papers* 16 (1867-68) : 72.

11. Comdr. William Dawson, "*Glatton* and *Hotspur* Experiment," *Proceedings of the Junior Naval Professional Association* 3 (1873) : 217-44; Edward Simpson (United States Navy Department), *Report on a Naval Mission to Europe,* 3 vols. (Washington, 1873) 1:195-96, 285-92; Nathaniel Barnaby, "Lessons from the *Hotspur-Glatton* Experiment," *Journal of R.U.S.I.* 22 (1873) : 293-309.

12. For faults of Palliser shells, see Comdr. William Dawson, "Naval Guns," *Journal of R.U.S.I.* 16 (1872) : 343-400. The Ordnance Select Committee reported that out of 150 shells of nine-inch caliber, twenty jammed in the bore on one occasion. Admiralty, Extracts from the Reports of Minutes and Proceedings of the Ordnance Select Committee 3 (London, 1866). The principle was originally adopted from the French.

13. Admiralty, *A Manual of Gunnery for Her Majesty's Fleet* (London,

1868), p. 165. Such was definitely the case in the American Civil War. Col. Henry Brackenbury, *European Armaments* in 1867 (London, 1867), p. 109.

14. For battles of the *Huascar*, cf. chap. 5, n. 2.

15. Admiralty, *Report on Bombardment of Alexandria* (London, 1882). Only Captain Fisher, of the *Inflexible*, called somewhat obliquely for better gunnery (p. 2).

16. Lt. Comdr. Casper F. Goodrich, *Report of the British Naval and Military Operations in Egypt, 1882* (Washington, 1882), p. 66.

17. Adm. Sir Percy Scott, *Fifty Years in the Royal Navy* (London, 1919), p. 48. In a detailed War Office appreciation of Alexandria, Capt. George S. Clarke concluded that "experience at Alexandria seems to show that even at moderate ranges, the fire of a fleet is not greatly to be feared." "Report on the Defences of Alexandria and the Result of the Action of July, 1882" (War Office, 1883), p. 90.

18. Admiralty, *A Manual of Gunnery* (1873).

19. "Naval Gunnery Training," *Naval Science* 2 (1873): 314–31.

20. *Times* (London), 24 May 1869, p. 10. Cf. also comments of the perfector of the mechanical gun carriage, Captain R. A. E. Scott, *Journal of R.U.S.I.* 15 (1871): 434. Targets were not even mentioned in the 1868 *Manual of Gunnery*.

21. Percy Scott, *Fifty Years*, pp. 26–28.

22. *A Manual of Gunnery* (1868) recommended Admiral Ryder's method of ascertaining distance, namely, an observer in the cross trees subtends angle between horizon and an enemy's waterline, p. 49.

23. Comdr. Wallace B. Hardy, "The Heavy Gun *vs.* the Ram and Torpedo," *Proceedings of the Junior Naval Professional Association* 3 (1873): 280.

24. Capt. W. H. Noble, *Report on Various Experiments Carried out Under the Direction of the Ordnance Select Committee* (London, 1866), p. 36; *Times* (London), 6 August 1863, p. 10; 22 August 1863, p. 12. Later experiments seemed to indicate that French armor was practically equal in resistance to British plates. Admiralty *Report of the Special Committee on Iron* 4 (1864): xii, 4.

25. Noble, *Report*, p. 25.

26. Ibid., pp. 30, 31. Cf. also article by Captain F. S. Stoney, "A Brief Historical Sketch on Our Rifled Ordnance from 1858 to 1868," *Proceedings of the Royal Artillery Institution* 6 (1870): 115–18. The American *Naval Mission to Europe* admitted that the British twelve-inch rifle would wreak more destruction upon thicker plate than could the Federal fifteen-inch smooth-bore, at identical distances, p. 185. Another official American source, Charles B. Norton and W. J. Valentine, *Report on Munitions of War* (Washington, 1868), p. 267, maintained that the inferior performance of the American giant guns

was due to a limitation on the powder charge to fifty pounds in Admiralty experiments. But a nine-inch, twelve-ton, rifle pierced the *Lord Warden* target using a charge of only forty-four pounds of powder. Noble, *Report,* p. 48; Admiralty, *Epitome of Various Guns that Have Been Tried Against Targets and Armour Plates, With the Results* (1866), pp. 2–3. The Assistant Superintendent of the Royal Laboratory, Woolwich, pointed out that all of the minor ironclad powers, including Italy, Austria, and Spain, were arming with British Armstrong guns. Capt. Vivian T. Majendie, "English Guns and Foreign Critics," *Proceedings of the Royal Artillery Institution* 7 (1871): 60–126.

27. E. J. Reed, *Our Iron-Clad Ships* (London, 1869), p. 63. Lieutenant Colonel Reilly, in a War Office publication, thought that French artillery was powerful, but lacking in endurance. Admiralty *Report on the French Artillery* (London, 1873), p. 3.

28. The commander in chief of the Mediterranean Squadron examined vessels of both the Austrian and the Italian fleets, "and was much struck with the absence of any serious damage from either shot or shell." Lord Clarence Paget to Board, Adm. I, 6049 (n.d.). Cf. also detailed articles in the *Standard* 9 and 10 August 1866.

29. P. H. Colomb, *Memoirs,* pp. 324–25.

30. A perusal of Admiralty ordnance publications shows that powder charges would be increased or decreased to simulate varying ranges. This was to ensure accuracy, but even at the common two hundred yards the target was sometimes missed.

31. Report of Captain Phillimore of H.M.S. *Defence,* Adm. I, 5816 (26 January 1863). Admiral Milne reported that the gun and carriage were lifted bodily from the deck upon firing, and that the piece was far too complicated for sea service. Adm. I, 5821 (25 December 1863).

32. Noble, *Report,* pp. 49, 50; Admiralty, *Epitome,* pp. 8–10; Admiralty, *Report of the Special Committee on Iron,* pp. 101–2.

33. The Duke of Somerset, Captain Coles, and Capt. R. A. E. Scott agreed that the sixty-eight pounder was a superior weapon against ironclads. Testimony before Select Committee on Ordnance, *Parl. Papers* 11 (1863): 251, 58, 198. The conclusion was sustained by the Committee, ibid., p. vii.

34. Since round shot from smoothbores had considerably greater initial velocity than an elongated shell from a rifle, the sixty-eight-pounder smoothbore seemed ideal for close-in naval fighting. Capt. Francis Stoney, *Proceedings of R.A.I.* 6 (1870): 107.

35. Capt. Francis Stoney, "The Progress of Our Heavy Ordnance," *Journal of R.U.S.I.* 14 (1870): 230–54; idem, "The Construction of Our Heavy Guns", *Proceedings of R.A.I.* 6 (1870): 406–32; Simpson, *Naval Mission to Europe,* 1:14–50; Dawson, "Naval Guns," p. 370.

36. P. H. Colomb, *Memoirs*, pp. 331–33.
37. E. W. Lloyd and A. G. Hadcock, *Artillery, Its Progress and Present Position* (London, 1893), p 35; Capt. W. H. Noble, "Rise of Rifled Naval Artillery," *Transactions of the Institution of Naval Architects* 40, (1899) : 236.
38. Robinson to Board, Adm. I, 5840 (11 February 1863).
39. "Report of an Experiment Carried on by the Ordnance Select Committee," *Proceedings of R.A.I.* 4 (1865) : 277.
40. Somerset to Palmerston, 17 December 1863, Palmerston MSS.
41. P. H. Colomb, *Memoirs*, p. 340.
42. Capt. Francis Stoney and Lt. Charles Jones, *Textbook of the Construction and Manufacture of the Rifled Ordnance in the British Service* (London, 1872), p. 156. Key's reluctance to change to more advanced models of artillery may be explained partially by his belief that gunnery accuracy rested more on steadiness of the ship, distance judgment, and the skill of the gunners than on the quality of the gun itself. Quoted by Dawson, "Naval Guns," p. 353.
43. "Report on Experiment," *Proceedings of R.A.I.* 4 (1865) : 39, and app.; Admiralty, *Statement of Results Obtained against Iron Plates with Shot and Shell of Various Calibres* (1865), p. 3.
44. Admiralty, *Epitome*, p. 8. The sixty-eight pounder failed to penetrate this target at two hundred yards. E. J. Bruce, "Experiment Carried out at Shoeburyness," *Proceedings of R.A.I.* 4 (1865) : 147.
45. *Proceedings of R.A.I.* 4 (1865) : 147; Admiralty, *Epitome*, p. 8; Admiralty, *Statement*, p. 3.
46. Hansard, *Parliamentary Debates*, 3d ser., 173 (1864) : 1123.
47. Somerset to Lord Russell, 6 September 1864, Russell MSS, P.R.O. 30/22 (26).
48. Somerset to Palmerston, 9 September 1864, Palmerston MSS.
49. Admiralty, *Extract from the Quarterly Report of Ordnance Select Committee* 3 (1865) : 154.
50. Robinson to Board, Adm. I, 5981 (13 September 1866). The Admiralty Armaments Book for 1865 indicates that the *Scorpion* was also armed with the nine-inch rifle.
51. Admiralty, *Epitome*, p. 2; Admiralty, *Extract from Quarterly Report*, pp. 347–51.
52. P. H. Colomb, *Memoirs*, p. 341.
53. Admiralty, *Extracts from Quarterly Report*, p. 351.
54. Ibid., p. 391.
55. Captain Noble testified that the ten-inch gun would do more work at two thousand yards than the nine-inch could do with its muzzle against the target. Committee on the 'Gibraltar' Shield, *Parl. Papers* 16 (1867–68) : 129.
56. Admiralty, *Epitome*, p. 2.

57. P. H. Colomb, *Memoirs*, pp. 349–56.

58. Robinson to Board, Adm. I, 5891 (26 August 1864) ; Adm. I, 6079 (20 January 1868).

59. P. H. Colomb, *Memoirs*, p. 354–58.

60. Comdr. R. A. E. Scott bitterly complained of such "improvements." "Modern Carriages for Heavy Naval Ordnance," *Journal of R.U.S.I.* 10 (1866) : 499.

61. Key to Controller, Adm. I, 6082 (27 November 1865).

62. Admiralty, "Report of Committee on Carriages for Twelve-Ton Guns" from *Experiments with Naval Ordnance* (London, 1866), pp. 66–77; *Times* (London), 3 May 1866, p. 11; ibid., 14 May 1866, p. 12.

63. See testimony of Admiral Robinson before Lords' Committee on Admiralty, *Parl. Papers*, 7 (1871) : 58; Reed, *Our Iron-Clad Ships*, pp. 57–58, 224.

64. *Times* (London), 9 September 1868, p. 10. The previous year Robinson had written to the board in some agitation that "this year is fast slipping away without our most powerful broadside ships being made efficient" through Scott mountings. Adm. I, 6019 (14 August 1868). Before the Turret Ship Committee, Reed had complained of the "extremely unsatisfactory state of existing arrangements for working heavy guns at the broadside." Minutes of Evidence, *Parl. Papers* 47 (1866) : 71.

65. Scott, "Modern Carriages," pp. 500–550.

66. P. H. Colomb, *Memoirs*, p. 375. One authority notes that Key "was an essentially conservative man. . . . His mind instinctively recoiled from large and general questions to take refuge in detail." N.A.M. Rodger, "The Dark Ages of the Admiralty, 1869–1885," pt. 3, *Mariner's Mirror* (May 1976), p. 125; pt. 2 (February 1976), p. 40.

67. P. H. Colomb, *Memoirs*, pp. 376–80.

68. Ibid., pp. 380–82. Even after Key had left the *Excellent*, Fisher complained that "the great failing of the *Excellent* is an aversion to change. I mean large changes. She has seldom led the way, and this is but natural." Marder, *Fear God*, 1:72.

69. Oscar Parkes, *British Battleships, 1860–1950* (London, 1957; 1966), pp. 287–89. Reed was in favor of adopting the breech-loader in 1871, just about the time when its advantages over muzzle-loading became obvious. He thought that this development would drive out the turret because of the great size of the gun barrel in breech-loaders. The exact opposite course was taken. Committee on Designs, *Parl. Papers* 14 (1872) : 130.

70. Reed "On Iron-Clad Ships," *Proceedings of the Royal Institution of Great Britain* 6 (1870–72). Admiral Robinson circulated a printed confidential memorandum showing that the French, in 1870, were behind in numbers of guns as well. 4 August 1870, Milne MSS, MLN P/B/1.

British ordnance may have declined vis-à-vis Prussia by 1868. According to Lt. E. W. Very, a basic authority for the early ironclad era, Krupp's breech-loader of nine-inches caliber enjoyed a slight advantage over comparable Armstrong-Woolwich pieces. *Proceedings of the United States Naval Institute* 9 (1883) : 441.

71. Her designer deemed protection of boilers, magazine, and machinery as far more vital than providing "cowardly protection to the men at their guns." John Scott Russell, *The Modern System of Naval Architecture*, 3 vols. (London, 1865), 1:551.

72. One of the best official sources for armor distribution in early British ironclads, other than the plans themselves, is Admiralty, *Steamships of England, 1868–1884* (1884). Smith was a Fellow of the Royal School of Naval Architecture.

73. *Times* (London), 11 February 1868, p. 10.

74. Reed to Robinson, Adm. I, 5981 (31 July 1866).

75. See John Bourne, "Ships of War," *Proceedings of the Institution of Civil Engineers* 26 (1866–67) : 166–79.

76. *United Service Gazette*, 18 September 1866, p. 4. Cf. statement by Nathaniel Barnaby on similar opinions in the 1870s and 1880s. *Naval Development of the Century* (London, 1904), pp. 174–75.

77. Report of the Committee on Designs, *Parl. Papers* 14 (1872) : x.

78. Report on Passive Obstructions for the Defence of Harbours and Channels, *Parl. Papers* 5 (1866) : v. U.S.S. *Cairo* was the first warship sunk by mine warfare. *Civil War Naval Chronology* (Washington, D.C., 1971), pp. 349–53.

79. See "Offensive Torpedo Warfare," *Naval Science* 2 (1873) : 148; C. Sleeman, *Torpedoes and Torpedo Warfare* (London, 1880), p. 5.

80. Robinson to Board, Adm. I, 5991 (16 March 1866).

81. Controller's Sumbission, Adm. I, 6018 (22 May 1867).

82. Admiralty, *A Manual of Gunnery* (1868), pp. 156–58. A writer, who may have been E. J. Reed, commented that "No wise officer would follow such instructions." "Offensive Torpedo Warfare," *Naval Science* 2 (1873) : 151; Comdr. William Dawson, "Offensive Torpedo Warfare," *Journal of R.U.S.I.* 15 (1871) : 92.

83. In the closing days of the American Civil War the Federals had introduced a torpedo vessel that could, it was claimed, shoot javelin-like torpedoes underwater by mechanical means for a distance of over 100 feet. Lieutenant Comdr. J. S. Barnes, *Submarine Warfare* (New York, 1869), p. 154–59.

84. Herbert C. Fyfe, *Submarine Warfare, Past, Present and Future* (London, 1902), pp. 214–33; Admiralty, *Report of the Committee on Whitehead's Torpedo* (London, 1870), passim: F. M. Barber, *Lecture on the Whitehead Torpedo*, (Newport, R. I., U.S. Torpedo Station, 1874); Simpson, *Naval Mission to Europe*, 1:175–76, termed the Whitehead torpedo "remarkably successful," but limited its effectiveness to coast

and harbor defenses because of its range of only six hundred feet. Cf. "Guns," *Autobiography of a Whitehead Torpedo* (London, 1876) ; Maj. R. H. Stotherd, *Torpedoes Offensive and Defensive* (Washington, D.C., Government Printing Office, 1872) ; F. Harvey, *Introduction to the Harvey Torpedo*, (London, 1875).

85. Comdr. G. H. U. Noel, *The Gun, Ram, and Torpedo* (London, 1874), pp. 83-91; Dawson, "Offensive Torpedo Warfare," pp. 86-110; Comdr. Philip H. Colomb, *Essays on Naval Defence* (London, 1893), pp. 293-95. The perfecting of the Whitehead torpedo may well have been also retarded by the opinion expressed by Noel, who won the Junior Naval Professional Association's Gold Medal for his essay: "I am sure that many generous hearts would gladly spare even the foe so dire an affliction." Noel, *Gun, Ram, and Torpedo*, p. 8

86. "Offensive Torpedo Warfare," *Naval Science* 2 (1873) : 139. Reed also doubted the practicability of the Whitehead torpedo at sea, an opinion shared by Dawson, "Offensive Torpedo Warfare," pp. 105-6; Robert Mallet, F.R.S., "Subaqueous Torpedos," *Naval Science* 1 (1872) : 271; "Naval Tactics in England," *Naval Science* 3 (1874) : 422.

87. Comdr. John A. Fisher, *A Treatise on Electricity* (Portsmouth, 1871).

88. Admiralty, *Torpedo Manual for Her Majesty's Fleet* 2 (London, 1877).

89. See Maj. R. H. Stotherd, "Defensive Submarine Warfare," *Journal of R.U.S.I.* 15 (1871) : 707.

90 Simpson, *Naval Mission to Europe*, 1:171-74; Fisher, *Treatise on Electricity*; Stotherd, *Torpedoes, Offensive and Defensive*.

91. Maj. R. H. Stotherd, "Defensive Torpedo Warfare," *Journal of R.U.S.I.* 15 (1871) : 713.

92. Foreign Office Memorandum, 23 May 1862, Palmerston MSS.

93. Reed, *Our Iron-Clad Ships*, p. 85.

94. Admiralty, *Torpedo Manual* 2: 181-90.

95. Mallet, "Subaqueous Torpedoes," p. 273.

96. In the succinct words of Fisher (writing in 1869), "As yet there has been no real torpedo warfare." *Treatise on Electricity*, p. 1. Yet the Confederates sank four Union monitors in the Civil War. R. H. Webber, ed. *Monitors of the U.S. Navy, 1861-1937* (Washington, D.C., 1969), p. 24.

97. As late as 1880, Sleeman, *Torpedoes and Torpedo Warfare*, p. 9, wrote of the "moral effect of torpedoes which is, undoubtedly, the very essence of the vast power of those terrible engines of war." The automobile torpedo was first used by the *Shah* in her clash with the *Huascar*, 1877. The attack was unsuccessful.

98. See chap. 5.

Chapter 5 : Tactics and the Ram

1. For a vivid description of ironclad construction see Charles Dickens,

Uncommercial Traveller, Hawarden Press ed. (London, 1899), pp. 347-51.

2. British naval observers almost completely ignored tactics in their reports on the American Civil War. Cf. chaps. 2, 7. For early ironclad engagements in South America, cf. Official Dispatches from Rear-Admiral De Horsey Reporting the Encounter Between H.B.M.S. Shah and Amethyst, and the Peruvian . . . Huascar, 1877, *Parliamentary Papers* 52 (1877): 717-42; H. W. Wilson, *Ironclads in Action* (London, 1896), 1:307-12; W. L. Laird Clowes, *The Royal Navy* (London, 1903), 7:285-89; W. L. Laird Clowes, *Four Modern Naval Campaigns* (London, 1902), pp. 73-131; Lieutenant T. B. Mason, *The War . . . Between Chile and the Allied Republics of Peru and Bolivia* (Washington, 1883); Admiralty, *Official Report of the Action Between the Peruvian Ironclad Huascar and the Chilean Fleet* (1880); *Army and Navy Gazette* 14 and 21 July 1877.

3. Comdr. Philip H. Colomb, "Modern Naval Tactics," *Journal of the Royal United Service Institution* 9 (1865): 2. As late as 1893 Colomb could complain that as yet no book existed dealing with the whole field of naval tactics and strategy. *Essays on Naval Defence* (London, 1893), p. iii.

4. *Army and Navy Gazette,* 2 October 1869, p. 1.

5. For example, cf. Admiralty I, 5816 (18 April 1863), and publications noted below.

6. Adm. Sir Cyprian Bridge, "The Past and Future of Naval Tactics," *Edinburgh Review,* 18 October 1872, p. 560. Also his "Fifty Years' Architectural Expression of Tactical Ideas," *Transactions of the Institution of Naval Architects* 53 (1911): 32-45. Bridge noted that this unsatisfactory tactical situation coincided with "a particularly brilliant period in the history of Naval architecture." p. 40.

7. Adm. Sir Cyprian Bridge, "Fleet Evolutions and Naval Tactics," *Naval Science* 2 (1873): 341. Cf. same article, plus service reactions, in *Journal of R.U.S.I.* 17 (1873): 227-49.

8. "Naval Autumn Manoeuvres," *Naval Science* 2 (1873): 1-12.

9. Gen. Sir Howard Douglas, *On Naval Warfare With Steam* (London, 1858). Four years previous, a Captain Moorsom had formulated *Suggestions for the Organization and Manoeuvers of Steam Fleets* (London, 1854), in which he had made provision for a number of echelon formations. But his work was more concerned with steam evolutions than tactics, and seems to have wielded little influence on service opinion or the Admiralty.

10. Lieutenant Duncan Stewart, *Notes on Steam Evolutions and their Bearing on Naval Gunnery* (Edinburgh, 1862), private printing.

11. D. M. Schurman, *The Education of a Navy* (London and Chicago, 1965), pp. 36-59.

12. P. H. Colomb, "Modern Naval Tactics," pp. 1–28.

13. Lieutenant A. H. Alston, "Remarks on the New Steam Tactics," British Museum, Add. MSS 41411, vol. 569, pp. 264–67.

14. Adm. William Fanshawe Martin, *Observations on the Scheme for Screw Evolutions* (Malta, 1863), p. 14. Cf. also Martin MSS, British Museum, Add. MSS 41411, vol. 569.

15. Douglas, *On Naval Warfare With Steam*, p. 116.

16. Bridge, "Fleet Evolutions and Naval Tactics," p. 333. Admiral Phipps Hornby (ca. 1870) still preferred line-ahead formation since it was the easiest to maintain. But it suffered from the disadvantages of all ships repeating the leader's mistakes and of delay, and from the necessity of repeating all signals from the flagship. Although clearly superior, in Admiral Hornby's view, to other formations, line-ahead suffered the further defect that ships could not cover each other with gunfire. Phipps Hornby MSS, National Maritime Museum, Greenwich, PHI 111 (n.d.); cf. also testimony on the other side of Admiral Robinson before the Committee on Designs, terming line-ahead "the very worst arrangement possible for ironclad steamships." *Parl. Papers* 14 (1872): 67.

17. Comdr. John A. Fisher, *Naval Tactics* (London, 1871), private printing. Arthur J. Marder, *Fear God and Dreadnought* (London, 1952), 1:80, 338–39.

18. That is, for boarding. British Museum, Add. MSS 41441 (18 July 1867). This advice must have been well received, for as late as 1873, ships' companies were still organized into boarding parties. Admiralty, *A Manual of Gunnery for Her Majesty's Fleet* (1873), p. 5.

19. Adm. I, 5981 (11 August 1866). At least one Admiralty lord, Lord John Hay, agreed with Key on the peculiar moral value of sail. Ibid.

20. See "Turret and Broadside Ironclads," *Colburn's United Service Magazine* (1867) pt. 1, p. 249; "Turret Ships," ibid. (1866) pt. 1, p. 97; Report of Admiralty Committee on Turret Ships, *Parl. Papers* 47 (1866); Reed to Robinson, Adm. I, 5891 (3 August 1864).

21. *Times* (London), 14 August 1866, p. 8.

22. "Naval Tactics," *Colburn's United Service Magazine* (1867), pt. 2, p. 165. Although general Service opinion seemed to agree that fleet actions would consist of close-action melees, there were exceptions. Cf. *Standard*, 25 January 1865; [M. H. Jansen], *The Revolution in Naval Warfare* (London, 1867), p. 3; John Scott Russell, *The Modern System of Naval Architecture*, 3 vols. (London, 1865), 1:551.

23. Adm. I, 6020 (6 December 1867).

24. Admiralty, *Naval Evolutions* (1867). The fighting instructions were reproduced in Admiralty, *Manual of Fleet Evolutions* (1875).

25. Capt. E. A. Inglefield, "Naval Tactics," *Journal of R.U.S.I.* 12 (1868): 483–97.

26 Adm. I, 6097 (19 January 1869).

27. Bridge, "Fleet Evolutions and Naval Tactics," pp. 332-43.

28. "Naval Tactics," *Naval Science* 1 (1872) : 15-25.

29. P. H. Colomb, "Modern Naval Tactics," p. 4.

30. "Tactical Results of Recent Naval Construction," *Naval Science* 2 (1873) : 138.

31. For the earliest steam ram projects, some from France and the United States dating from the 1820s, see James P. Baxter III, *Introduction of the Ironclad Warship* (Cambridge, Mass., 1933 ; 1968) pp. 337-41.

32. *Times* (London), 14 September, p. 7 ; ibid., 11 November 1858, p. 10 ; *Journal of R.U.S.I.* 16 (1872) : 75-76.

33. *Times* (London), 9 October 1858, p. 4 ; ibid., 12 July 1859, p. 12 ; Duncan Campbell, *Steam Rams* (Edinburgh, 1870), private printing. A search of Admiralty records fails to substantiate Campbell's claims.

34. Adm. Gregorie Boutakov, *Nouvelles Bases de Tactique*, trans. H. de la Planche (Paris, [1867]).

35. Adm. S. S. Robison, *A History of Naval Tactics* (Annapolis, 1942), p. 681; Comdr. Philip H. Colomb, "The Attack and Defence of Fleets," *Journal of R.U.S.I.* 15 (1871) : 426.

36. Adm. G. R. Satorius, "On the Forms, Armaments, Materials, and Construction of Vessels of War," *Transactions of IN.A.* 5 (1864) : 134-45.

37. Ibid., p. 141. The Admiralty was not nearly so charitable to Satorius's projects, mainly because of the controller's adverse reports. Cf. Robinson to Board, Adm. I, 6079 (15 January 1868).

38. Persano's main qualification seemed to be, in the words of a contemporary, that he was "connu dupuis longtemps dans les salons de Turin et de Gênes." C. E. Lullier, *Essai sur l'Histoire de la Tactique Navale* (Paris, 1867), p. 283.

39. For the Battle of Lissa, cf. Admiralty (Intelligence Department), *Modern Naval Operations* (1901), pp. 6-14 ; Clowes, *Four Modern Naval Campaigns*, pp. 1-72 ; Adm. Sir Reginald Custance, *The Ship of the Line in Battle* (London, 1912), pp. 47-73 ; Edward Kirk Rawson, *Twenty Famous Naval Battles* (London, 1900), pp. 533-65 ; Wilson, *Ironclads in Action*, 211-51 ; F. von Attlmayr, *Der Krieg im der Adria im Jahre 1866* (Pola, 1896) ; *Osterreichs Kampfe im Jahre 1866* (Official Austrian Staff History), vol. 5 (Vienna, 1869) ; H. R. Steyskal, *Die Seeschlacht bei Lissa 1866/1966* (Vienna, 1966), (excellent photographs of entire Austrian fleet at Lissa) ; A. Iachino, *La Campagna Navale Di Lissa, 1866* (Milan, 1966), (good illustrations of ships and personnel, maps and diagrams) ; G. Randaccio, *Storia della Marina Militare Italiano dal 1860 al 1870* (Rome, 1881) ; Lullier, *Essai*, pp. 283-300 ; Ufficio Storicio Della Marina Militare, *Le Navi Di Linea Italiane 1861-1961* (Rome, 1962 ; 1969), pp. 41-154 ; Cf. also A. Sokol, *The Imperial and Royal Austrian-Hungarian Navy* (An-

napolis, 1968) ; Ing. Petar Mardešic, "Viska Bitka," pp. 21–69, in *Dvištvo Za Proučavanje I Unapredenje Pomorstva Jugoslavije U Zadru* (Zadar, 1967), (contains diagrams and drawings of warships involved) ; J. R. Coutts-Smith, "Document: The Battle of Lissa," *Mariner's Mirror* (August 1965), pp. 265–69. The order of objectives presented to Persano by the Italo-Sardinian Minister of Marine is instructive: "As soon as the *Affondatore* rejoins the squadron, you will put out to sea, and direct the fleet against the fortresses, the coast, and the fleet of the enemy." Lullier, *Essai*, p. 284.

40. Adm. I, 5977 (September 1866).
41. "The Naval Action off Lissa," *Colburn's United Service Magazine* (1866), pt. 3, pp. 77–78.
42. Comdr. Philip H. Colomb, "Lessons From Lissa," *Journal of R.U.S.I.*, 11 (1867) : 104–26.
43. Pownell Pellew, "Fleet Manoeuvring," *Journal of R.U.S.I.* 11 (1867) : 527–41.
44. Ibid., p. 543.
45. Reports, etc. Relative to Trials of the Channel Fleet in 1868, *Parl. Papers* 45 (1867–68) : 405.
46. Paget to Board, Adm. I, 6049 (25 August 1868). Cf. also Admiral Symonds to first lord expressing similar opinions. Adm. I, 6104 (20 January 1869).
47. Adm. I, 6020 (6 December 1867).
48. E. J. Reed, "On Iron-Cased Ships of War," *Transactions of I.N.A.* 4 (1863) : 35; Reed, *Our Iron-Clad Ships* (London, 1869), pp. 255–90.
49. *Times* (London), 8 August 1870, p. 10.
50. Robinson to Board, Adm. I, 6138 (3 February 1869).
51. Adm. I, 6079 (15 January 1868). Three years previous Reed had noted in exasperation: "Now in the first place we all know that it is very easy to talk about small high speed ships, but that it is very difficult to produce them. Every shipbuilder knows that it is much easier to get high speed in a large ship than in a small one." *Transactions of I.N.A.* 6 (1865) : 89.
52. Adm. I, 6049 (n.d., filed under *1868*).
53. Inglefield, "Naval Tactics," p. 500.
54. Ibid., pp. 497–98.
55. John Scott Russell, "The Fleet of the Future: For Commerce—for War", *Transactions of I.N.A.* 11 (1870) : 72–73. For another fanciful account of a naval battle of the future, also written in 1870, cf. *The Battle of the Ironclads* (London, 1871). In this tale of naval battles between Britain and France, and the United States and Prussia, the victory goes to the former through the power of the gun, torpedo, boarding and, most important, the ram.
56. *Naval and Military Gazette*, 15 February 1868, p. 105.

57. *Journal of R.U.S.I.* 12 (1868) : p. 499.
58. Adm. Sir Edward Belcher, "Naval Construction," *Transactions of I.N.A.* 9 (1868) : 162-76.
59. "Foreign Navies," *Colburn's United Service Magazine* (1869), pt. 3, p. 555. Lullier agreed that Lissa's lesson was "de plus clairement et nettoyment: que le personnel d'un flotte ne s'improvise pas." *Essai*, p. 297.
60. Disraeli to Lord Derby, January 1868, in Buckle and Monypenny, *Life of Disraeli*, 4: 579.
61. *Times* (London), 27 July 1870, p. 4; ibid., 13 July 1870, p. 4; ibid., 19 August 1870, p. 3. Strangely, a number of Admiralty warships of the time, including some of the large armored designs that Admiral Sartorius so scorned were fitted with 'flooding devices to increase their immersion, but to what purpose even the authoritative Oscar Parkes could give no definite answer, although the idea was presumably to present a smaller target. Parkes, *British Battleships, 1860-1950* (London, 1957; 1966) p. 172.
62. Adm. I, 6097 (18 January 1869).
63. Report of the Committee on Designs, *Parl. Papers* 14 (1872) : xix.
64. Ibid., p. 73.
65. Ibid., p. 130.
66. Ibid., p. 83.
67. Ibid., p. 86.
68. Report of Admiral George Elliot and Rear Admiral A. P. Ryder . . . Dissenting from the Report of the Committee on Designs, *Parl. Papers* 14 (1872) : 993-1060.
69. P. H. Colomb, *Essays on Naval Defence*; idem, "Attack and Defence of Fleets," pp. 405-37; *Journal of R.U.S.I.* 16 (1872) : 1-24.
70. Staff Comdr. Philip Going, "Ramming as a Mode of Naval Warfare," *Proceedings of the Junior Naval Professional Association* 3 (1873) : 245-58.
71. Comdr. Wallace B. Hardy, "The Heavy Gun *vs.* the Ram and Torpedo," *Proceedings of Junior Naval Professional Association* 3 (1873) : 272.
72. Comdr. G. H. U. Noel, *The Gun, Ram, and Torpedo* (Portsmouth, 1874), pp. 73-82.
73. John K. Laughton, "Essay on Naval Tactics," in Noel, *Gun, Ram, and Torpedo*, pp. 42-50. A French author, C. Chabaud-Arnault, called for *sang-froid et un coup d'oeil* in ramming. *Histoire des flottes militaires* (Paris, 1889), p. 452.
74. Thomas Brassey, *The British Navy* (London, 1882), 1:267.
75. Nathaniel Barnaby, *Naval Development of the Century* (London, 1904), p. 89.
76. W. L. Laird Clowes, "The Ram in Action and in Accident," *Journal of R.U.S.I.* 38 (1894) : 223-33.
77. Bridge, "Fifty Years," p. 40.

Chapter 6: Deployment

1. L. G. Carr Laughton, "The Writing of Naval History," *Mariner's Mirror* 10 (1924) : 19.
2. Somerset to Palmerston, 11 January 1862, Palmerston MSS. As late as 1865 Somerset asserted that "it seems the best policy to place the iron-clads in reserve, and use our old wooden ships during a time of peace." Somerset to Gladstone [1865?], Gladstone MSS, Additional MSS 44304.
3. Robinson to Board, Admiralty I, 6138 (3 February 1869).
4. Ibid., Adm. I, 5840 (11 February 1863).
5. Iron-hulled ironclads posed a particular problem in fouling. The wooden warships of the Royal Navy had been protected against the under-water growth of marine organisms on their hulls by the attachment of copper sheathing. But copper attached to iron produced a galvanic action that ate away both metals. An expensive and complicated solution was to line the hull with two courses of timber, to which insulation was affixed the copper. Experiments with zinc and Muntz-metal sheathing led to bottoms that resembled "a lawyer's wig." Event-ually, the age-old method of docking and scraping was returned to. See Oscar Parkes, *British Battleships, 1860-1950* (London, 1957; 1966), p. 160.
6. For examples of the influence of this philosophy on naval writing, see Patrick Barry, *Dockyard Economy and Naval Power* (London, 1863), pp. 183-85; Capt. J. C. R. Colomb wrote that "a pirate or privateer is a common enemy, and unheard of in those days except in the China seas." *The Protection of Our Commerce and Distribution of our Naval Forces Considered* (London, 1867), p. 17.
7. Palmerston to Somerset, 6 September 1864, Somerset MSS. Six years later Admiral Robinson made the identical point. Robinson to Board, Adm. I, 6177 (22 January 1870) ; ibid., (9 April 1870).
8. Reed to Controller (Admiral Robinson), "Constructor's Report on *In-constant*," Committee on Designs, *Parliamentary Papers* 14 (1872), App. A, IV, p. 291.
9. Lennox to Disraeli, 12 January 1867, Disraeli MSS, B/XX/LX/256. It must be remembered that the United States was not a signatory of the Treaty of Paris, outlawing privateering. Cf. statement of Admiral Robinson, Trials of the Channel and Mediterranean Squadrons, *Parl. Papers* 44 (1870) : 13.
10. Dacres memorandum to Board, 1 December 1866, Milne MSS, MLN/P/B1.
11. Lennox to Disraeli, 27 October 1866, Disraeli MSS, B/XX/LX/45; 13 December 1866, B/XX/LX/249.
12. Committee on Designs, *Parl. Papers* 14 (1872) : 317. Reed and Robin-son had powerful forces opposing them. The *Times* called for fast, wooden, unarmored ships, 14 February 1868, p. 7; the influential Capt. J. C. R. Colomb advocated the protection of commerce by small cruisers

in time of peace. *On the Distribution of Our War Forces* (London, 1869), p. 27. A further consideration for the board was that wooden cruisers would not be subject to fouling, as would iron ships.

13. Capt. W. Horton, "The Necessity for Building Unarmoured Ships of War," *Journal of the Royal United Service Institution* 10 (1866): 1–26.

14. Speech by the First Lord H. T. L. Corry, Hansard, *Parliamentary Debates* 192 (1868): 37.

15. Milne MSS. December 1866, MLN P/B/1/c.

16. Ibid., December 1867.

17. Disraeli to Lord Derby, 28 January 1868, George E. Buckle and William F. Monypenny, *The Life of Benjamin Disraeli, Earl of Beaconsfield*, 6 vols. (London, 1916), 4: 572.

18. Lennox to Disraeli, 5 January 1868, Disraeli MSS, B/XX/LX/270 (Lennox's italics).

19. Hansard, *Parl. Debates* 185 (1867): 1838. A similar proposal had been advanced by the *Naval and Military Gazette* the year previous. 8 December 1866, p. 777.

20. Objections to the Admiralty's policy of employing unarmored cruisers were summarized by Capt. Jasper Selwyn, who wondered about the outcome of a battle between such cruisers and "one of those wretched little armoured tubs" that could be found in American waters. Here was a precise foreshadowing of the *Shah-Huascar* clash. "The Necessity for Building Unarmoured Ships," *Journal of R.U.S.I.* 10 (1866): 31.

21. The concept of convoy protection was considered useless at this time. Cf. *Transactions of the Institute of Naval Architects* 11 (1870): 76 for views on this.

22. Somerset to Palmerston, April 1862, Palmerston MSS.

23. Naval Defence of the Colonies, *Parl. Papers* 1 (1865): 189.

24. J. C. R. Colomb, *Distribution of Our War Forces*, p. 27. Nathaniel Barnaby, while chief constructor, called for seagoing colonial defense ironclads as well as harbor monitors. Not until the twentieth century did any first-class colonial ironclads materialize. "English Naval Policy," *Naval Science*, 1 (1872): 39–40.

25. W. G. Romaine (Admiralty Second Secretary) to Sir John Pakington, Adm. I, 5977 (19 September 1866). J. C. R. Colomb assumed that all important colonies would be defended "from home." *Distribution of Our War Forces*, p. 5.

26. Testimony of Admiral Robinson, Committee on Designs, *Parl. Papers* 14 (1872): 169–70, 316.

27. As with each one of Reed's designs, the *Audacious* class came in for violent criticism. *Blackwood's* termed the class "the most miserable failure which has yet been made by any naval architect in the Kingdom." "The British Navy, What We Have, and What We Want," *Blackwood's* (March 1871), p. 362. Cf. also C. F. Henwood, "Ironclads

Present and Future," *Journal of R.U.S.I.* 14 (1870) : 148-74, for violent criticism of the design.

28. Committee on Designs, *Parl. Papers* 14 (1872) : xiv, xvi.

29. Report of Admiral George Elliot and Rear Admiral A. P. Ryder . . . Dissenting from the Report of the Committee on Designs, *Parl. Papers* 14 (1872) : 1017.

30. "Report of the Committee on Admiralty Designs," *Naval Science* 1 (1872) : 166-67. This criticism, of course, ignored the committee's recommendation that unarmored cruisers contend with commerce raiders.

31. *Proceedings of the Institution of Civil Engineers* 33 (1871-72), pt. 1, p. 337.

32. Early demands for a consistent policy of global mercantile and colonial defense came from Capt. J. C. R. Colomb, "General Principles of Naval Organization," *Journal of R.U.S.I.* 15 (1871) : 270, and W. Drummond Jervois, *Defensive Policy of Great Britain* (London, 1871) : 9-10.

33. Lt. Col. F. J. Soady, "Observations on the Defence of England," *Journal of R.U.S.I.* 14 (1870) : 570

34. Minute by the Defence Committee, *Parl. Papers* 41 (1860) : 2; J. C. R. Colomb agreed that "Our outposts are safe from the attacks of European powers so long as we command the Channel and Mediterranean." *The Protection of Our Commerce and Distribution of Our Naval Forces Considered* (London, 1867), p. 24; cf. also [M. H. Jansen], *The Revolution in Naval Warfare* (London, 1867), p. 56; "Our Coast Defences," *Macmillan's Magazine* (September 1870), p. 564.

35. Arthur J. Marder, *British Naval Policy* (London, 1940), p. 45.

36. J. C. R. Colomb, *Distribution of Our War Forces*, p. 27; *Nautical Magazine* concluded: "Our insular position requires a defensive rather than an aggressive warfare." "Our Unprotected Harbour and Coast Defences," *Nautical Magazine* 40 (1871) : 283.

37. "A General Outline of the Wants of the Navy at the Present Moment with Reference to Ships," Adm. I, 5981 (23 August 1866).

38. Robinson to Board, Adm. I, 6138 (3 February 1869).

39. Adm. G. A. Ballard, "The Black Battlefleet," *Mariner's Mirror* 15 (1929) : 112. Cf. "Turret Ships," *Colburn's United Service Magazine* (1866), pt. 1, p. 93.

40. *Engineer*, 22 November 1867, p. 435.

41. "Our Unprotected Harbour and Coast Defences," *Nautical Magazine* 40 (1871) : 281. Cf. also the *Standard*, 21 August 1866: "The enemy might send out one or two fleets for the special purpose of occupying the attention of our large ships while his monitors ran up the Thames and laid London under tribute." Cf. also *Naval and Military Gazette*, 21 March 1868, for even more farfetched fears.

42. Hansard, *Parl. Debates* 205 (1871) : 678; cf. also Barry, *Dockyard*

Economy and Naval Power, p. 163; "Letter to Arthur W. Peel, Esq., M.P." (Dundee, 1871), p. 4, and W. Drummond Jervois, *The Defensive Policy of Great Britain* (London, 1871), p. 11, which voice identical alarms.

43. Robinson to Board, Adm. I, 5848 (11 February 1863). Reed's views on coastal defenses are summarized in his *Our Naval Coast Defences* (London, 1871), and in idem, "The Navy," *Macmillan's Magazine,* November 1870, pp. 8-9, and before the Committee on Designs.

44. Admiralty, "Correspondence on New Designs for Armor-clads," p. 3. Cf. Chap. 7.

45. See testimony of Admiral Robinson before Committee on Designs, p. 71; J. C. R. Colomb, *Protection of Our Commerce*, pp. 11-12; "Naval Warfare," *Colburn's United Service Magazine* (1870), pt. 3, pp. 493-505.

46. *Times* (London), 29 November 1866, p. 6.

47. Capt. A. B. Tulloch, "On the Protection of London Against an Invading Force Landing on the East Coast," *Journal of R.U.S.I.* 14 (1870): 357; Lt. Col. F. J. Soady, "Observations on the Defence of England," ibid., 14 (1870): 570-84. I. F. Clarke, *Voices Prophesying War* (London and New York, 1966), pp. 30-63.

48. William Vernon Harcourt, "Our Naval and Military Establishments With Reference to the Dangers of Invasion," *Journal of R.U.S.I.* 16 (1872): 575-93.

49. Memorandum by Adm. Sir Sidney Dacres, Adm. I, 6159 (8 August 1870). Cf. similar memorandum by Admiral Symonds, Adm. I, 6014 (20 January 1869).

50. Robinson to Board, Adm. I, 6138 (2 March 1869).

51. E. J. Reed, *Modern Ships of War* (London, 1889), p. 16. Cf. also his statement before the Committee on Designs, *Parl. Papers* 14 (1872): 151: "She was designed strictly upon orders which I received, the source and object of which I was never acquainted with."

52. Committee on Designs, *Parl. Papers* 14 (1872): 151.

53. Ibid., p. 312. Perhaps the best explanation for the *Glatton* was given by Lord Lennox in a letter to Disraeli "The argument in favour of this ship is that it would be popular with the general public, as showing that the Admiralty were anxious to make use of the latest invention, 'America model.'" 12 January 1867, Disraeli MSS, B/XX/LX/256.

54. Childers to Gladstone, 19 December 1870, Add. MSS 44128, f. 197.

55. Robinson to Dacres, 6 August 1870, Milne MSS, MLN/P/B/1.

56. Parkes, *British Battleships*, p. 212. For a defense of these ships by their designer, see Nathaniel Barnaby, "Modern Ships of War," *Journal of R.U.S.I.* 16 (1872): 67.

57. Reed, *Modern Ships of War*, p. 34.

58. Unfortunately, E. J. Reed was the author of this scheme. Cf. his *Our*

Naval Coast Defences, and *Broad Arrow*, 20 May 1871, p. 611. It was taken up by *Blackwood*'s. "The British Navy, What We Have, What We Want," *Blackwood*'s (March 1871), p. 373.

59. Milne to Board, 5 February 1873, Milne MSS, MLN P/B/1/(c). A useful contemporary explication of the need for coastal defense-offense ironclads is to be found in William Fairbairn's "The Present and Past Construction of the Navy," *Transcriptions of I.N.A.* 12 (1871): 208–11. In the discussion following, E. J. Reed agreed with Fairbairn's call for more coastal ironclads.

60. Committee on Designs, *Parl. Papers* 14 (1872): xvii.

61. *Transactions of I.N.A.* 9 (1868): 215. For the post-Reed coastal iron-clad policy, see speech by J. G. Goschen, Hansard, *Parl. Debates* 205 (1871): 706.

62. Admiralty, *Steam Ships of the Navy* (1868–1884); Admiralty, *Ships' Covers*.

63. John Scott Russell, *The Fleet of the Future, 1862* (London, 1862), p. 40. One of the rare criticisms of coastal ironclads is found in "On a Further Reconstruction of the Navy," *Cornhill Magazine* (December 1861), p. 718.

64. Robinson to Board, Adm. I, 6138 (2 March 1869).

65. "A Review of the Present Conditions of Naval Design," *Annual of the School of Naval Architecture* (January 1872), p. 34.

66. Hansard, *Parl. Debates* 79 (1899): 1362.

Chapter 7: Captain Coles and the Turret Warship

1. W. L. Burn, *The Age of Equipoise* (London, 1964), p. 233.

2. James P. Baxter III, *The Introduction of the Ironclad Warship* (Cambridge, Mass., 1933; 1968), pp. 185–95.

3. Capt. Cowper Phipps Coles, *English versus American Cupolas: A Comparison Between Captain Coles' and Captain Ericsson's Turrets* (Portsea, 1864). Ericsson's claims to priority and superiority are found in U.S. National Archives Record Group 45, Microcopy 124 (1861–66); Ericsson MSS, Library of Congress, and Fox Papers, New York Historical Society. Ericsson particularly objected to the "gingerbread" machinery below deck of the Coles turret. Ericsson to John Bourne, 16 January 1866, Ericsson MSS. The great engineer I. K. Brunel proposed, also during the Crimean War, a small iron warship, carrying a hemispherical turret in which was mounted a single twelve-inch gun, with ammunition hoisted from a submerged hull and loaded into the breech mechanically. Apparently the turret did not revolve, for elaborate arrangements were proposed for forward and lateral movement

by means of steam jets. Numbers of these intriguing craft were to be carried within a screw steamship with bow doors, and floated out for battle. L. T. C. Rolt, *Isambard Kingdom Brunel, a Biography* (London, 1957), p. 170. Note should be made of the startlingly sophisticated and successful turrets developed by James Eads during the American Civil War and mounted in four Union monitors. Although the general structure resembled the Coles turret principles, the entire floor of the Eads turret dropped to the bearth deck for gun loading, below the waterline. The floor was then raised by steam power and the guns run out by the same agency. Upon discharge of the guns, recoil dropped the turret floor to the bearth deck to repeat the cycle. At the battle of Mobile Bay, the Eads-turreted *Chickasaw* and *Winnebago* hammered most effectively at the Confederate ironclad *Tennessee*. R. H. Webber, *Monitors of the U.S. Navy, 1861–1937* (Washington, D.C.: Department of the Navy, 1969) ; Thomas Brassey, *The British Navy* 5 vols. (London, 1882), 1:293–94.

4. For turret ship arguments, see Capt. Cowper Phipps Coles, "Shot-Proof Gun-Shields as Adapted to Iron-Cased Ships," *Journal of the R.U.S.I.* 4 (1860): 280; idem "Iron-clad Sea-Going Turret Ships," ibid., 7 (1863): 128; idem, "The Turret *vs.* the Broad-Side System," ibid., 11 (1867): 236–54; Report of the Admiralty Committee on Turret Ships, *Parliamentary Papers* 47 (1866). Voluminous material extolling the virtues of the turret ship are to be found in Coles's many pamphlets, letters to the Admiralty, and correspondence in the *Times* and in that of his supporters. These will be indicated in the text or in the bibliography.

5. For some of the arguments against turret ships, particularly for ocean cruising, see discussion following lectures by Captain Coles printed in *Journal of R.U.S.I.*, noted in n. 4 above; Papers Relating to Turret Ships (Navy), *Parl. Papers* 45 (1867–68) ; Report of Committee of Naval Officers on the Design of a Sea-Going Turret Ship, *Parl. Papers* 47 (1866) ; Admiral Sir F. W. Grey, *The Turret System* (London, 1868).

6. Admiralty, "Précis of Correspondence Between the Admiralty and Captain C. P. Coles," Admiralty I, 6108 (7 June 1869).

7. Coles, a half-pay officer, had agreed to an arrangement with the navy whereby he had received five thousand pounds for the Admiralty's exclusive right to his turrets, plus one hundred pounds for each turret built for a period of fourteen years. He also received three guineas expenses when employed as a consultant. "Duplicate Deed of Covenant, the Lords Commissioners of the Admiralty and Captain Coles," 19 November 1862, Admiralty Library. Coles could make his own arrangements with private builders, but these had to be approved by the board.

8. Coles to Admiralty, Adm. I, 5827 (15 July 1863) ; see also Adm. I, 5842 (21 October 1863) ; *Times* (London), 6 November 1863.

9. Admiralty to Coles, Adm. I, 5841 (24 July 1863).

10. Coles to Board, Adm. I, 5840 (18 February 1863).

11. Adm. I, 5840 (24 February 1863).

12. Admiralty to Controller, Adm. I, 5983 (6 March 1863).

13. Correspondence . . . Relative to the Design of a Sea-Going Turret Ship, *Parl. Papers* 47 (1866): 20.

14. Admiralty, Controller's Submission, Adm. I, 5841 (14 April 1863), 5, 7 May 1863). For sketch of Coles's turret ship of 1863, see pamphlet by Coles, *Letters from Capt. C. Coles to the Secretary of the Admiralty on Sea-Going Turret Ships* (London, 1865), and Correspondence *Parl. Papers* 47 (1866) : 156.

15. Admiralty to Coles, Adm. I, 5840 (5 March 1863). This offer was repeated to Coles on 30 June and 27 July 1863, ibid.

16. Coles to Admiralty, Adm. I, 5842 (2 October 1863) ; see also ibid., Adm. I, 5840 (19 March 1863).

17. Coles to Admiralty, Adm. I, 5840 (14 April 1863). Reed had, in fact, proposed that Coles be put in charge of a turret department in the Admiralty. E. J. Reed, *Modern Ships of War* (London, 1888), pp. 33-34.

18. *Times* (London), 26 March 1863, p. 7, and below.

19 *Punch*, 30 June, 7 July, and 25 August 1866; ibid, 27 June 1867.

20. Hansard, *Parliamentary Debates* 169 (1863): 695-98; ibid., 176 (1864): 1929; John Morley, *The Life of Richard Cobden* (London, 1883), pp. 875-76.

21. John Scott Russell, *The Modern System of Naval Architecture*, 3 vols. (London, 1865), 1:xxvii.

22. *Times* (London), 30 June 1864, p. 8; ibid., 9 August 1864, p. 6. Portraits of the Queen and Prince Consort occupied a prominent place in the *Royal Sovereign*'s captain's cabin.

23. Oscar Parkes, *British Battleships, 1680-1950* (London, 1957; 1966), p. 72.

24. Vansittart to Milne, Adm. 128, 60 (10 December 1862).

25. McKay to Robinson, Adm. I, 5859 (21 April 1863).

26. Milne to Board, Adm. I, 5820 (22 May 1863).

27. Rear Adm. Alexander Milne, "Memoranda Relative to the Civil War in America," Adm. I, 5871 (15 March 1864). Cf. similar reports by British Captains in America. Capt. R. Vesy Hamilton to Board, Adm. 128, 60 (1863) ; Captain Kennedy to Milne, Adm. I, 5820 (13 July 1863). Living conditions aboard federal monitors are vividly described in R. B. Ely, "This Filthy Ironpot," *American Heritage* 19, no. 2 (1968): 46-111. Less negative is W. F. Keeler, *Aboard the USS Monitor* (Annapolis, Md., 1964).

28. Foreign Office, "Occasions in the Civil War in America on which Forts and Guns have had the Best of it against Iron-Clad Ships." Palmerston MSS, 24 June 1863.

29. United States Executive Department, *Armoured Vessels in the Attack on*

Charleston (Washington, D.C., n.d.). Doubts were expressed about the monitor's seaworthiness as well (p. 175).

30. Admiralty, Controller to Board, Adm. I, 5892 (23 October 1863).

31. Admiralty to Coles, Adm. I, 5827 (15 July 1863); Controller's Submission, Adm. I, 5841 (9 June 1863); *Correspondence, Parl. Papers* 47 (1866): 22–23.

32. Controller's Submission, Adm. I, 5892 (5 November 1863).

33. Adm. I, 5840 (20 February 1863).

34. James D. Bullock, *The Secret Service of the Confederate States in Europe* (London, 1883), 1:390.

35. Lord John Russell, *The Later Correspondence of Lord John Russell*, ed. G. P. Gooch (London, 1925), 2:334.

36. Brooks Adams, "The Seizure of the Laird Rams," *Proceedings of the Massachusetts Historical Society* 45 (1911–12), p. 297. Cf. also Admiralty, *Correspondence between Her Majesty's Government and Messrs. Laird Bros. . . . Respecting the Ironclad Vessels Building at Birkenhead, 1863–64* (1864). The most authoritative account of the Laird rams episode is found in Frank Merli, *Great Britain and the Confederate Navy* (Bloomington, Ind., 1965; 1970), pp. 178–217. Also W. D. Jones, *The Confederate Rams at Birkenhead; A Chapter in Anglo-American Relations* (Tuscaloosa, Ala., 1961).

37. Palmerston to Somerset, 13 September 1863, Somerset MSS. He was just as determined that the confederates should not have the rams. Ibid., 19 September 1863.

38. Ibid., 16 September 1863.

39. Somerset to Palmerston, 15 September 1863, Palmerston, MSS.

40. Ibid., 18 September 1963.

41. Ibid., 19 September 1863.

42. *Times* (London), 12 October 1863, p. 11. The Duke of Somerset admitted that "the vessels are not good for much," in letter to Lord Russell, 18 February 1864, Russell MSS, PRO 30/22/26. Reed had previously inspected the rams and pointed out their weaknesses, but had felt that they might prove a "useful addition" for testing turret ships. Adm. I, 5842 (17 September 1863). A perusal of the Russell MSS indicates that a nervous foreign secretary pressured Somerset into buying two vessels of very problematical worth. Robinson believed them useless even for coastal defense. Channel Fleet, *Parl. Papers* 44 (1867): p. 15. Also Adm. I, 5943 (20 December 1865).

43. Adm. I, 6111 (16 September 1869). Further information on this intriguing chapter in mutiny is missing.

44. Captain James Graham Goodenough, "Report on Ships of United States," Adm. I, 5879 (21 October 1864); Donald McKay to Robinson, 15 March 1865, 18 April 1865, Somerset MSS.

45. McKay to Robinson, 14 February 1865, Somerset MSS. McKay main-

tained that hardly any federal naval officer could be found in favor of the monitor or the turret principle, and that even American naval constructors agreed with him. Ibid., 18 April 1865. Cf. report of naval attaché Captain Bythsea, critical of the seagoing and coastal monitors. Adm. I, 128 (25 July 1865). That year Reed termed the American monitor a "wretched, low-lying, ill-ventilated, wave-washed, unseaworthy abortion—'monitors' forsooth.'" E. J. Reed, "On Iron-Cased Ships of War," *Transactions of the Institution of Naval Architects* 4 (1863): 34.

46. *Journal of R.U.S.I.* 7 (1863): 150.
47. Controller's Submission, Adm. I, 5891 (7 September 1864).
48. Coles to Admiralty, Adm. I, 5891 (5 September 1864).
49. Correspondence, *Parl. Papers* 47 (1866): 18.
50. Hansard, *Parl. Debates* 182 (1866): 10.
51. Controller's Submission, Adm. I, 5935 (2 November 1865).
52. Coles to Admiralty, Adm. I, 5879 (10 October 1864).
53. Correspondence, *Parl. Papers* 48 (1866): 116; Reed to Board, Adm. I, 5892 (29 October 1864).
54. Coles to Board, Adm. I, 5892 (5 November 1864).
55. Reed to Board, Adm. I, 5892 (10 November 1864).
56. Coles to Admiralty, Adm. I, 5892 (22 November 1864).
57. Admiralty to Coles, Adm. I, 5892 (24 November 1864).
58. Ibid. Cf. also Adm. I, 5983 (30 October 1865).
59. Controller's Submission, Adm. I, 5942 (25 January 1865).
60. Hansard, *Parl. Debates* 177 (1865): 1379.
61. Ibid., p. 1184.
62. Ibid., p. 1414.
63. *Times* (London), 16 March 1865, p. 6.
64. Correspondence, *Parl. Papers* 47 (1866): 126; Controller's Submission, Adm. I, 5944 (28 June 1865); Adm. I, 5941 (3 April 1865).
65. Reed to Admiralty, Adm. I, 5841 (11 April 1865).
66. Ibid., Adm. I, 5942 (22 May 1865).
67. Controller's Submission, Adm. I, 5941 (26 April 1865).
68. Ibid. (8 April 1865).
69. Correspondence, *Parl. Papers* 47 (1866): 130–32. The *United Service Gazette* insisted that "nothing but the pressure of Parliament and the Press will induce the Admiralty to act honestly in the matter" (22 April 1865). The *Daily News* quoted Coles as writing that his enemies were taking advantage of his illness and would "like to crush me" (15 August 1865).
70. Report of the Admiralty Committee on Turret Ships, *Parl. Papers* 47 (1866): 42–44.
71. Ibid., pp. 49–51.
72. Ibid., pp. 54–59.

73. Ibid., p. 71.
74. Ibid., p. 87; also Controller's Submission, Adm. I, 5942 (28 June 1865).
75. Report of the Admiralty Committee on Turret Ships, *Parl. Papers* 47 (1866): 8, 76.
76. Admiralty to Coles, Adm. I, 5960 (5, 8 June 1865).
77. Correspondence, *Parl. Papers* 47 (1866): 131–34.
78. Admiralty, "Precis of Corresuondence," Adm. I, 6108 (11 July 1865).
79. Controller's Submission, Adm. I, 5942 (13 July 1865).
80. "Report of Trial and Turrets and Guns of the *Royal Sovereign.*" A. Cooper Key to Admiralty, Adm. I, 5943 (11 July 1865).
81. Admiralty, "Precis of Correspondence," Adm. I, 6018 (14 September 1865).
82. Correspondence, *Parl. Papers* 47 (1866): 138.
83. Cowper to Coles, *Report by Capt. C. P. Coles to Lord Charles Paget on Sea-Going Turret Ships* (London, 1865).
84. Adm. Sir Frederick Grey to Board, Adm. I, 5935 (n.d.).
85. Controller to Board, Adm. I, 5983 (30 October 1865).
86. Board of Admiralty to Controller, Adm. I, 5943 (9 October 1865).
87. Admiralty to Coles, Adm. I, 5983 (30 October 1865).
88. Correspondence, *Parl. Papers* 47 (1866): 171–77. In discussing the fact that Reed was to design the Admiralty's new turret ship, "A Conservative" wondered whether the chief constructor's name had been confounded with Coles's, or Reed had changed his opinion of turret ships, or the Admiralty had "gone stark, staring mad." *Standard*, 29 December 1865.
89. Controller's Submission, Adm. I, 5943 (27 October 1865).
90. Controller's Submission, Adm. I, 5983 (4 January 1866).
91. *Standard*, 10 January 1866.
92. Controller's Submission, Adm. I, 5980 (13 January 1866); Board Minute, Adm. I, 5980 (13, 16, and 19 January 1866). A depressed Captain Coles wrote to W. B. Ferrand, M.P.: "I feel, sir, from the first, that the Admiralty have merely been playing with me, and so long as they can keep me quiet and hide their own blunders, they care not." Cowper-Coles MSS, January 1866.
93. Controller's letter to Board, Adm. I, 5980 (10 January 1866).
94. Coles to Admiralty, Adm. I, 5980 (24 January 1866).
95. Ibid. (30 January 1866).
96. Correspondence, *Parl. Papers* 47 (1866): 6.
97. Ibid.; cf. Adm. I, 5980 (20, 22 February 1866).
98. *Transactions of I.N.A.* 7 (1865): xxii.
99. Hansard, *Parl. Debates* 182 (1866): 5.
100. Controller's Submission, Adm. I, 5980 (7 January 1865); ibid., Adm. I, 5981 (22 August 1866). Not that Robinson had any higher an appre-

ciation of the two rams than the Duke of Somerset. Adm. I, 5943 (20 December 1865).

101. Hansard, *Parl. Debates* 181 (1866): 1878.

102. Reed to Robinson, Adm. I, 5980 (10 and 30 January 1866).

103. Among these were the *Engineer, Standard, Daily News,* and *Naval and Military Gazette.* Henwood's proposals are contained in his *Textbook to the Turret and Tripod System of Captain Cowper P. Coles* (Paris, 1867); *Ironclads, Present and Future* (London, 1870); "Conversion of Our Screw Line-of-Battle Ships into Armoured Turret Ships," *Journal of R.U.S.I.* 13 (1869).

104. Robinson to Board, Adm. I, 5981 (6 July 1866).

105. Reed to Board, Adm. I, 5982 (20 October 1866). Robinson noted Henwood's "very erroneous calculations," Adm. I, 6017 (25 January 1867), and later expressed exasperation at the designer's "tendency to guess at, instead of ascertaining what the facts really are." Adm. I, 6018 (May 1867). Cf. statement by Lord Henry Lennox outlining Admiralty objections to Henwood's proposals, Hansard, *Parl. Debates* 185 (1867): 1847–48. Robinson's alternate scheme for utilizing the line-of-battleships is found in Adm. I, 5981 (6 July 1866). The bulk of the Henwood proposals and Reed and Robinson's criticisms are found in Adm. I, 6400 (17 December 1876).

106. Reed, "On the Stability of Monitors Under Canvas," *Transactions of I.N.A.* 9 (1868): 198–207; *Proceedings of the Institute of Civil Engineers* 26 (1867): 188; Reed, "On Iron-Clad Ships," pp. 98–99. John Scott Russell agreed with Reed on the probable inefficiency of the Henwood wooden monitors. *The Fleet of the Future, 1862* (London, 1862), p. 42. Cf. also Admiralty, *Correspondence on the Henwood Monitor* (1868).

107. *Army and Navy Gazette,* 21 March 1868.

108. Henwood, *Textbook,* contains Halsted's plans for multi-turret warships; Adm. E. Pellew Halsted, *A Turret Navy for the Future* (London, 1866); "The Turret and Tripod Systems of Captain Coles, R.N., C.B., as Exhibited at Paris," *Transactions of I.N.A.* 9 (1868): 115–45. The chairman of the institution told Pellew's audience that "his plan is perfect" (p. 153). The author of the official history of the institution remarks: "Such were the methods by which the public was being taught to believe that Reed and the other Admiralty Constructors were wilfully obstructing the brilliant ideas of Coles." Kenneth C. Barnaby, *The Institution of Naval Architects* (London, 1960), p. 57. Cf. also Robinson to Halsted, Adm. I, 6081 (14 July 1868). Admiralty, *Correspondence on the Henwood Monitor* (1868).

109. Plans in National Maritime Museum under "Duncan" (January 1867).

110. Hansard, *Parl. Debates* 181 (1866): 1160; see also ibid., 184 (1866): 1198.

111. Ibid., 182 (1866): 1330; ibid., p. 1329.
112. Ibid., p. 8.
113 *Times* (London), 1 January 1866, p. 7; cf. also ibid., 12 December 1865, pp. 8–9, and ibid., 30 October 1866, p. 7.
114. *United Service Gazette*, 13 January 1866, p. 4. Cf. also *Naval and Military Gazette*, 6 January 1866, p. 9. *London Review*, 3 February 1866.
115. Controller's Submission, Adm. I, 5983 (8 March 1866). This action was taken on the initiative of the controller, who recommended that "notwithstanding all that has passed," a tracing of the plans be sent to Coles. Adm. I, 5983 (11 January 1866).
116. Coles to Admiralty, Adm. I, 5983 (23 March 1866). Coles also objected that "as Mr. Reed has so signally failed in the speed of all his vessels" he would be no fit designer of the turret ship. Coles to Ferrand, 3 March 1866, Cowper-Coles MSS.
117. Admiralty, "Precis of Correspondence," Adm. I, 6018 (24 April 1866); Coles to Admiralty, Adm. I, 5970 (29 April 1866).
118. Admiralty to Coles, Adm. I, 5974 (24 April 1866).
119. Coles to Admiralty, Adm. I, 5983 (8 May 1866).
120. Reed to Board, Adm. I, 5983 (20 July 1866).
121. Controller's Submission, Adm. I, 5983 (20 July 1866).
122. Minute of the First Lord of the Admiralty with Reference to H.M.S. *Captain, Parl. Papers* 42 (1871): 662.
123. Coles to Admiralty, Adm. I, 5970 (24 July 1866).
124. *Times* (London), 16 June 1866, p. 9; [William H. White], "The Story of the Captain," *Gentleman's Magazine* (November 1870).
125. E. J. Reed, *Our Iron-Clad Ships* (London, 1869), p. 237.
126. Robinson to Board, Adm. I, 5983 (3 July 1866).
127. Reed to Board, Adm. I, 5983 (2 August 1866). Reed had privately complained that the Coles turret ship was "an unconcealed imitation" of the many structural advances made in shipbuilding since the *Bellerophon*. Reed to Robinson, Adm. I, 5997 (28 July 1866).
128. Admiralty to Messrs. Laird, Adm. I, 5983 (9 August 1866).
129. Messrs. Laird to Admiralty, Adm. I, 5983 (15 August 1866).
130. Minute of the First Lord, *Parl. Papers* 42 (1871): 707.
131. Ibid., pp. 716–17. Robinson urged "that great pains should be taken to conciliate Captain Coles and inform him of what had been done." Robinson to Board, Adm. I, 6027 (30 January 1867). Sir John Pakington, then First Lord, later explained that he had "shrunk very much" from Coles's proposed eight feet of freeboard, but "I did consent to it on this ground, that the principle on which I was acting was that Captain Coles should solve his own problems, and that as he pressed to have a ship with that freeboard, it would not have been consistent with the principle on which I was acting to interfere further than to express my doubts and fears with regard to the success of so low a

freeboard." President's Introductory Remarks, *Transactions of I.N.A.* 12 (1871): xxv. Pakington's First Sea Lord, Admiral Milne, voiced identical views. Letter to Pakington, 13 October 1870, Milne MSS, MLN P/A/1.

132. Controller to Board, Adm. I, 5942 (10 May 1865).

133. Coles to Admiralty, Adm. I, 5983 (19 November 1866).

134. Controller to Board, Adm. I, 5983 (12, 23 November 1866).

135. Admiralty to Coles, Adm. I, 5983 (11 December 1866).

136. Ibid.; Controller's Submission, Adm. I, 6017 (10 January 1867).

137. *Journal of R.U.S.I.* 11 (1867): 475

138. Admiralty, "Copy of the Reply made by Sir Robert Spencer Robinson to the Minute of the First Lord of the Admiralty," Adm. 116, 190 #12, (17 February 1871); printed copy in *Parl. Papers* 40 (1871).

139. Controller's Submission, Adm. I, 6017 (10, 14 January 1866).

140. Coles to Admiralty, Adm. I, 6017 (14, 19 January 1867).

141. Controller's Submission, Adm. I, 6917 (24 January 1867).

142. For contract giving details of arrangement of responsibility, see Admiralty, "Iron-plated, Twin-Screw Turret Ship," Adm. I, 5983 (n.d.).

143. Admiralty to Messrs. Laird, Adm. I, 6017 (25 January 1867).

144. Admiralty to Coles, Adm. I, 6018 (9 March 1867).

145. Capt. Cowper Phipps Coles, "The Turret vs. the Broadside System," *Journal of R.U.S.I.* 11 (1867): 434–53.

146. *Times* (London), 19 November 1867, p. 10. The Prince of Wales seemed to array his prestige behind the anti-Reed agitation when he stated: "Last year, or the year before, we might have supposed that our ships were as perfect as they needed to be; but now we find that very much more is wanting." *Times*, 27 March 1868, p. 9.

147. Admiralty Minute, Adm. I, 6018 (12 April 1867).

148. Ibid.

149. Reed to Admiralty, Adm. I, 6018 (27 July 1867).

150. Controller's Submission, Adm. I, 6079 (8 February 1868).

151. Robinson's reports on the submitted designs, and letter to the competitive firms informing them of the results of the competition are found in Adm. I, 6013 (October 1867). This Admiralty Board contained a strong turret party, consisting of Sir John Pakington (First Lord), Sir Sidney Dacres, and Sir John C. Hay. Yet the board unanimously agreed on the fairness of the reports of the controller and constructor on the turret designs. The *Times* termed the competition results a triumph of "prejudice and vanity." 27 March 1868, p. 9.

152. Papers Relative to Navy Designs for Ships, *Parl. Papers* 45 (1867-68).

153. Hansard, *Parl. Debates* 193 (1868): 1135–40.

154. Controller's Submission, Adm. I, 6081 (22 August 1868).

155. Minute of the First Lord, *Parl. Papers* 42 (1871): 869. Correspondence in Adm. I, 6068 (28 August; 1, 4 September 1868).

156. Adm. I, 6068 (28 August; 1, 4 September 1866).

157. *Standard,* 29 March 1869.
158. Minute of the First Lord, *Parl. Papers* 42 (1871): 668.
159. Ibid., p. 720.
160. Ibid., p. 669.
161. Reed to Admiralty, Adm. I, 6219 (3 February 1870).
162. *Times* (London), 12 February 1870, p. 4.
163. Minute of the First Lord, *Parl. Papers* 42 (1871): 670-71.
164. Ibid., p. 728. Lairds later excused the increased draught as something that often occurred in shipbuilding. They went on to assert that the deeper immersion could be considered as of positive benefit' as affording that much more protection against shot and ramming! *Times,* 24 August 1870, p. 4.
165. Spencer Childers, *The Life and Correspondence of the Rt. Hon. Hugh C. E. Childers, 1827–1896* (London, 1901), 1:215.
166. For naval administration in the 1860s, see Sir John Briggs, *Naval Administrations, 1827–1892* (London, 1897); Adm. Sir Richard Vesy Hamilton, *Naval Administration* (London, 1896); W. L. Laird Clowes, *The Royal Navy* (London, 1903), 7:1-11; Sir Oswey Murray, "The Admiralty," pt. viii, *Mariner's Mirror* 24 (October 1938); Select Committee on the Board of Admiralty, *Parl. Papers* 7 (1871); Robinson, *Results of Admiralty Organization* (London, 1871); Thomas Brassey, *Recent Naval Administration* (London, 1872).
167. Adm. G. A. Ballard, "The First Mastless Capital Ship," *Mariner's Mirror* 32 (1946): 12. Also cf. Norman McCord, "The Loss of H.M.S. *Magaera,*" ibid., 52 no. 2 (1971): 115-33. One recent authority asserts that Childers was the most mistrusted and disliked first lord of the nineteenth century. But Childers's positive achievements yet rank him as one of the great Victorian administrators: the officer's retirement scheme and the seagoing training squadron. Leslie Gardner, *The British Admiralty* (Edinburgh and London, 1968), pp. 278-82. On Childers, cf. also N. A. M. Rodger, "The Dark Ages of the Admiralty, 1869–1885," pt. 1, *Mariner's Mirror* (November 1975), pp. 335, 36, 344, and passim. Rodger notes that, with Childers, Reed and Robinson were Liberals among a largely and traditionally Conservative Board, and that Childers looked to Reed and Robinson as allies. Thus his chagrin at his deteriorating relations with these officials was the greater. Just when the break occurred cannot be pinpointed, for as late as 1869 Reed's *Our Ironclad Ships* carried a dedication to Childers.
168. Minute of the First Lord, *Parl. Papers* 42 (1871): 674. Robinson later explained to Childers that this request of Messrs. Laird was merely "made on the ground that it was an interesting piece of statistical science to obtain" for purposes of comparison with other ships. Ibid., App. p. 763.
169. Ibid., p. 670.

170. Controller to Board, Adm. I, 6178 (7 October 1870).
171. Minute of First Lord, *Parl. Papers* 42 (1871) : 720-51.
172. Ibid.
173. Ibid., p. 755.
174. *Times* (London), 9 July 1870, p. 9; ibid., 18 July 1870, p. 9. The *United Service Gazette* termed Robinson's report on the turret ships' cruises "a barefaced trick" (28 July 1870, p. 5), and an "untrue and garbled report absolutely transparent in its dishonesty," and accused him of tampering with Admiral Symonds's report (13 August 1870), p. 4).
175. Minute of the First Lord, *Parl. Papers* 42 (1871) : 753, 754.
176. Ibid., p. 675.
177. Ibid.
178. Quoted in Hansard, *Parl. Debates* 203 (1870) : 413; Minutes of Evidence, H.M.S. Captain Court Martial, *Parl. Papers* 62 (1871) : 839. Reed in December 1870 asserted that his post had been offered to Coles. *Times* (London), 21 December 1870, p. 12.
179. Letter in the *Times* (London), 12 August 1870. Reed was later more explicit. "The construction of the British Navy had obviously passed out of my hands into the hands of Captain Coles." "The Navy," *Macmillan's Magazine*, November 1870. Apparently internal Admiralty dissension had as much to do with Reed's resignation as did turrets. Adm. Sir Michael Seymour wrote to Admiral Milne that Reed, "whose impudence passes all belief," had engaged in a dispute over Whitworth guns. "The Controller was violent beyond measure," as well, with Reed "trying to make terms such as no one with an atom of self respect could listen to for an instant, in which he is backed up by Robinson." Milne MSS, 5 February and 5 May 1870. MLN/p/a/1.
180. Cf. the *Standard*, 12 and 19 July 1870; *Broad Arrow*, 16 July 1870; *Times* (London), 11 July 1870. The exception to this restraint was, predictably, the *United Service Gazette*, which termed Reed the Admiralty's "Obstructor" rather than constructor, and his close relationship with Robinson an "insult to the Service" (25 June and 23 July 1870).
181. *Times* (London), 8 August 1870, p. 10.
182. Ibid., 3 August 1870, p. 4. Cf. also 20 and 24 August 1870.
183. Adm. I, 6178 (30 August 1870).
184. Controller's Submission, Adm. I, 6178 (30 August 1870); Minute of First Lord, *Parl. Papers* 42 (1871) : 680. Another reason adduced by the controller for accepting the ironclad was the avoidance of political trouble with the Lairds "because their father is in Parliament." Adm. I, 6178 (30 August 1870).
185. Admiralty, "Copy of the Reply Made by Sir Robert Spencer Robinson," Adm. 116, 190, # 12 (17 February 1871), pp. 13-14.

186. Minute of First Lord, *Parl. Papers* 42 (1871): 773. Robinson somewhat contradicted Reed here, for the latter apparently stated that he had approved only the calculations, which Robinson said he (Reed) had never seen.

187. "Loss of the *Captain*. Remarks on the Evidence," Admiral Robinson to Board, Adm. I, 6160 (16 October 1870); printed copy in British Museum, Add. MSS, 44428, dated 20 October 1870. Gladstone Papers.

188. Although never publicly revealed, this cruise with what Childers termed "the most powerful fleet which has as yet been brought together," was to make a demonstration of force at the outbreak of the Franco-Prussian War. Childers to Milne, Milne MSS, 18 August and 12 July 1870, MLN/P/A/1. For Milne's secret orders cf. Adm. I, 6159 (27 August 1870).

189. Minutes of Evidence, *Parl. Papers* 42 (1871): 799.

190. Private notebook of Admiral Milne, n.d., but obviously entries made while he was on board the *Captain* or just after disembarkation. MLN P/B/3c.

191. 11 August 1870, Cowper-Coles MSS.

192. Vice Admiral Sir Robert Hastings Harris, *From Naval Cadet to Admiral* (London, 1913), p. 108.

193. Minutes of Evidence, *Parl. Papers* 42 (1871): 773.

194. Ibid., p. 790; letter from Captain Osborne in The *Times*, 14 September 1870, p. 10, a startling admission for the most consistent of Coles supporters.

195. The First Sea Lord, Admiral Dacres, unwittingly provided confirmation of Reed's assertion when he wrote to Lord Northbrook: "you must take Mr. Reed's evidence with a great deal of dilution. He never in his life expressed fear of the Captain's safety to anyone." Gladstone MSS, 8 October 1870, Add. MSS. 44266, p. 15. It must be remembered that the *Captain* was the first ship to have her curve of stability plotted and, in this light, Reed's misgivings appear remarkably prescient.

196. Minutes of Evidence, *Parl. Papers* 42 (1871): p. 830. Admiral Symonds who had favorably reported on the *Captain* after her cruise in company with the *Monarch*, also thought that the *Captain* was overmasted. Minute of First Lord, *Parl. Papers* 42 (1871): 746. Even before the foundering of the *Captain*, Milne had noted: "She appeared to be overmasted and in every way aloft especially with very heavy topmasts. Milne MSS (n.d.) P/B/3/c. Cf. James May, *Narrative of the Loss of H.M.S. Captain* (Brompton, 1872), p. 3.

197. Minutes of Evidence, *Parl. Papers* 42 (1871): 809, and passim.

198. *Times* (London), 10 September 1870, p. 9; ibid., 11 October 1870, p. 9.

199. Admiralty Board Minute, *Parl. Papers* 42 (1871): 931.

200. Adm. G. A. Ballard, "British Battleships of 1870," *Mariner's Mirror* 17 (1931): 256.

201. Parkes, *British Battleships*, p. 137.

202. Harris, *From Naval Cadet*, p. 109.

203. Minutes of Evidence, *Parl. Papers* 42 (1871) : 799.

204. Committee on Designs, *Parl. Papers*, p. xlvii. The same point was made in "The Stability of the *Captain, Monarch,* and some other Iron-clads," *Naval Science* 1 (1872). Cf. also "The Loss of the Captain," *Annual of the Royal School of Naval Architecture* 1 (1871) : 49.

205. Admiralty, "Loss of the *Captain,*" Adm. I, 6160 (15 October 1870), p. 156; Henry Laird testified that he thought that the *Captain* "ought not on any occasion to be permanently inclined to her gunwale, although I knew that there was a large reserve of stability beyond that." Minutes of Evidence, *Parl. Papers* 42 (1871) : 826.

206. Minutes of the First Lord on the Loss of H.M.S. Captain, *Parl. Papers* 42 (1871) : 657-767.

207. Reply Made by Sir Spencer Robinson, *Parl. Papers* 40 (1871). The original, Adm. I, 6178 (30 August 1870), confirms Robinson's interpretation. Childers's supporters claimed that the discrepancy was due to a printer's mistake. Hansard, *Parl. Debates* 208 (1871) : 1211. *Broad Arrow,* 11 March 1871, p. 301. According to Admiral Dacres, he "never saw a line" of the Childers Minute, nor was he ever consulted upon it, although holding the post of first sea lord. *Committee on Admiralty, Parl. Papers* 7 (1871) : 36. One authority declares that the Board had become a "rubber stamp" under Childers, and that there could no longer be any doubt about who was responsible for any decision. Rodger, "Dark Ages," pt. 1, *Mariner's Mirror* (November 1975), p. 337. Childers had undoubtedly made his own bed, but he refused now to lie in it.

208. Constructor's Department to Board, Adm. I, 6177 (10 December 1870). Cf. Reports of the Council of Construction, Committee on Designs, *Parl. Papers* 14 (1872) : 827, 911.

209. *Times* (London), 21 December 1870, p. 12. The Royal Commission investigating the foundering of H.M.S. *Magaera* reported that "we feel bound also to state that, in the course of the inquiry, it has been clearly shown to us that the system of administration at the Admiralty is defective in some important points. Its secretariat arrangements are insufficient, and its mode of registration defective." The *Magaera* went down in September 1871. Again Reed and Robinson were blamed, while the ill Childers escaped censure. Further evidence of the chaotic state of Admiralty administration could be seen in the case where Reed's survey of the rusty plates of H.M.S. Magaera, drawn up in 1866, were not located until 1871. Norman McCord, "Loss of H.M.S. *Magaera,*" *Mariner's Mirror* 52, no. 2 (May 1971) : 115-33.

210. Hansard, *Parl. Debates* 207 (1871) : 1147-1244.

211. Ballard, "First Mastless Capital Ship," p. 28; Parkes, *British Battle-ships,* p. 191.

212. Briggs, *Naval Administration,* pp. 191-93; *Army and Navy Gazette*

9 (10 February 1871): 2. Childers thought that the *Gazette*'s report, which noted Admiral Robinson's stubbornness, "put the case in its true light." Childers to Algernon West (Gladstone's Private Secretary) 11 February 1871, Gladstone MSS, British Museum, Add. MSS. 44128, f. 212. Gladstone admitted that the loss of the *Captain* had led to "most grave practical disagreements between Sir Spencer Robinson" and other board members. Hansard, *Parl. Debates* 205 (1871): 1329.

Chapter 8: H.M.S. *Devastation*

1. Fred T. Jane, *The British Battle-Fleet* (London, 1912), p. 312.
2. E. J. Reed, *Modern Ships of War* (London, 1888), p. 24.
3. E. J. Reed, *Our Iron-Clad Ships* (London, 1869), p. 227; Admiralty, "Correspondence Respecting New Designs for Armoured Ships" (1869), p. 6.
4. Letter by Reed, in *Times* (London), 24 August 1870, p. 4.
5. Committee on Designs, *Parliamentary Papers* 14 (1872): 70.
6. William C. Church, *Life of John Ericsson* (New York, 1891), 1:105–6. Unimpressed, Ericsson told Bourne that Reed would draw out of him all he could, then, "he will assuredly cut you." Ericsson to Bourne, 21 December 1866, Ericsson MSS, Library of Congress.
7. Reed to Robinson, Adm. I, 5982 (21 November 1866).
8. "Armour-Plated Ships," *Nautical Magazine* 36 (1867): 23.
9. Reed to Robinson, Adm. I, 6018 (26 July 1867).
10. Coles, "The Turret *vs.* the Broadside System," *Journal of the Royal United Service Institution*, 11 (1867): 480.
11. *Proceedings of the Institute of Civil Engineers* 26 (1867): 192. John Bourne praised the concept of Reed's but still insisted that the breast-work deviated from the "grand" pure monitor design. Ibid., p. 238.
12. Cf. MSS letter (1870) by Coles in his pamphlet *Iron-Clad Sea-Going Shield Ships* (1863) to Spencer Butler (Admiralty Library P485). Coles attempted to show from his 1863 lecture that he was the inventor of the breastwork, but the evidence he cited is unimpressive. He concluded that his letter was to be treated as "confidential so far as my enemies are concerned." Coles's strongest supporter, Sherard Osborne, admitted that he believed the breastwork to be Reed's idea, and concluded: "I am bound to tell you that Captain Coles objected to the breastwork, as he thought that projectiles might strike through the deck." Committee on Designs, *Parl. Papers* 14 (1872): 90.
13. Robinson to Board, Adm. I, 6058 (17 October 1868).
14. Ibid.
15. Letter quoted in The *Times,* 14 September 1870, p. 14.

16. Coles to Admiralty, Adm. I, 6058 (7 March 1868).

17. Committee on Designs, *Parl. Papers* 14 (1872): 315.

18. Reed to Robinson, Adm. I, 6138 (3 March 1869).

19. Committee on Designs, *Parl. Papers* 14 (1872): 137.

20. Ibid., p. 316. Cf. also *Transactions of the Institution of Naval Architects* 14 (1873): 9. According to Robinson, Childers limited the *Devastation*'s tonnage without consulting the board. Lord's Committee on Admiralty Administration, *Parl. Papers* 7 (1871): 59.

21. Committee on Designs, *Parl. Papers* 14 (1872): 308-10. Minute of the First Lord of the Admiralty with Reference to H.M.S. *Captain, Parl. Papers* 42 (1871): 699. Hansard, *Parliamentary Debates* 195 (1869): 103.

22. Admiralty, "Correspondence Respecting New Designs for Armoured Ships" (1869), p. 3.

23. *Times* (London), 16 November 1869, p. 4.

24. *United Service Gazette*, 20 November 1869.

25. Hansard, *Parl. Debates* 195 (1869): 117.

26. Ibid., p. 111.

27. Ibid., pp. 102-3.

28. Ibid., 205 (1871): 670. Identical sentiments were voiced by Sir John Hay, a former Lord of the Admiralty. Ibid., 208 (1871): 1170.

29. "X," "Our Armoured Fleet," *Annual of the Royal School of Naval Architecture* 1 (1871): 19-20.

30. Hansard, *Parl. Debates* 208 (1871): 1165-66.

31. Ibid., 215 (1873): 582; cf. Ibid., p. 338.

32. Oscar Parkes, *British Battleships, 1860-1950* (London, 1957; 1966) p. 200. Nathaniel Barnaby later remarked ruefully: "It must have been well known to all who have been concerned in introducing this type of ship into the English Navy that they were incurring great responsibility in departing so far from well known types, and that they would show a greater regard for their own security and peace of mind, if they adhered to the old ways." Milne MSS, 20 January 1873, MLN/P/B/3.

33. Reed to Robinson, Adm. I, 6177 (22 January 1870).

34. "The Late Admiralty Committee on Designs," *Naval Science* 1 (1872): 305. Although this article was anonymous, the internal evidence strongly suggests the pen of Reed. Cf. also his "The Navy," *MacMillan's* (November 1870), p. 7.

35. Committee on Designs, *Parl. Papers* 14 (1872): 308. Cf. Reed's testimony, ibid., pp. 142, 149.

36. *Ship's Covers, Devastation* class. Nathaniel Barnaby estimated that using sail and steam combined, at a speed of nine knots, the *Monarch* would have a radius of only fifty-four hundred miles. "Modern Ships of War," *Journal of R.U.S.I.* 16 (1872): 65.

37. Nathaniel Barnaby, "On the Unmasted Sea-Going Ships," *Transactions of I.N.A.* 14 (1873) : 2-3.
38. Letter from John Ericsson, *Engineering*, 18 February 1870, p. 108.
39. *Transactions of I.N.A.* 14 (1873) : 14. On this occasion Reed said that the ships were "orphans and have not any real parentage" due to "very objectional circumstances." Reed was very probably referring to the extension of the ships' sides up the level of the breastwork, but may also have had in mind the tonnage restrictions that cramped his original designs (p. 15). Cf. also Committee on Designs, *Parl. Papers* 14 (1872) : 142. Reed, in fact, informed the committee that "if it had not been to meet what had become an imperative demand from the outside, I would not have proposed a low freeboard vessel at all" (P. 141).
40. Testimony of Admiral Robinson, Committee on Designs, *Parl. Papers* 14 (1872) : 167; Barnaby, "On the Unmasted Sea-Going Ships," p. 5.
41. The Admiralty found itself under heavy fire, required to defend its policies in the light of the loss of the *Captain* and the *Magaera*, and the inexplicable grounding of the giant *Agincourt* within the space of a year.
42. Letter of Admiral Sir Spencer Robinson to the First Lord of the Admiralty, *Parl. Papers* 29 (1872) : 563.
43. Reed, "The Late Admiralty Committee on Designs," *Naval Science* 1 (1872) : pp. 316, 301.
44. Committee on Designs, *Parl. Papers* 14 (1872) : xiv. The committee's recommendations are found in pp. i-xx. The "Digest on Evidence," ibid., is the best source for the evidence given before the committee.
45. *Transactions of I.N.A.* 155 (1903) : 137. Reed, on the other hand, severely criticized some of the most important reconmmendations of the committee. He could see little strategic sense in the suggestion that the *Devastation* class operate anywhere in the world from "centres of naval power." "The Late Admiralty Committee on Designs," p. 303. He further called for a continuation of the *Monarch* type, with the addition of twelve-inch armor, for oceanic cruising. "Report of the Committee on Admiralty Designs," p. 166.
46. Parkes, *British Battleships*, pp. 23-33.
47. N. A. M. Rodger, "The Dark Ages of the Admiralty, 1869-1885," pt. 1, *Mariner's Mirror* (November 1975), p. 36.
48. Nathaniel Barnaby, *Naval Development of the Century* (London, 1904), p. 25. Barnaby also bemoaned "the decline in the character of the British seaman . . . brought about partly by the suppression of sails. . . ." (p. 26). In addition, Barnaby was a true believer in the ram, designing his ironclads to be "full buttocked" (in his words) for maneuverability in ramming jousts in what Rodger terms Barnaby's "entirely theoretical, not to say fantastic conception of naval warfare." Rodger, "Dark Ages," pt. 2, *Mariner's Mirror* (February 1976), pp. 5-6.

Bibliography

Manuscripts

The Admiralty Papers. Public Record Office. London (weeded with with what may sometimes seem to be mere capriciousness). Papers dealing with the rolling of the ironclads or the painting of gun carriages are preserved, while those pertaining to the *Captain* catastrophe, for example, have been destroyed in many instances. The Admiralty digests, massive folio volumes for each year, help to fill in the gaps, or at least point out the gaps.

United States Navy Records. National Archives. Most valuable here, although again erratically weeded, are Record Groups Nos. 19 and 45. Herein are found the correspondence of the Secretary of the Navy, Chief of Bureau of Construction and Repair, the Assistant Secretary of the Navy, and the Chief Engineer on matters of warship design in the 1860s.

Private Manuscript Collections

Cowper-Coles MSS. London. Contains a few letters from Captain Coles, but more important, numerous drawings and plans of his turret ship proposals.

Dahlgren MSS. Library of Congress.

Disraeli MSS. Hughenden Archives. High Wycombe, Bucks. Scattered throughout this collection are a small number of letters pertaining to naval policy from Disraeli, Lord Lennox, and H. C. L. Corry.

Ericsson MSS. Located in the main in the New York Historical Society, but some material in the Swedish-American Historical Society, Philadelphia, and U.S. National Archives, R.G. 45.

Fox MSS. New York Historical Society. G. V. Fox was assistant Secretary of the Federal Navy under Lincoln.

Gladstone MSS. British Museum. 1862–71. The statesman's concern here, in the few pieces that bear upon the navy, is almost exclusively with economy. The most important correspondent is Hugh C. E. Childers.

Phipps Hornby MSS. National Maritime Museum. There is very little here in the field of naval design, but a wealth of material on the day-to-day operation of the fleet.

Milne MSS. National Maritime Museum. The papers of Adm. Sir Alexander Milne contain much material dealing with Admiralty policy and personalities. Letters from practically every naval officer and Admiralty official of importance can be found in this collection. Milne's out-letters are in copy letter books, but these hold little of value for a study of naval design.

Palmerston MSS. National Registry of Archives. London. There is some political correspondence here dealing with the navy; some including his own ideas on design and strategy are to be found in Viscount Palmerston's copy letter book.

Russell MSS. Public Record Office. London. Lord Russell's correspondence with Hugh Childers and Edward Cardwell contains some items of naval interest.

Somerset MSS. County Record Office. Aylesbury, Bucks. The papers of the twelfth Duke of Somerset contain much of interest in naval design and policy but not so much as their bulk might indicate. Of more importance are letters from Donald McKay, Palmerston, and principal naval officers.

United States Naval Historical Foundation. Library of Congress.

Admiralty Papers, Printed and Manuscripts

Ships' Covers. National Maritime Museum. A volume issued for each ship of the Royal Navy, dealing with the vessel from its earliest conception to its scrapping.

Ships' Plans. National Maritime Museum. There is no substitute for examining the official plans upon which the ironclads were constructed. However, their bulk (often six feet in length) makes their perusal awkward. Oscar Parkes, *British Battleships,* closely follows the official plans, and is reliable in details.

"Duplicate Deed of Covenant, the Lords Commissioners of the Admiralty and Captain Coles," 19 November 1862 Admiralty Library.

"Armaments of H.M. Ships," 1862, 1865, 1873.

Transactions and Reports of the Special Committee on Iron, vols. 1–4. (1862–64).

Extracts from the Reports of Minutes and Proceedings of the Ordnance Select Committee, vols. 1–6 (1862–68).

Noble, W. H. *Report on Ballistic Experiments* (1963).

Complete List of the Steam Ships, Steam Launches, and Sailing Ships on the List of the Navy (1863–70). In this series are the MSS volumes "List of the Navy" (1863–70). Valuable for dimensions, and so on.

Correspondence Between Her Majesty's Government and Messrs. Laird Bros . . . Respecting the Ironclad Vessels Building at Birkenhead, 1863–64 (1864).

Statement of Results Obtained Against Iron Plates with Shot and Shell of Various Calibres (1865).

Epitome of Various Guns That Have Been Tried Against Targets and Armor Plates, with the Results (1866).

Experiments with Naval Ordnance. H.M.S. *Excellent* (1866).

Noble, W. H. *Report on the Various Experiments Carried Out under Direction of the Ordnance Select Committee* (1866).

Iron-Cased Ships of France (1867). A confidential report on the ironclads of the Royal Navy's main rival.

Naval Evolutions (1867). Official Admiralty publication on naval tactics.

Results of Trials Made in Her Majesty's Screw Ships and Vessels (1867, 1868, 1870). The most reliable source for the speed and steam economy of the ironclads.

Correspondence on the Henwood Monitor (1868).

A Manual of Gunnery for Her Majesty's Fleet (1868). The earliest extant manual dealing with the new ordnance, armor, and gunnery of the early ironclad age.

Steamships of the Navy (1868–84). A useful reference source for particulars, speed, costs, and times of completion of the ironclads.

"Correspondence Respecting New Designs for Armoured Ships" (1869). Valuable correspondence among Robinson, Reed, and Childers relating to the *Devastation* in particular.

Ward, Capt. James. "Report of the Condition of the United States Navy in 1869" (1869). A melancholy chronicle of the decay of a great naval power.

Report of the Committee on Whitehead's Torpedo (1870).

Goodenough, Captain James Graham. "Report on Foreign Navies" (1871–72). A detailed compilation of England's naval rivals, collated from attaché's reports.

Instructions for the Management of Harvey's Sea Torpedo (1872).

Stoney, Capt. Francis, and Jones, Lt. Charles. *Textbook of the Construction and Manufacture of the Rifled Ordnance in the British Service* (1872). Probably the most useful single source for the design, construction, working, power, and history of the artillery of the Royal Army and Navy.

A Manual of Gunnery for Her Majesty's Fleet (1873).

Manual of Fleet Evolutions (1875).

Torpedo Manual for Her Majesty's Fleet (1877).

Official Report of the Action Between the Peruvian Ironclad Huascar and the Chilean Fleet (1880).

Report on the Bombardment of Alexandria (1882).

Modern Naval Operations (1901).

Russia, War Vessels, 1906 (1906). Translated from information captured from Russian fleet at Tsushima by Japan, and turned over to the Royal Navy.

Unless otherwise indicated, the above entries are found in the Admiralty Library.

Government Printed Papers

Extensive information as to naval policy, ironclad design, and weapons, along with Opposition reaction, can be found in Hansard's *Parliamentary Debates*, 1863–72. The following *Parliamentary Papers* deal with naval matters bearing upon design.

Copy of the Minute by the Defence Committee Relative to the Report of the Royal Commissioners for National Defence. Vol. 41 (1860).

Statement Relating to the Advantages of Iron and Wood in Construction of Ships (Navy). Vol. 36 (1863).

Estimates, Navy. Vol. 35 (1863–64).

Report from Select Committee on Ordnance. Vol. 11 (1864).

Iron-Plated Ships and Batteries. Vol. 35 (1865).

Naval Defence of the Colonies. Vol. 1 (1865).

Correspondence Between the Admiralty and Captain Cowper Coles, and Papers Relating Thereto Relative to the Design of a Sea-Going Turret Ship. Vol. 47 (1866).

Report of the Admiralty Committee on Turret Ships. Vol. 47 (1866).

Report on Passive Obstructions for the Defence of Harbours and Channels. Vol. 5 (1866).

Reports of Trials of Speed of Scorpion and Wyvern in 1865. Vol. 44 (1866).

Channel Fleet. Vol. 44 (1867).

Committee on the 'Gibraltar' Shield. Vol. 16 (1867–68).

Navy (Channel Fleet), 1868. Vol. 45 (1867–68).

Papers Relative to Navy (Designs for Ships). Vol. 45 (1867–68).

Reports, Etc. Relative to Trials of the Channel Fleet in 1867. Vol. 45 (1867–68).

Channel and Mediterranean Squadrons, 1869. Vol. 44 (1870).

Copy of Report from the Institution of Naval Architects to the Board of Trade in April, 1867, Respecting the Construction, Equipment, and Freeboard of Ships. Vol. 60 (1870).

Reports of the Performance of the Ships of the Combined Channel and Mediterranean Squadrons during the Cruise Between the Twenty-Third Day of August and the Second Day of October, 1869. Vol. 44 (1870).

Minutes of Evidence, H.M.S. Captain Court Martial. Vol. 62 (1871).

Copy of the Reply Made by Sir Robert Spencer Robinson to the Minute of the First Lord of the Admiralty. Vol. 40 (1871).

Detached Squadron (Cruise Around the World). Vol. 41 (1871).

Minute of the First Lord of the Admiralty with Reference to H.M.S. Captain with the Minutes of the Proceedings of the Court Martial, and the Board Minute Thereon. Vol. 42 (1871).

Report from the Select Committee of the House of Lords on the Board of Admiralty; Together with the Proceedings of the Committee, Minutes, Appendix, and Evidence. Vol. 7 (1871).

Report of Admiral George Elliot and Rear Admiral A. P. Ryder . . . Members of the Committee Appointed by the Lords Commissioners of the Admiralty to Examine the Designs Upon Which Ships of War Have Recently Been Constructed, Dissenting from the Report of the Committee on Designs. Vol. 14 (1872).

Report of the Committee to Examine the Designs Upon Which Ships of War Have Recently Been Constructed with Analysis of Evidence. Vol. 14 (1872).

Royal Commission on Unseaworthy Ships. Vol. 36 (1873).

Final Report of Royal Commission on Unseaworthy Ships. Vol. 34 (1874).

Nominal Lists of all Ironclads and Date of Their First Completion for Sea. Vol. 38 (1874).

Official Dispatches from Rear Admiral De Horsey Reporting the Encounter Between H.B.M.S. Shah and Amethyst and the Peruvian . . . Huascar, 1877. Vol. 52 (1877).

Other Printed Sources

Adams, Ephraim D. *Great Britain and the American Civil War.* 2 vols. New York. 1925.

Admiralty Administration, Its Faults and Defaults. London, 1861.

American Iron and Steel Association. *History of the Manufacture of Armor Plate for the United States Navy.* Philadelphia, 1899.

Arem, E. *Rol' Flota v Voem 1877–1878 gg.* St. Petersburg, 1903. Russo-Turkish naval war, 1877–78.

Attlmayr, F. von. *Der Krieg im der Adria im Jahre 1866*. Pola, 1896.

Barber, F. M. *Lecture on the Whitehead Torpedo*. Newport, R. I., 1874.

Barnaby, Kenneth C. *The Institution of Naval Architects, 1860–1960*. London, 1960. A valuable condensation of a century of naval architecture and development.

Barnaby, Sir Nathaniel. *Naval Development of the Century*. London, 1904.

Barnes, Lt. Comdr. T. S. *Submarine Warfare, Offensive and Defensive, Including a Discussion of the Offensive Torpedo system*. New York, 1869.

Barrett, Edward. *Gunnery Instructions*. New York, 1862. A brief manual.

Barry, Patrick. *Dockyard Economy and Naval Power*. London, 1863. Contains some of the earliest photographs of shipbuilding facilities.

———. *The Dockyards, Shipyards, and Marine of France*. London, 1864.

Bartlett, C. B. *Great Britain and Seapower, 1815–1867*. London, 1963. Good background.

The Battle of the Ironclads. London, 1871. A fantasy of future ironclad warfare.

Baxter, James Phinney III. *The Introduction of the Ironclad Warship*. Cambridge, Mass. and London, 1933; 1968. The basic modern source for this topic.

Bennett, Frank M. *The Steam Navy of the United States*. Pittsburgh, Pa., 1896. A basic source to this day.

Bigelow, John. *France and the Confederate Navy*. New York, 1888. A reply to James Bullock.

Bourgeoise, M. *Études sur les manoeuvres des combats sur mer*. Paris, 1876.

Boutakov, Adm. Gregorie. *Nouvelles Bases de Tactique*. Translated from the Russian by H. de la Planche. Paris, 1867. An influential work on naval tactics emphasinzing the ram.

Boynton, The Reverend C. B. *The Navies of England, America, France, and Russia*. New York, 1865. A work more distinguished for its chauvinism than for its accuracy, but valuable for an insight into contemporary American opinion on the monitor.

———. *The History of the Navy During the Rebellion.* N. Y., 1862–68.

Brackenbury, C. B. *European Armaments in 1867.* London, 1867.

Brandt, John D. *Gunnery Catechism as Applied to the Service of Naval Ordnance.* London, 1864.·

Brassey, Thomas. *The British Navy.* 5 vols. London, 1882. Brassey is an invaluable source for the British Navy in the mid-nineteenth century. Plans, particulars, and armament of British and foreign ironclads are extensive. Brassey may be considered in many ways to have been the British Mahan, the first writer to deal with the major questions of the ironclad age in detail.

———. *Papers and Addresses.* London, 1894.

———. *Recent Naval Administrations.* London, 1872.

Breyer, Siegfried. *Battleships and Battlecruisers, 1905–1970.* Munich, 1973. The definitive source for twentieth-century battleships.

Briggs, Sir John H. *Naval Administration, 1827–1892.* London. 1897. An important source for the administration and administrators of the Royal Navy. Briggs had served most of his life in the Admiralty.

Brodie, Bernard. *Seapower in the Machine Age.* Princeton, N. J., 1941. London, 1944.

Brown, A. Crosby. "Monitor Class Warships of the United States Navy." Society of Naval Architects and Marine Engineers, *Historical Transactions 1893–1943.* New York, 1945.

Buckle, George Earle, and Monypenny, William F. *The Life of Benjamin Disraeli, Earl of Beaconsfield.* 6 vols. London, 1910–20.

Buh, Lance Buhl. "The Smooth Water Navy: American Naval Policy and Politics, 1865–1876." Ph.D. dissertation, Harvard University, 1969.

Bullock, James D. *The Secret Service of the Confederate States in Europe, or How the Confederate Cruisers were Equipped.* London, 1883. Written by the chief Confederate agent in Europe.

Burn, W. L. *The Age of Equipoise.* London, 1964.

Campbell, Duncan. *Steam Rams.* Edinburgh, private printing.

Canfield, Eugene. *Civil War Naval Ordnance.* Washington, D.C.: Department of the Navy. 1969.

―――. *Notes on Naval Ordnance of the American Civil War.* Washington, D.C., 1960.

Captain Coles and the Admiralty. London, 1886.

Chabaud-Arnault, C. *Histoire des flottes militaires.* Paris, 1889.

Chalmers, James. *Armour for Ships and Forts.* London, 1865.

Chatfield, Henry. *Remarks on the Proposed Changes at the Admiralty.* London, 1863.

Chevalier, Edouard. *La Marine Française et la marine allemande pendant la guerre de 1870–71.* Paris, 1873.

Childers, Lt. Col. Spencer. *The Life and Correspondence of the Rt. Hon. Hugh C. E. Childers, 1827–1896.* 2 vols. London, 1901.

Church, W. C. *The Life of John Ericsson.* 2 vols. New York, 1891. Must be used with caution.

Clarke, I. F. *Voices Prophesying War.* London and New York, 1966.

Clowes, W. L. Laird. *Four Modern Naval Campaigns.* London, 1902.

―――. *The Royal Navy.* Vol. 7. London, 1903. Another basic source for the ironclads and navy of nineteenth century Britain. In addition to technical information, the volume contains most useful compilations of the service of naval officers and administrators. The bulk of the volume is devoted to the operational history of the navy, 1857–1900.

Coles, Capt. Cowper Phipps. *A Comparison Between Ironclad Ships with Broadside Ports, and Ships with Revolving Shields.* Portsea, 1863.

―――. *Captain Coles' Correspondence with the Admiralty on Giving Free Publication to His Views on Ironclads.* Ventnor, 1866.

―――. *English versus American Cupolas: A Comparison Between Captain Coles' and Captain Ericsson's Turrets.* Portsea, 1864.

―――. *Iron-Clad Sea-Going Shield Ships.* London, 1863.

―――. *Letters from Captain Cowper Coles to the Secretary of the*

Admiralty on Sea-Going Turret Ships. Portsea, 1865. Contains Coles's answers to the Turret Ship Committee's objections to his design for a seagoing turret ship.

————. *Letters . . . and the Opinion of the Press on Turrets.* London, 1861.

————. *Our National Defences.* London, 1861.

————. *Shot-Proof Gun Shields as Adapted to Iron-Cased Ships for National Defence.* London, 1860.

————. *The Turret versus the Broadside System.* London, 1867.

Colomb, Capt. J. C. R. *On the Distribution of Our War Forces* London, 1869.

————. *The Protection of Our Commerce and Distribution of Our Naval Forces Considered.* London, 1867.

Colomb, Comdr. Philip H. *Essays on Naval Defence.* London, 1893.

————. *Memoirs of Admiral the Rt. Hon. Sir Astley Cooper Key.* London, 1898.

Custacne, Sir Reginald. *The Ship of the Line in Battle.* London, 1912.

Dahlgren, F. H. *Shells and Shell Guns.* Philadelphia, 1856.

Daly, Robert. *Aboard the USS Monitor, 1862.* Annapolis, Md., 1964. Excellent, balanced account of life aboard a monitor.

Department of the Navy, U.S. *Dictionary of American Fighting Ships III.* Appendix 2. Washington, D.C., 1968.

Dislere, P. *La Guerre d'escadre et la guerre des côtes.* Paris, 1826.

Douglas, Gen. Sir Howard. *On Naval Warfare with Steam.* London, 1858.

Eads, James. *System of Naval Defenses.* New York, 1868. Report to Hon. Gideon Welles.

Egerton, Mrs. Fred. *Admiral of the Fleet, Sir Geoffrey Phipps. Hornby,* London, 1896.

Ellett, Charles, Jr. *Coast and Harbor Defences; or, The Substitution of Steam Battering Rams for Ships of War.* Philadelphia, 1899.

Elliot, Arthur D. *Life of Lord Goschen.* London, 1911.

Elliot, Adm. George. *Flotilla. Coast and Harbour Defence.* London, 1871.

Eskew, G. L. "Our Navy's Ships and Their Builders, 1775–1883." Washington, D.C., 1962. Typescript composed under the auspices of Bureau of Ships, U.S. Navy.

Fairbairn, William. *Treatise on Iron Shipbuilding; its History and Progress.* London, 1865.

Farenholt, O. W. *The Monitor Catskill: A Year's Reminiscence!* Military order of the Loyal Legion of the United States. War Paper 23. San Francisco, 1912.

Fishbourne, F. Gardiner. *Loss of H.M.S. Captain.* London, 1870; 1871.

Fisher, Comdr. John A. *A Treatise on Electricity.* Portsmouth, 1868; 1871.

———. *Naval Tactics.* London, 1871.

Fleischer, J. *Geschichte der K. K. Kriegsmarine wahrend der Kriegs im Jahr 1866.*

Fox, Gustavus Vasa. *Confidential Correspondence of Gustavus Vasa Fox, Assistant Secretary of the Navy, 1861–1865.* 2 vols. New York, 1920.

Fyfe, Herbert C. *Submarine Warfare, Past, Present and Future.* London, 1915.

Gardiner, Leslie. *The British Admiralty.* Edinburgh and London, 1968. Lacks notes.

Grey, Adm. Sir Frederick W. *Admiralty Administration, 1861–1866.* London, 1866.

———. *On the Organization of the Navy.* London, 1860.

Halley, A. L. *A Treatise on Ordnance and Armor,* New York, 1865.

Halsted, Rear Adm. E. Pellew. *A Turret Navy for the Future.* London, 1866.

Hamilton, Rear Adm. Sir R. Vesey. *Naval Administration.* London, 1896.

Harris, Vice Adm. Sir Robert Hastings. *From Naval Cadet to Admiral.* London, 1913.

Hawkey, Arthur. *H.M.S. Captain.* London, 1963. Excellent popular account.

Henwood, Charles F. *Ironclads, Present and Future.* London, 1870.

―――. *Textbook to the Turret and Tripod Systems of Captain Cowper P. Coles, R.N., C.B., as Designed for Future Navies by S. C. F. Henwood, Esq., Naval Architect.* Paris, 1867.

―――. *Sir Robert Spencer Robinson et al Arraigned at the Bar of Public Opinion.* London, 1874.

Hornby, Rear Adm. Geoffrey Phipps. *The Cruise Round the World of the Flying Squadron.* London, 1871.

Hovgaard, William. *Modern History of Warships.* London, 1920.

Iachino. *La campagna navale di Lissa, 1866.* Milan, 1866.

I. N. *The Monitor Ironclads.* Boston, 1864.

Instructions for the Management of Harvey's Sea Torpedo. London, 1872.

Italy, Marina. *Officio Storico. Le Navi di dinea Italiane, 1861–1961.* Rome, 1962.

Jane, Fred T. *The British Battlefleet.* London, 1912. Authoritative.

―――. *The Imperial Russian Navy.* London, 1899.

[Jansen, M. H.] *The Revolution in Naval Warfare.* London, 1867.

Jervois, W. F. Drummond. *Defensive Policy of Great Britain.* London, 1871.

Johnson, John. *The Defence of Charleston Harbor.* Charleston, 1890. Johnson was a Confederate Major of Engineers.

Jones, V. C. *The Confederate Rams at Birkenhead.* Tuscaloosa, 1961.

―――. *The Civil War at Sea.* 3 vols. New York, 1960–62.

Keeler, W. F. *Aboard the U.S.S. Monitor.* Annapolis, Md., 1964.

Kiddle, W. W. *The Loss of H.M.S. Captain.* London, 1870.

King, Chief Engineer J. W., U.S.N. *The War-Ship and Navies of the World.* London, 1878. Boston, 1880. A useful compilation containing plans and descriptions of ironclads. Written to draw attention to the stagnant state of the United States Navy in comparison to the great strides in naval architecture in Europe.

Kraevskii, A. A. *Sbor'nik statei okrugukh Sudakh.* St. Petersburg, 1875.

Kronenfels, J. F. von. *Das Schummends Floten-Material.* Vienna, 1881.

Letter to Arthur W. Peel, the Defence of our Harbours. Dundee. 1871.

Lewal, M. L. *Traite practique d'Artillerie Naval et Tactique des Combats de Mer.* Paris, 1863.

Lewis, Berkeley. *Notes on Ammunition of the American Civil War.* Washington, D.C., 1959.

Lewis, Gene D., and Ellett, Charles, Jr. *The Engineer as Individualist 1810–1862.* Urbana, Ill., 1968.

Lewis, Michael. *The Navy in Transition.* London, 1966. Excellent for personnel and organization of the R.N., 1815–64.

Lloyd, E. W., and Hadcock, A. G. *Artillery, Its Progress and Present Position.* London, 1893.

Lullier, C. E. *Essai sur L'Histoire de la Tactique Navale.* Paris, 1867.

McDougall, Neil. *Relative Merits of Simple and Compound Engines as Applied to Ships of War.* London, 1874.

Mann, K. A., ed. *Obzop deiatel'nosti Morskoſo upravleniia h. Rossi| y. Pervoe dvadsatiletie B. Imp. Alexsandra Nikolaevicha, 1855–1880 gg.* 2 vols. St. Petersburg, 1880.

Manning, Frelerick. *Life of Sir William White.* London, 1923.

Marder, Arthur J. *British Naval Policy.* London, 1940.

———. *Fear God and Dreadnought, The Correspondence of Admiral of the Fleet Lord Fisher of Kilverstone.* Vol. 1. London, 1952.

———. *From the Dreadnought to Scapa Flow.* Vol. 1, London, 1961.

Markham, Clements. *The War Between Peru and Chile.* London, 1882.

Martin, Adm. W. Fanshawe. *Observations on a Scheme for Screw Ship Evolutions.* Malta, 1863.

Mason, Lt. T. B. *The War on the Pacific Coast of South America Between Chile and the Allied Republics of Peru and Bolivia.* Washington, D.C., 1883.

May, James. *Narrative of the Loss of H.M.S. Captain.* Brompton, 1872. Personal recollection of the disaster by the only officer to survive.

Merli, Frank. *Great Britain and the Confederate Navy*. Blooming-ton, Ind., 1970.

Merrill, James. *The Rebel Shore, The Story of Union Sea Power During the Civil War*. Boston, 1957.

Moorsom, Capt. W. *Suggestions for the Organization and Manoeu-vres of Steam Fleets*. London, 1854.

Morley, John. *The Life of Richard Cobden*. London, 1883.

Murray, Robert. *Shipbuilding in Iron and Wood*. Edinburgh, 1863.

Noble, W. H. *Report on Various Experiments Carried Out under the Direction of the Ordnance Select Committee*. London, 1866.

Noel, Comdr. G. H. U. *The Gun, Ram, and Torpedo; Manoeuvers and Tactics of a Naval Battle in the Present Day*. Portsmouth, 1874.

On Armour-Plated Ships of War. London, [1864?].

Osbon, Bradley S. *Handbook of the United States Navy*. New York, 1864. A dictionary of naval material.

Osborne, Sherard. *Our Admiralty*. London, 1867.

Österreichs Kampfe im Jahre 1866. Vol. 4. Vienna, 1869. The offi-cial staff history of the Austro-Italian war.

Otway, Sir Arthur. *Autobiography and Journals of Admiral Lord Clarence E. Paget*. London, 1896.

Paget, John C. *Naval Powers and Their Policies*. London, 1876.

Paris, E. *On a Sea-Going Turret Ship*. London, 1868.

Parker, Foxhall A. *Squadron Tactics Under Steam*. New York. 1864.

———. *Fleet Tactics under Steam*. New York, 1870.

Parkes, Oscar. *British Battleships*. London, 1957. A most useful reference work dealing with the ironclads themselves. Plans and technical data are generally reliable. This book, by a former editor of *Jane's Fighting Ships*, was thirty years in the making and will probably remain the standard source for the layman for British capital ship information.

Paullin, C. O. *A Half Century of Naval Administration in America: The Naval Department in the Civil War*. U. S. Naval Institute, *Proceedings* 38, 39. December 1972, March 1973.

Pellew, Comdr. Pownell. *Fleet Manoeuvring*. London, 1868.

Penn, G. *Up Funnel, Down Screw*. London, 1955.

Peterson, Harold L. *Notes on the Ordnance of the American Civil War*. Washington, D.C., 1959.

Plimsoll, Samuel. *Our Seamen, An Appeal*. London, 1873.

Randaccio, C. *Storia della marina militare Italiano dal 1860 al 1870*. Rome, 1881.

Rawson, Edward Kirk. *Twenty Famous Naval Battles*. Vol. 2. London, 1900.

Reed, Edward James. *Modern Ships of War*. London, 1888. Reed's long absence from office, during which period ironclads were built of which he almost entirely disapproved, gives a sharp tone to this later work.

———. *Our Iron-Clad Ships*. London, 1869. This is the best source for the design policy of Reed. Written the year before the *Captain* disaster (and dedicated to Childers), the work is useful for revealing Reed's opinion on turret ships.

———. *Our Naval Coast Defences*. London, 1871. Outlining a scheme for miniature coastal-defense ironclads that could be manned by volunteers and hauled up on shore when not required.

———. *Shipbuilding in Iron and Steel*. London, 1869. The standard work on this subject until superseded by William White in the 1880s.

———. *Theory and Practice of Hydro-Mechanics*. London, 1885. The theoretical basis for Reed's hull designs.

———. *Treatise on the Stability of Ships*. London, 1885.

Robertson, Frederick Leslie. *The Evolution of Naval Armament*. London, 1921.

Robinson, Sir Robert Spencer. *On the State of the British Navy*. London, 1874.

———. *Remarks on H.M.S. Devastation*. London, 1873.

Robinson, Rear Adm. S. S. *A History of Naval Tactics from 1530 to 1930*. Annapolis, Md., 1942.

Rowland, K. T. *Steam at Sea*. New York, 1970.

Russell, John Scott. *The Fleet of the Future. 1862*. London, 1862.

———. *The Modern System of Naval Architecture*. 3 vols. London,

1865. Contains important plans and comments on the new developments in naval architecture, to which Russell was unsympathetic. Massive.

Russell, Lord John. *The Later Correspondence of Lord John Russell.* Edited by G. P. Gooch. Vol. 2. London, 1925.

Sartorius, Sir G. R. *The Ram Used Simply as a Projectile Without Armour Plating or Artillery.* London, n.d.

Scott, Adm. Sir Percy. *Fifty Years in the Royal Navy.* London, 1919.

Scharf, Thomas. *History of the Confederate States Navy from Its Organization to the Surrender of Its Last Vessel.* 2 vols. Albany, N. Y., 1894; 1969.

Schurman, D. M. *The Education of a Navy.* London and Chicago, 1965.

Sennett, Richard, and Oram, Sir Henry. *The Marine Steam Engine.* London, 1900.

Shapack, Arnold R. "Oak to Iron-Monitors in United States Naval History." M.A. thesis, University of Maryland, 1973.

Simpson, Edward. *Report of a Naval Mission to Europe.* 3 vols. Washington, D.C., 1873. Excellent official account of contemporary European ordnance developments.

Sleeman, C. *Torpedoes and Torpedo Warfare.* London, 1880; Portsmouth, 1889.

Sloan, William. *Benjamin Franklin Isherwood, Naval Engineer.* Annapolis, Md., 1965.

Smith, E. C. *A Short History of Marine Engineering.* London, 1938.

Smith, W. E. *The Distribution of Armour in Ships of War.* London, 1885.

Smith, Adm. W. H. *The Sailor's Word Book.* London, 1867. This nautical dictionary is invaluable for translating now-obsolete naval terms. As with Dr. Johnson's work, however, opinion is sometimes confused with definition.

Sokol, Anthony. *The Imperial and Royal Austro-Hungarian Navy.* Annapolis, Md., 1968.

[Duke of Somerset.] *The Naval Expenditure from 1860 to 1866.* London, 1867.

The Stevens Ironclad Battery. New York, 1874.

Stewart, Duncan. *Notes on Steam Evolutions and their Bearing on Naval Gunnery.* Edinburgh, 1862.

Steyskal, H. R. *Die seeschlacht dei Lissa 1866/1966.* Vienna, 1966.

Still, William N. *Confederate Shipbuilding.* Athens, Ga., 1969.

————. *Iron Afloat: The Story of Confederate Ironclads.* Nashville, Tenn., 1970.

Swann, K. *John Roach, Maritime Entrepreneur: The Years as Naval Contractor, 1862–1886.* Annapolis, Md., 1965.

Thompson, Robert M., ed. *Confidential Correspondence of Gustavus V. Fox, Assistant Secretary of the Navy, 1861–1865.* New York, 1918.

Todd, Herbert H. *The Building of the Confederate States Navy in Europe.* Nashville, Tenn., 1941.

U. S. Navy. *Civil War Naval Chronology.* Washington, 1971. Exhaustive and invaluable.

Very, Lt. Thomas. *The Navies of the World.* New York, 1880. A work very similar to that of King's, also written by an American naval officer, and possibly for a similar purpose.

Webber, R. H. *Monitors of the U.S. Navy, 1861–1937.* Washington, D.C., Department of the Navy, 1969.

Wheeler, F. B. *John F. Winslow, L.L.D. and the Monitor.* Poughkeepsie, N.Y., 1893

[Willis, William.] *Remarks on Naval Administration.* London, 1871.

Wilson, H. W. *Ironclads in Action.* 2 vols. London, 1896.

————. *Battleships in Action.* London, 1926. Wilson remains the best authority for the naval battles of the early ironclads.

General and Service Periodicals

American Neptune. A current United States periodical with authoritative information and articles on nineteenth-century naval technology.

Annual of the Royal School of Naval Architecture, 1871–74.

Colburn's United Service Magazine, 1863–72.

Journal of the Royal United Service Institution, 1863–72. An excellent source for Service proposals and opinion. The discussion following the articles is often of as much interest as the article itself.

Mariner's Mirror, 1929–35. Primarily utilized for the excellent series by Admiral G. A. Ballard, "British Battleships of 1870."

Nautical Magazine, 1863–72. An invaluable journal of naval and mercantile opinion.

Naval and Military Gazette, 1863–71. The voice of militant service conservatism.

Naval Science, 1872–75. A short-lived Reed venture notable for the caliber of its contributions and its acerbic comments on post-Reed naval policies.

Proceedings of the Institution of Civil Engineers, 1863–71. Contains a small number of articles of naval interest. Again the discussions may be as valuable as the article itself.

Proceedings of the Junior Naval Professional Association, 1873–74. An interesting, but short-lived vehicle for the naval writer on scientific subjects.

Scientific American, 1862–65. Some excellent contemporary accounts of U.S. ironclads.

Standard, 1863–71. A violent pro-Coles, anti-Reed, Conservative journal.

Times (London), 1863–71. The *Times*'s "Military and Naval Intelligence" section is a valuable source for the entire policy of the Royal Navy. Its leaders and letters to the editor furnish valuable information, and reveal the paper's increasing support of Captain Coles.

Transactions of the Institution of Naval Architects, 1862–73. This is the most important secondary source for a study of the developments in naval architecture. Reed, Robinson, or Coles could be expected to attend the reading of articles on ironclad design, and to forward vigorously their reactions and opinions.

Transactions of the Society of Naval Architects and Marine Engineers. U.S. counterpart to the *Transactions of the Institution of Naval Architecture*. An invaluable source.

Transactions of the Royal Artillery Institution, 1863–70.

United Service Gazette, 1863–71. This most violent of Coles's partisans brutally ignored the most elementary amenities of public controversy.

United States Naval Institute *Proceedings,* a respected journal, with authoritative articles on early U.S. ironclads.

Miscellaneous Official Printed Material

Armoured Vessels in the Attack on Charleston. Washington, D.C., 1864. United States Executive Document #69.

Correspondence Between Her Majesty's Government and Messrs. Laird Bros . . . Respecting Iron-Clad Vessels Building at Birkenhead, 1863–64. London, 1864.

Report of the Secretary of the Navy in Relation to Armoured Vessels. Washington, D.C., 1864. A valuable collection of opinions of the United States Navy officers on ironclads.

King, W. R. *Torpedoes: Their Invention and Use, from the First Application to the Art of War to the Present Time.* Washington, D.C.: War Department, 1866.

Liste de la Flotte. Paris, 1868. Paper by the French Ministry of Marine.

National Research Council. Committee on Undersea Warfare. *An Annotated Bibliography of Submarine Warfare, 1552–1952.* Washington, D.C., 1954.

Norton, Charles B., and Valentine, W. J. *Report to the Government of the United States of the Munitions of War Exhibited at the Paris Universal Exhibition, 1867.* New York and London, 1868.

Robinson, Sir Robert Spencer. "Loss of the *Captain,* Remarks on the Court Martial." 1870. Robinson's unpublished memorandum, reflecting adversely on Captain Burgoyne. Reference Division, British Library. Add. MSS. 44429 (4 February 1871).

Morgan, Maj. J. P. *Causes of Inaccurate Shooting with Smooth-Bore and Rifled Guns.* London, 1873. War Office.

Majendie, Capt. Vivian J. *Report on the French Artillery*. London, 1873. War Office publication.

Report on a Naval Mission to Europe. 2 vols. Washington, D.C., 1873. United States Navy Department publication.

The Armed Strength of Italy. Translated from the German by Lt. W. H. Hare, R.E., for the Intelligence Branch of the Quartermaster General's Department. London, 1875.

Goodrich, Lt. Comdr. Casper. *Report of the British Naval and Military Operations in Egypt, 1882*. Washington, D.C., 1882.

Clarke, Capt. George S. "Report on the Defences of Alexandria and the Result of the Action of July, 1882." London, 1883. War Office publication.

Official Records of the Union and Confederate Navies in the War of the Rebellion. 31 vols. Washington, D.C., 1894–1922.

U.S. Congress, 40th Senate, 3d Sess., Rep. Comm. 266. *Report of Joint Committee on Heavy Ordnance*. Washington, D.C., 1869.

U.S. Navy Department. *Ordnance Instructions for the United States Navy*. Washington, D.C., 1866.

———. Naval History Division. *Civil War Naval Ordnance*. Washington, D.C., 1969.

U.S. War Department. Ordnance Bureau. *A Collection of Annual Reports and Other Important Papers Relating to the Ordnance Department . . . from Records of the Office of the Chief of Ordnance, from Public Documents, and from Other Sources*. Washington, D.C., 1878; 1880; 1890.

Index